The Illustrated Principles of

Pool *and* Bil

WITH:

- **Over 250 illustrations and photographs**

- **Over 80 clearly presented principles of the game**

- **Thorough Index and Glossary**

- **Page-number-based cross-referencing throughout the book**

- **Supplemental website at www.engr.colostate.edu/pool**

CONTAINING:

- Over 90 digital video clips

- Over 60 special high-speed video clips

- Over 20 technical proofs of pool principles

- Links to additional information and resources

The Illustrated Principles of
Pool *and* Billiards

by

David G. Alciatore, PhD ("Dr. Dave")

Sterling Publishing Co., Inc.
New York

10 9 8 7 6 5 4 3 2 1

Published by Sterling Publishing Co., Inc.
387 Park Avenue South, New York, NY 10016

© 2004 by David G. Alciatore
Photo and Illustration © 2004 by David G. Alciatore

Distributed in Canada by Sterling Publishing
c/o Canadian Manda Group, One Atlantic Avenue, Suite 105
Toronto, Ontario, Canada M6K 3E7
Distributed in Great Britain by Chrysalis Books Group PLC
The Chrysalis Building, Bramley Road, London W10 6SP, England
Distributed in Australia by Capricorn Link (Australia) Pty. Ltd.
P.O. Box 704, Windsor, NSW 2756, Australia

Text design by Lundquist Design, New York

Manufactured in China

ISBN 1-4027-1428-9

Preface

There are many pool and billiards books and videos on the market already. Why yet *another* book? Following are qualities that distinguish this book from others currently available on the market:

- **Comprehension development:** This book develops comprehension of basic principles. Many pool and billiards books are "cookbook" style, telling you what to do but not always why or how it works. Some also contain countless examples of different kinds of shots. These examples are useful, but often do not produce a level of understanding that can truly make someone a better pool player. This book contains examples and many illustrations, but the main goal is to present the fundamental principles of the game. By developing an understanding of these principles, you can anticipate and predict all types of shots that you might face, not just limited examples that might be presented. If you understand a few basic principles, you can figure out shots on your own without being shown examples of every possible shot.

- **Illustrations:** This book contains numerous well-illustrated graphics and photographs that visually explain all of the principles. Also, unlike many books on the market, all figures are drawn precisely to scale.

- **Supplemental material:** This book is supplemented by a website that provides additional resources. The website, located at **www.engr.colostate.edu/pool**, includes the following:

  1. cross-referenced video clips that help illustrate concepts in the book. Visual clip art markers throughout the book indicate where clips are available to reinforce the topics being described. The video clips were taken with two types of cameras: a sophisticated high-speed camera and a digital-video camcorder. The high-speed camera captures some motion that is impossible to see with normal vision or with a standard video camera. Seeing the stick, ball, and cushion dynamics in slow motion will help you understand the principles. The numerous video clips are valuable because:

     a) They are easily accessible on the Internet with the click of a mouse, for quick viewing while you are reading or practicing.

b) They are closely tied to the content in the book, to help reinforce your learning.

c) They allow you to see something in action, which is much better than just reading something with still illustrations. However, doing is even better, so you should duplicate and practice everything you see in the book and video clips.

d) There is no need to buy a separate videotape, which may or may not directly parallel the book.

2. Technical proofs that provide technical background and mathematical formulas to support many of the principles in this book. This information might not be of interest to nontechnical readers, but those of you with engineering or physics backgrounds (i.e., the nerds and geeks out there) might enjoy it.

3. links to additional information and resources available on the Internet.

A CD-ROM can be purchased on the website, to allow you to access all the resources listed above quickly and without an Internet connection.

- **Organization:** This book is well organized, has an easy-to-read format and layout, and is not overly verbose. The clip art markers; the lists of figures, principles, and video clips at the beginning of the book; and the glossary and index at the end of the book make it easy to use the book and website for learning and quick reference. Also, cross-references to principles, figures, and sections appear throughout the book (with page numbers). This makes it very easy to find what you want and need with minimum effort.

So what qualifications do I have to write this book? My qualifications and inspiration come from my enthusiasm for and experience with the game and from my analytic and intuitive nature. Being a professor of mechanical engineering, I have a thorough knowledge and understanding of physics and motion-analysis principles. I also have many years of teaching experience and have written a university-level textbook. The textbook experience helped me develop my skills for presenting and illustrating difficult concepts in a concise and understandable way. I have been around pool since I was four years old, when my parents purchased an inexpensive pool table. I have always enjoyed playing pool and have always been a student of the game. My most productive experience came from being in an 8-ball pool league in the Washington, DC area. I learned a lot from the players in the league, many of whom were frequent tournament players (and serious gamblers). My inspiration and knowledge also come from my experience teaching advanced dynamics to engineering graduate students. For more than ten years, I have often used pool examples to motivate my students to learn some very difficult motion-analysis techniques.

This book is appropriate for novice players who want to learn efficiently. It is equally appropriate for experienced league and tournament players who want to strengthen their games with an improved understanding and an expanded arsenal of shots. If you are new to the game, you might want to refer to the glossary to familiarize yourself with some of the lingo. The book website also provides useful links if you want to browse the Internet and better experience the world of pool.

You will not find any "trick shots" in this book. If you want to see those, watch the ESPN trick-shot tournaments on TV. Learning canned trick shots is simply a distraction and really doesn't serve any meaningful purpose for normal players, unless you are desperate to try to "impress" your friends or you have an ambition to become a trick shot tournament player in the future. However, once you master all of the principles in this book, some of the real shots you will be able to make will inspire the same kind of awe and delight that a skillful trick shot can.

I hope you will enjoy the book and find it useful. I also encourage you to become or continue to be a student of the game by reading other books, watching instructional videos, viewing pool and billiard events (on TV and in person), and discussing the intricacies of the game with experienced players and friends. But most importantly, play a lot and have fun. That's what it's all about.

Good luck with your game,
Dr. Dave

PS: If you have kids, start them early!

Acknowledgments

I dedicate this book to all of my past Advanced Dynamics graduate students in mechanical engineering, who put up with my enthusiasm for pool by enduring countless examples of pool physics—even though the examples often had little to do with engineering applications.

I also want to express my appreciation to Alan Propp, Carolyn Yalin, Frank Rogers, Diane Reiser, Horizon Gitano-Briggs, and Varo Maldonado. Al, Carolyn, and Frank proofread my first complete draft and provided valuable input that helped me significantly improve the book. Diane is a great friend who provided much input as a novice player and contributed some creative ideas (e.g., the rack-of-balls figure presented in Chapter 1). She also helped me with the photo shoots. Horizon, a PhD student in mechanical engineering, helped me refine some of my ideas and was a tremendous help with shooting the high-speed-video clips, available on the book website. Finally, Varo has been my reliable pool buddy who has given me countless hours of enjoyable practice and provided useful feedback on the book.

I also want to thank Jordan Radin and Ashley Harvey for letting me include a photograph of their son Isaac in the preface.

Table of Contents

Figures xi

Principles xviii

Normal Video Clips xxi

High-speed Video Clips xxiv

Technical Proofs xxvii

Chapter 1   Introduction 1

Section 1.01 Pyramid of Progress 2

Section 1.02 Terminology 4

Section 1.03 8-ball and 9-ball rules 6

Section 1.04 Using the book 11

Chapter 2   Fundamentals 15

Section 2.01 Cue stick and tip 16

Section 2.02 Grip 19

Section 2.03 Bridge 21

Section 2.04 Stance 25

Section 2.05 Stroke 27

Chapter 3   Executing Basic Shots .33

Section 3.01 Introduction 33

Section 3.02 Aiming methods 35

Section 3.03 Cue ball path—the 90° rule 41

Section 3.04 Cue ball path—the 30° rule 48

Section 3.05 Basic shot planning .56

Section 3.06 Effective pocket size and center 60

Section 3.07 Shot margins of error 72

Chapter 4   Spin and English 79

Section 4.01 Introduction 80

Section 4.02 Draw shot 86

Section 4.03 Follow shot 90

Section 4.04 English (sidespin) 95

Section 4.05 Cut-shot effects 105

Section 4.06 Rail cut shots 109

Section 4.07 Controlling the cue ball path 115

Section 4.08 English examples and advice 120

Chapter 5   **Position Play and Strategy** **125**

   Section 5.01 Introduction 125

   Section 5.02 Position-play fundamentals 126

   Section 5.03 The makable region .137

   Section 5.04 Ball groupings 143

   Section 5.05 Break-up and avoidance shots 147

   Section 5.06 Safeties and defensive play 152

Chapter 6   **Bank and Kick Shots** **169**

   Section 6.01 Introduction 169

   Section 6.02 Bank-shot aiming methods 173

   Section 6.03 Kick-shot aiming methods 182

   Section 6.04 Speed effects 186

   Section 6.05 English effects 194

   Section 6.06 Cut-angle effects 197

   Section 6.07 Bank- and kick-shot advice 200

Chapter 7   **Advanced Techniques (Shot Making)** **203**

   Section 7.01 Combination shots 203

   Section 7.02 Carom shots 205

   Section 7.03 Frozen-ball throw shots 209

   Section 7.04 Using throw for position 214

   Section 7.05 Power break 217

   Section 7.06 Two-rail kick and bank shots 225

   Section 7.07 Frozen-ball bank shots 231

   Section 7.08 Kick shot-vertical plane spin 233

   Section 7.09 Massé shots 235

   Section 7.10 Jump shots 240

   Section 7.11 That's all, folks 245

Bibliography 247

Glossary 249

Index 264

Figures

Figure 1.1 Pyramid of Progress 2

Figure 1.2 Rack of skills 4

Figure 1.3 Pool-table terminology .5

Figure 1.4 Cue-stick terminology 5

Figure 1.5 Proper 8-ball and 9-ball racks 7

Figure 1.6 Example of terminology and
symbols used in illustrations 12

Figure 1.7 Format for principle boxes 13

Figure 1.8 Supplemental clip-art markers
used throughout the book 14

Figure 2.1 Ideal cue-tip shape 17

Figure 2.2 The effect of cue tip shape on ball contact 18

Figure 2.3 Cue-tip preparation tools 18

Figure 2.4 Good grip 20

Figure 2.5 Bad grips 20

Figure 2.6 Various hand bridges 21–22

Figure 2.7 Various rail bridges 22

Figure 2.8 Mechanical-bridge technique 25

Figure 2.9 Good stance 27

Figure 2.10 Stroking-plane alignment 32

Figure 3.1 Basic shot terminology 34

Figure 3.2 Various cut angles and levels of difficulty 34

Figure 3.3 Aiming line and contact point 36

Figure 3.4 Undercutting a cut shot 37

Figure 3.5 Shot illustrating the ghost-ball aiming method 38

Figure 3.6 Ghost-ball aiming method 38

Figure 3.7 Example shot showing how to
use the cue stick to help you aim 39

Figure 3.8 Using the cue stick to help visualize the impact line . .40

Figure 3.9 Using the cue stick to help visualize the aiming line .40

Figure 3.10 90° rule 42

Figure 3.11 Types of shots where the 90° rule applies 44

Figure 3.12 Using your hand to visualize
the 90° rule impact and tangent lines 44

Figure 3.13 Object ball and cue ball speeds versus cut angle 46

Figure 3.14 Three cut shots for Figure 3.13 46

Figure 3.15 Stop-shot example 47

Figure 3.16 Using the 90° rule to check
for and prevent a scratch 48

Figure 3.17 30° rule 50

Figure 3.18 Half-ball hit 50

Figure 3.19 Large margin of error for 30° rule 51

Figure 3.20 Various ball-hit fractions (top view) 51

Figure 3.21 Types of shots where the 30° rule applies 52

Figure 3.22 Using your hand to visualize the 30°
rule cue-ball paths 53

Figure 3.23 Using a drafting triangle to
visualize the 30° rule cue-ball paths 54

Figure 3.24 30° angle proportions 54

Figure 3.25 Example shot illustrating the 30° rule 55

Figure 3.26 Using the 30° rule to check
for and prevent a scratch 56

Figure 3.27 Shot examples with various levels of difficulty 58

Figure 3.28 Margin of error of object-ball
angle, based on distance to the pocket 60

Figure 3.29 Angle to the pocket, and
error in angle to the pocket 61

Figure 3.30 Effective target size and center for a side pocket 62

Figure 3.31 Effective target size and center for a corner pocket . .62

Figure 3.32 Side-pocket near-point speed effect 64

Figure 3.33 Avoiding side-pocket near-point for fast shots 65

Figure 3.34 Corner-pocket near-rail speed effect 66

Figure 3.35 Avoiding corner-pocket near-rail for fast shots 67

Figure 3.36 Example corner-pocket shot
using slow speed off the near rail .68

Figure 3.37 Effective pocket target sizes for a
slow shot, based on the angle to the pocket 69

Figure 3.38 Example points from the graph in Figure 3.37 70

Figure 3.39 Effective pocket target sizes for a
fast shot, based on the angle to the pocket 71

Figure 3.40 Side-pocket margin-of-error
regions for a slow shot 73

Figure 3.41 Corner-pocket margin-of-error
    regions for a slow shot 73
Figure 3.42 Side-pocket margin-of-error regions for a fast shot . .74
Figure 3.43 Corner-pocket margin-of-error
    regions for a fast shot 74
Figure 3.44 Choosing a shot based on the margins of error 75
Figure 3.45 Deciding whether to shoot at
    the side or corner pocket 76
Figure 3.46 Cut-angle error and object-ball angle error 77
Figure 4.1   Types of English 80
Figure 4.2   Effect of vertical-plane English
    (viewed from the side) 81
Figure 4.3   Effect of horizontal-plane English
    (viewed from above) 81
Figure 4.4   Elephant Practice Ball with an English circle 82
Figure 4.5   Example of how English is illustrated 82
Figure 4.6   Conversion of vertical-plane
    spin to normal roll (side view) 84
Figure 4.7   Sliding forces due to vertical-plane spin 84
Figure 4.8   Impact height for normal roll 85
Figure 4.9   Draw shot 86
Figure 4.10 Using a draw shot to prevent a scratch 87
Figure 4.11 Follow shot 90
Figure 4.12 Using a follow shot to prevent a scratch 90
Figure 4.13 Following a ball through another 92
Figure 4.14 Rail dribble follow shot 94
Figure 4.15 Normal follow shot into a rail 94
Figure 4.16 Sidespin deflection off a rail 95
Figure 4.17 Sidespin interaction with rail 96
Figure 4.18 Using English for position control 97
Figure 4.19 Cause of English deflection 99
Figure 4.20 English deflection 99
Figure 4.21 English curve 100
Figure 4.22 Throw action 101
Figure 4.23 English throw 102
Figure 4.24 Using throw to make a partially blocked shot 104
Figure 4.25 Deflection and throw cancellation 104

Figure 4.26 Cut-shot throw 105
Figure 4.27 Example of overcutting a cut
    shot to compensate for throw 106
Figure 4.28 Using outside English to eliminate cut throw 108
Figure 4.29 Increased throw with inside English 108
Figure 4.30 Rail cut shot (recommended method) 110
Figure 4.31 Rail cut shot throw cancellation 110
Figure 4.32 Rail cut shot (common mistake) 112
Figure 4.33 Rail cut shot (gap too large) 113
Figure 4.34 Rail cut shot (too fast) .114
Figure 4.35 Effect of cut angle on draw shot 115
Figure 4.36 Effect of cut angle on follow shot 116
Figure 4.37 Effect of speed on draw
    shot-tangent line persistence .117
Figure 4.38 Effect of speed on follow
    shot-tangent line persistence .117
Figure 4.39 Avoiding a tangent-line scratch using slow speed . .118
Figure 4.40 Cue-ball path control for a cut shot next to a rail . .119
Figure 4.41 Effect of speed on 30° rule 120
Figure 4.42 Achieving position with English (slow speed) 122
Figure 4.43 Achieving position with English (medium speed) . .122
Figure 4.44 Achieving position with English (fast speed) 123
Figure 5.1   Favorable angle for position control 128
Figure 5.2   Unfavorable angle for position control 129
Figure 5.3   Speed- and angle-control example 130
Figure 5.4   Another speed- and angle-control example 131
Figure 5.5   Example using draw and side English 133
Figure 5.6   Using reverse English to kill
    the cue-ball motion off a rail .134
Figure 5.7   Hitting the rail first, for position 135
Figure 5.8   Hitting the rail first, to avoid an obstacle ball 136
Figure 5.9   Cheating the pocket to achieve position 137
Figure 5.10 Example shot with several position-play alternatives 138
Figure 5.11 The makable region 139
Figure 5.12 Example of poor position and a difficult shot 139
Figure 5.13 Example of great position
    from a risky and difficult shot 140

Figure 5.14 Example of good position
from a safe and easy shot 141
Figure 5.15 Keep the cue ball away from the rail 142
Figure 5.16 Example table layout with ball groupings 144
Figure 5.17 Pocketing the first grouping of balls 145
Figure 5.18 Getting up-table for the second grouping of balls . .145
Figure 5.19 Pocketing the second grouping of balls 146
Figure 5.20 Overlap of makable regions in a ball grouping 147
Figure 5.21 Example break-up opportunity 148
Figure 5.22 Using the 90° rule to break up problem balls 149
Figure 5.23 Possible table layout after a break-up shot 150
Figure 5.24 Running the table after a break-up shot 150
Figure 5.25 Example table layout requiring an avoidance shot . .151
Figure 5.26 Using the 30° rule to plan an avoidance shot 152
Figure 5.27 Running the table after an avoidance shot 152
Figure 5.28 Example shot where you should
block the pocket if you miss 155
Figure 5.29 Missed shot leading to blocked pocket 155
Figure 5.30 Opportunity for a position safety 157
Figure 5.31 Executing a position safety 157
Figure 5.32 End result of a position safety 158
Figure 5.33 Opportunity for a frozen-ball safety 159
Figure 5.34 Executing a frozen-ball safety 159
Figure 5.35 End result of a frozen-ball safety 160
Figure 5.36 Opportunity for a two-way shot 161
Figure 5.37 Executing a two-way shot 161
Figure 5.38 End result of a two-way shot 162
Figure 5.39 Opportunity for an 8-ball in-and-safe 163
Figure 5.40 Executing an 8-ball in-and-safe 163
Figure 5.41 End result of an 8-ball in-and-safe 164
Figure 5.42 Running the table after an 8-ball in-and-safe 164
Figure 5.43 Example ball layout after a well-executed safety . . .166
Figure 5.44 Possible reply to a well-executed safety 167
Figure 5.45 End result of a reply to a well-executed safety 167
Figure 6.1   Bank-shot terminology 170
Figure 6.2   Kick shot 171
Figure 6.3   Aiming a bank shot with a mirror 173

Figure 6.4   Equal rail-distance bank method 174

Figure 6.5   Equal rail-distance error—aim
      point too far to the right 176

Figure 6.6   Equal rail-distance error—aim point
      too far to the left 176

Figure 6.7   Corner pocket imaginary-diamond locations 177

Figure 6.8   Using the diamonds to measure equal rail distances 178

Figure 6.9   Aim at the rail-grove points, not the diamonds 179

Figure 6.10 Equal extended-rail-distance bank method 180

Figure 6.11 Parallel midpoint-line bank method 181

Figure 6.12 Equal rail-distance kick shot 183

Figure 6.13 Mirror-image kick-shot method 184

Figure 6.14 Mirror-image kick-shot with a cut angle 184

Figure 6.15 Equal separation-distance kick-shot method 186

Figure 6.16 Rail throwback at high speed 187

Figure 6.17 Rail deformation and throwback 188

Figure 6.18 Using the bank high-speed
      effect to avoid an obstacle ball 189

Figure 6.19 Curved rebound path due to slow-speed roll 190

Figure 6.20 Using the bank low-speed-roll
      effect to help avoid an obstacle ball 191

Figure 6.21 Effect of distance from the rail on rebound angle . .192

Figure 6.22 Ideal bank speed 193

Figure 6.23 Natural-English effect 194

Figure 6.24 Reverse-English effect 195

Figure 6.25 Using sidespin to create an angled kick shot 196

Figure 6.26 Using reverse English to straighten a kick shot 197

Figure 6.27 Bank outside cut, creating reverse English 198

Figure 6.28 Bank inside cut, creating natural English 199

Figure 7.1   Aiming a combination shot 204

Figure 7.2   Compounding errors in a combination shot 205

Figure 7.3   Cue-ball billiard shot 206

Figure 7.4   Object-ball carom shot .207

Figure 7.5   30° rule cue-ball billiard example 208

Figure 7.6   Throw due to frozen object balls 210

Figure 7.7   Cue-ball impact position resulting
      in no object-ball throw 210

Figure 7.8   Throw due to frozen cue-ball English 212

Figure 7.9   Throw due frozen cue-ball cut angle 213

Figure 7.10 Example shot requiring cheat and throw 214

Figure 7.11 Using pocket cheating to help position 215

Figure 7.12 Using English throw and
             pocket cheating to achieve better position 216

Figure 7.13 Differences in power-break
             stance, grip, and bridge 218

Figure 7.14 Making the 8-ball on the break 221

Figure 7.15 Power 9-ball break 223

Figure 7.16 Soft 9-ball break 224

Figure 7.17 Two-rail kick shot 226

Figure 7.18 Two-rail bank shot 227

Figure 7.19 Two-rail-kick shot aiming method 228

Figure 7.20 Two-rail parallel-line kick-shot method 229

Figure 7.21 Two-rail parallel-line kick
             rail-induced-English effect 230

Figure 7.22 Two-rail parallel-line kick speed effect 230

Figure 7.23 Straight-on bank of a ball frozen to a rail 231

Figure 7.24 Cut-angle bank of a ball frozen to a rail 232

Figure 7.25 Rail-impact height 234

Figure 7.26 Example kick shot requiring
             control of vertical-plane spin 235

Figure 7.27 Large-curve massé shot example 236

Figure 7.28 Large-curve massé shot stance and bridge options .237

Figure 7.29 Small-curve massé shot example 239

Figure 7.30 Small-curve massé shot stance and bridge 239

Figure 7.31 Executing a legal jump shot 240

Figure 7.32 Jump-shot example 242

Figure 7.33 Illegal jump shot 243

Figure 7.34 Legal jump shot 244

Principles

Principle 1.1   Fun, focus, and discipline 3
Principle 2.1   The "short game" 16
Principle 2.2   Treat your cue tip well 17
Principle 2.3   Grip "best practices" 19
Principle 2.4   Death grip 19
Principle 2.5   Best bridge 23
Principle 2.6   Bridge "best practices" 23–24
Principle 2.7   Beware of the mechanical bridge 24
Principle 2.8   Stance "best practices" 26
Principle 2.9   Stance "don'ts" .27
Principle 2.10 Stroke "best practices" 28–29
Principle 2.11 Don't move anything 29
Principle 2.12 Level stroke 30
Principle 2.13 Stroke "steer" 30
Principle 2.14 Additional stroke "best practices" 31
Principle 3.1   Ghost-ball aiming 35
Principle 3.2   Cut shots are often undercut 36
Principle 3.3   90° rule 42
Principle 3.4   Cut-angle speed .45
Principle 3.5   30° rule 49
Principle 3.6   The easiest and best shot 57
Principle 3.7   Slow accuracy 59
Principle 3.8   Closer to the pocket is better 61
Principle 3.9   The side pockets are bigger 63
Principle 3.10 The corner pocket is sometimes
      "bigger" than the side pocket 63
Principle 3.11 With a side pocket, avoid hitting the near point . .64
Principle 3.12 Corner-pocket rattle 66
Principle 3.13 Beware of large side-pocket angles 69
Principle 3.14 Slower speed, bigger pockets 71
Principle 3.15 Pocket center 72
Principle 3.16 Closer to the object ball is better 77
Principle 3.17 Smaller cut angle is much better 78
Principle 4.1   Normal roll 84
Principle 4.2   Immediate cue ball roll 86

Principle 4.3   Good draw 88

Principle 4.4   Minimum cue ball motion 89

Principle 4.5   Good follow 91

Principle 4.6   Blocked pocket; no problem 93

Principle 4.7   Tangent line and English independence 97

Principle 4.8   English is persistent 98

Principle 4.9   English deflection 99

Principle 4.10 English curve 101

Principle 4.11 English throw 102

Principle 4.12 Slow throw 103

Principle 4.13 You need to overcut cut shots 106

Principle 4.14 Eliminating cut throw 108

Principle 4.15 Cut spin 109

Principle 4.16 Rail cut shot 111

Principle 4.17 90° rule cut-angle effects 116

Principle 4.18 Cue-ball curve delay .118

Principle 4.19 Beware of English 121

Principle 5.1   The "Holy Grail" of pool 126

Principle 5.2   Ideal position control 127

Principle 5.3   Speed is key 127

Principle 5.4   Leave angles on shots 129

Principle 5.5   Always think three balls ahead 130

Principle 5.6   Follow and draw are often
better than sidespin English 132

Principle 5.7   Hitting the rail first 136

Principle 5.8   Cheating a pocket 137

Principle 5.9   Stay in the makable region 140

Principle 5.10 The best spot in the makable region 142

Principle 5.11 Keep the cue ball away from the rail 143

Principle 5.12 Aim for makable region overlaps 147

Principle 5.13 Defense and safeties are OK 153

Principle 5.14 Blocked pocket from soft defensive miss 154

Principle 5.15 The best offense is a good defense 156

Principle 5.16 Always look for safeties 165

Principle 5.17 Things you can do with ball-in-hand 165

Principle 5.18 Learn from your mistakes 168

Principle 6.1   Bank-shot geometry 172

Principle 6.2   Equal rail-distance bank method 174

Principle 6.3   Do not aim directly at the diamonds 179

Principle 6.4   Parallel midpoint-line bank method 182

Principle 6.5   Mirror-image kick-shot method 184

Principle 6.6   Rail throwback at high speed 187

Principle 6.7   Curved rebound path due to slow-speed roll 190

Principle 6.8   Smaller rebound angle when close to a rail 192

Principle 6.9   Ideal bank speed 193

Principle 6.10 Bank and kick English 195

Principle 6.11 Bank cut angle compensation 199

Principle 7.1   Combinations are tough 205

Principle 7.2   A billiard shot is sometimes
better than a combo or tough cut 209

Principle 7.3   Frozen object ball throw 211

Principle 7.4   Frozen cue ball throw 213

Principle 7.5   Cheat and throw for position 216

Principle 7.6   Break efficiency 217

Principle 7.7   Power break "best practices" 219–220

Principle 7.8   8-ball-break victory 221

Principle 7.9   The best 9-ball break 223

Principle 7.10 Rail-induced English 226

Principle 7.11 Frozen ball banked off a rail 233

Principle 7.12 Rail spin 234

Principle 7.13 Massé curve shot 238

Principle 7.14 Jump shot 241

Normal Video Clips

**These video clips are available for viewing online at the book
website: *www.engr.colostate.edu/pool***

NV 2.1   Miscue due to off-center hit with no chalk 17

NV 2.2   Close-up of the grip during a good stroke 20

NV 2.3   Mechanical-bridge stroke with elbow out 25

NV 2.4   Mechanical-bridge stroke with elbow vertical 25

NV 2.5   A good stroke 29

NV 2.6   Steering follow-through 30

NV 3.1   Practicing contact point and ghost-ball visualization . . .39

NV 3.2   Using the cue stick to help
visualize the impact and aiming lines 41

NV 3.3   Addressing the ball and taking your stance 41

NV 3.4   90° rule with various entering angles 43

NV 3.5   Using your hand to visualize
the 90° rule impact and tangent lines 44

NV 3.6   Stop shot 47

NV 3.7   Using the 90° rule to check for and prevent a scratch . .48

NV 3.8   Using your hand to visualize the 30° rule 53

NV 3.9   30° rule example 55

NV 3.10 Using the 30° rule to check
for and prevent a scratch 56

NV 3.11 Following the recommended
routine for planning and executing a shot 59

NV 3.12 Side-pocket near-point effects 65

NV 3.13 Corner-pocket near-rail effects 68

NV 3.14 Near-rail rattle 68

NV 3.15 Large target size for shallow-angle rail shots 68

NV 4.1   Stun shot 87

NV 4.2   Using a draw shot to prevent a scratch 87

NV 4.3   Straight-on draw shot 89

NV 4.4   Using draw to minimize deflected motion of cue ball . .89

NV 4.5   Using a follow shot to prevent a scratch 91

NV 4.6   Straight-on follow shot 92

NV 4.7   Following an obstacle ball into a pocket 93

NV 4.8   Rail-dribble follow shot 94

NV 4.9   Normal follow shot into a rail 94

NV 4.10 Effect of left English 96

NV 4.11 Effect of right English .96

NV 4.12 Using English for position control 97

NV 4.13 Squirt due to high-speed English 100

NV 4.14 English curve due to an elevated cue 101

NV 4.15 Using throw to make a partially blocked shot 104

NV 4.16 Overcutting a cut shot to compensate for throw 107

NV 4.17 Rail cut shot with natural (running) English 110

NV 4.18 Large cue-ball deviation from
        the tangent line with follow and small cut angle 116

NV 4.19 Large cue-ball deviation from
        the tangent line with draw and small cut angle 116

NV 4.20 Delay of follow tangent-line
        deflection with higher speed 118

NV 4.21 Delay of draw tangent-line
        deflection with higher speed 118

NV 4.22 Avoiding a tangent-line scratch
        using slow-speed roll 119

NV 4.23 Cue-ball path control for a cut shot next to a rail 119

NV 4.24 30° rule speed effects .120

NV 4.25 Positioning the cue ball at various
        spots on the table from an easy side-pocket shot 123

NV 5.1   Using speed and angle control
        to pocket a three-ball sequence 130

NV 5.2   Using speed and angle control
        to pocket another three-ball sequence 131

NV 5.3   Using side English to help run a four-shot sequence . .133

NV 5.4   Using reverse English to kill
        the cue-ball motion off a rail 134

NV 5.5   Hitting the rail first for position 135

NV 5.6   Hitting the rail first to avoid an obstacle ball 136

NV 5.7   Cheating a pocket 137

NV 5.8   Freeze the cue ball on an object ball for a safety 160

NV 6.1   Equal-distance bank method 175

NV 6.2   Equal extended-rail-distance bank method 180

NV 6.3   Parallel midpoint-line bank method example 182

NV 6.4   Mirror-image kick-shot method 185

NV 6.5   Equal separation-distance kick-shot method 186

NV 6.6   Bank high-speed effect 187

NV 6.7   Bank low-speed effect 191

NV 6.8   Kick shot with natural English 194

NV 6.9   Kick shot with reverse English 195

NV 6.10 Using sidespin to create an angled kick shot 196

NV 6.11 Using reverse English to straighten a kick shot 197

NV 6.12 Bank outside cut creating reverse English 198

NV 6.13 Bank inside cut creating natural English 199

NV 7.1   Aiming a combination shot 204

NV 7.2   Cue-ball billiard shot 206

NV 7.3   Object-ball carom shot 207

NV 7.4   30° rule cue ball billiard shot 208

NV 7.5   Frozen-object ball throw 210

NV 7.6   Frozen-cue ball throw 214

NV 7.7   Power-break stance and stroke 220

NV 7.8   Soft 9-ball break 225

NV 7.9   Two-rail parallel-line kick-shot method 229

NV 7.10 Double kiss of a ball frozen to a rail 231

NV 7.11 Large-curve massé shot 237

NV 7.12 Small-curve massé shot 239

NV 7.13 Jump shot 244

NV 7.14 see Bunjee Jumper demonstrations
online at *www.bunjeejump.com* 244

High-speed Video Clips

**These video clips are available for viewing online at the book
website: *www.engr.colostate.edu/pool***

HSV 2.1   Miscue due to off-center hit with no chalk 17

HSV 3.1   Stop shot showing loss of bottom spin over distance . .47

HSV 3.2   Stop shot to prevent a scratch 47

HSV 3.3   Side-pocket miss due to near-point deflection 65

HSV 3.4   Side-pocket miss off far-pocket wall 65

HSV 3.5   Side-pocket near miss due to wall rattle 65

HSV 3.6   Side-pocket rattle out 65

HSV 3.7   Corner-pocket in off near point 68

HSV 3.8   Corner-pocket miss due to near-rail deflection 68

HSV 4.1   Draw shot 89

HSV 4.2   Following an obstacle ball into a pocket 93

HSV 4.3   Rail-dribble follow shot 94

HSV 4.4   Squirt due to high-speed English 100

HSV 4.5   Squirt due to high-speed English (close-up) 100

HSV 4.6   Object ball throw at slow speed 103

HSV 4.7   Object ball throw at fast speed 103

HSV 4.8   Cut-shot throw at fast speed 107

HSV 4.9   Cut-shot throw at slow speed 107

HSV 4.10 Rail cut shot with natural (running) English 110

HSV 4.11 Rail cut with running English,
hitting the rail very early 113

HSV 4.12 Rail cut with running English,
hitting the rail early 113

HSV 4.13 Rail cut with running English,
hitting the rail late and too hard .114

HSV 4.14 Rail cut with reverse English,
with kiss away from the rail 114

HSV 4.15 Rail cut slightly away from
the rail exaggerating the effect of Figure 4.34 114

HSV 4.16 Rail cut slightly away from
the rail exaggerating the desired effects of Figure 4.30 114

HSV 6.1   Rail deformation during high-speed bank 188

HSV 6.2 Cue ball kicked off a rail at an angle with top spin . . .191

HSV 6.3 Cue ball kicked off a rail
at an angle with bottom spin 191

HSV 6.4 Cue ball kicked off a rail
at an angle with normal roll 191

HSV 6.5 Cue ball kicked off a rail at an angle with stun 191

HSV 6.6 Cue ball kicked off a rail
with fast speed and reverse English 197

HSV 6.7 Cue ball kicked off a rail
with fast speed and natural English 197

HSV 6.8 Cue ball kicked off a rail
with slow speed and reverse English 197

HSV 6.9 Cue ball kicked off a rail
with slow speed and natural English 197

HSV 6.10 Cue ball kicked straight
into a rail with side English 197

HSV 6.11 Cue ball kicked off a rail with reverse English 197

HSV 6.12 Cue ball kicked off a rail with natural English 197

HSV 6.13 Ball banked fast into the
rail with a cut angle and English 200

HSV 6.14 Ball banked slowly into
the rail with a cut angle and English 200

HSV 7.1 Throw of a frozen object ball at slow speed 212

HSV 7.2 Throw of a frozen object
ball at slow speed, with English 212

HSV 7.3 Throw of a frozen object ball at fast speed 212

HSV 7.4 Throw of a frozen object
ball at fast speed, with English .212

HSV 7.5 Frozen-cue ball throw 214

HSV 7.6 8-ball break with a square, center hit 220

HSV 7.7 9-ball break with a square, oblique hit 220

HSV 7.8 Making the 8-ball on the
break in the near side pocket 222

HSV 7.9 Making the 8-ball on the
break in the near corner pocket .222

HSV 7.10 Making the 8-ball on the
break in the near side pocket (with deflection assist) 222

HSV 7.11 Making the 8-ball on
the break in the far side pocket .222

HSV 7.12 Ball frozen to a rail banked
with a double-kiss near miss 231

HSV 7.13 Cue ball kicked off the rail with top spin 234

HSV 7.14 Cue ball kicked off the
rail with top spin (side view) 234

HSV 7.15 Cue ball kicked off the rail with roll 234

HSV 7.16 Cue ball kicked off the rail with roll (side view) 234

HSV 7.17 Cue ball kicked off the rail with stun 234

HSV 7.18 Cue ball kicked off the rail with stun (side view) 235

HSV 7.19 Cue ball kicked off the rail with bottom spin 235

HSV 7.20 Cue ball kicked off the
rail with bottom spin (side view) 235

HSV 7.21 Slight massé curve around a ball 239

HSV 7.22 Massé curve around a ball adjacent to a rail 239

HSV 7.23 Jump shot (slight bottom spin) 240

HSV 7.24 Jump shot (slight top spin) 240

HSV 7.25 Jump shot (tip slip and stun) 240

Technical Proofs

These analyses are available for viewing online at the book website: www.engr.colostate.edu/pool

TP 2.1   Minimum cue-tip friction
         required for no-slip horizontal impact 18
TP 3.1   90° rule 43
TP 3.2   Ball speeds after impact 46
TP 3.3   30° rule 51
TP 3.4   Margin of error based on distance 61
TP 3.5   Effective target sizes for slow
         shots into a side pocket at different angles 69
TP 3.6   Effective target sizes for slow
         shots into a corner pocket at different angles 69
TP 3.7   Effective target sizes for fast
         shots into a side pocket at different angles 71
TP 3.8   Effective target sizes for fast
         shots into a corner pocket at different angles 71
TP 3.9   Pocket-target center offsets
         based on angle to the pocket 72
TP 3.10 Pocket margin-of-error regions for a slow shot 73
TP 3.11 Pocket margin-of-error regions for a fast shot 74
TP 3.12 Object ball angle error based on cut angle 78
TP 4.1   Time and distance required to develop normal roll 85
TP 4.2   Center of percussion of the cue ball 85
TP 4.3   English-induced-throw effects 103
TP 4.4   Relationship between the
         amount of throw and cut angle 107
TP 6.1   Parallel midpoint-line bank method geometry 182
TP 6.2   Mirror-image kick-shot method geometry 185
TP 6.3   Increase in bank rebound
         angle due to the rail coefficient of restitution 191
TP 7.1   Two-rail parallel-line kick-shot geometry 229
TP 7.2   Multiple-rail diamond-system formulas 231
TP 7.3   Ball-rail interaction and the
         effects on vertical plane spin .235

Chapter 1
Introduction

Pool, the game of knocking spheres around a table into holes, has created delight for millions of people over many centuries. Pool is great for all ages and can be played year-round. A pool table can be a centerpiece of social activity anywhere—a family room, a bar, or a retirement home. Pool requires physical coordination; but speed, strength, and stamina are not requirements, like in many other sports. Pool can also be mentally challenging where chesslike strategy and planning can have a big impact on your chances for success.

Pool crosses all socioeconomic and national boundaries. From the aristocrats of the past to today's bar and pool-hall regulars, pool has been and continues to be enjoyed by all. It is a sport with true international appeal, with many followers around the globe. You can find a table practically anywhere, it costs practically nothing to play, and you don't even need to have your own equipment. I once played at a hole-in-the-wall bar in Boquillas, Mexico. It was a poor community without electricity, but not without a pool table. I could not communicate with the locals via spoken word, but we had a great time. (I think the tequila helped.) I also once played in a pub in Bristol, England. We *could* communicate with spoken word (barely), but we *still* had a good time. (I think the warm, thick beers helped.) Who knows, maybe pool can be an integral part of a world-peace solution.

Hopefully, you have already experienced and enjoyed the game. Pool is one game that can truly be enjoyed at all levels of ability. Even someone picking up and stroking a stick for the first time can feel like they know what they are doing and have fun.

Now it is time to start your journey with the book. This first chapter describes the book's organization and explains how to use the book as a learning and reference tool. It also presents a concise but fairly complete summary of the rules for 8-ball and 9-ball, the two most popular billiard games.

Section 1.01 *Pyramid of Progress*

Figure 1.1 shows what I call the pool-skills development pyramid, or **Pyramid of Progress**. The foundation layers of the pyramid (A–D) represent successive levels of competencies required to become a good pool player. There is a natural progression of ability from the bottom layer to the top. The pyramid illustrates the importance of building your level of ability from the bottom up. The inspiration for the pyramid idea comes from Maslow's "Hierarchy of Needs," from the world of psychology. It states that people cannot reach their full potential unless they progressively meet their physiological needs (food, water, air, shelter), safety needs (security, freedom from fear), belonging needs (friends, family, love), and esteem needs (self respect, reputation). If a lower-level need is not met, it is difficult, if not impossible, to satisfy higher-level needs. With the pool pyramid, you cannot reach your maximum competitive ability unless you first develop and master the lower-level fundamentals.

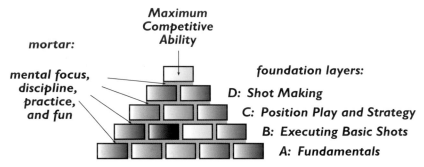

Figure 1.1 Pyramid of Progress

The mortar in **Figure 1.1**, required to build the pyramid and hold it together, represents the mental focus, discipline, practice, and fun that is required to develop and maintain your pool game (see **Principle 1.1**). Continual practice, self-analysis, and improvement are required throughout the entire development and maintenance process. Confidence and intuition can come only with a great deal of practice and experience. As pointed out in **Principle 1.1**, it is also important to enjoy the game and have fun. If you do not have fun with the game, you will not have a desire to improve.

Principle 1.1 **Fun, focus, and discipline**

The main purpose of pool is to have fun. Beyond having passion for the game, the most important attributes of a good pool player are mental focus and discipline.

- If you don't have fun, you will be less likely to dedicate energy to improve your game.
- You can play at the top of your game only when you have concentration and focus on fundamentals and on the execution of each shot.
- Intuition and confidence can come only with lots of practice.

The Pyramid of Progress also parallels the organization of the book. Layer A (Fundamentals) is covered in Chapter 2, which presents the important fundamental techniques involved with the cue stick and tip, the grip, the bridge, stance, and stroke. Layer B (Executing Basic Shots) is covered in Chapter 3, which presents the fundamentals of aiming methods, ball paths, shot planning, and pocket selection. Layer C (Position Play and Strategy) is covered in Chapter 4, which presents spin and English, and Chapter 5, which presents speed control, creating angles, defensive play, and safeties. Layer D (Shot Making) is covered in Chapter 6, which presents bank shots, and Chapter 7, which covers advanced techniques including power breaks, combinations, carom shots, throwing, massé shots, and jump shots. The top of the pyramid (Maximum Competitive Ability) represents the ultimate goals of being all that you can be, having confidence, and winning often. This can be achieved only by having a solid foundation, created by the lower layers.

I want to reiterate the importance of building the "pyramid" from the bottom up, resisting the urge to jump right into the glitzy "shot making" stuff. This requires discipline, but there is a payoff—you will develop better and faster! The lower "building blocks" must be developed, to the point where they are comfortable, natural, and automatic, before progressing to the more advanced skills. Even if you are an experienced player, you should still review the early material and try to improve upon the fundamentals. There are many good players who could be much better if they had stronger fundamentals and a better understanding of basic principles of pool. Many good players rely strictly on experience and do not truly understand pool principles. They have seen so many different shots, they often intuitively know what to do; but if they were armed with an understanding of principles, they could better plan many shots that would be difficult to execute relying strictly on experience and intuition. I do not want to undervalue the importance of experience and intuition—they are absolutely essential to being a great player. However, understanding can be extremely valuable in helping to accelerate your learning and intuition-building process.

Figure 1.2 shows what I call the **rack of skills,** which lists important pool elements and skills corresponding to the pyramid levels discussed above. Like the pyramid, the rack of skills has five levels, each with specific topics. Each chapter begins with a version of this figure, highlighting the topics covered by the chapter. This will help you understand where each topic fits; and hopefully, it will remind you to reinforce the lower-level topics before continuing.

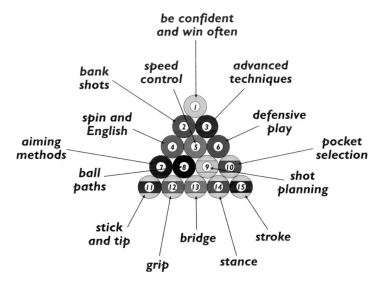

Figure 1.2 Rack of skills

Section 1.02   *Terminology*

Figure 1.3 and **Figure 1.4** illustrate some basic terminology used to refer to the table and cue-stick components. If you are unfamiliar with pool terminology, you might want to refer to the glossary at the end of the book whenever you come across an unfamiliar term. On the **break**, the first shot of the game, the **cue ball** (the white ball) can be placed anywhere in "the **kitchen,**" behind the **head string**. The front ball of the **rack** must be centered over the **foot spot**. The **diamonds** are equally spaced along the rails and are useful in aiming bank shots (see Chapter 6). The portion of the rail off which the balls rebound is called the **cushion,** or simply the rail. The ball being targeted by the cue ball is called the **object ball**. More generally, the term "object ball" can refer to any ball other than the cue ball. As shown in **Figure 1.4**, the terms **butt** and **shaft** are used to refer to the grip and tip halves of the cue stick. For a common 2-piece cue stick, the shaft and butt and separate pieces connected together via a threaded joint.

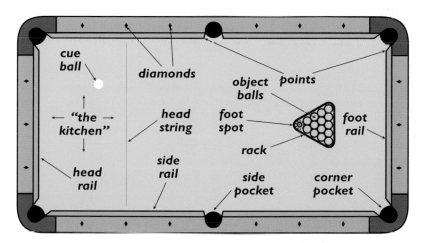

Figure 1.3 Pool table terminology

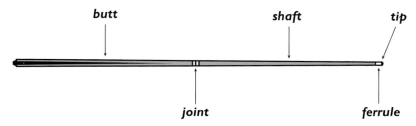

Figure 1.4 Cue-stick terminology

Section 1.03   *8-ball and 9-ball rules*

Billiards is a term used to describe all forms of cue games, including **pool** (aka pocket billiards) and **snooker,** played on tables with pockets, and **carom** games, played on tables without pockets. The most popular billiards games are 8-ball and 9-ball pool. 8-ball is the most popular game for casual and league play, and 9-ball is the most popular game for tournament play (especially on TV). This book presents examples for only 8-ball and 9-ball; however, many of the principles and techniques presented apply to all billiards games. The detailed rules for 8-ball and 9-ball can be found in the Billiard Congress of America (BCA) book *Billiards: The Official Rules and Records Book.* The rules are also available online at **www.bca-pool.com** in the "Play" section under "Rules." This section of the book presents a brief summary for the benefit of those that have not played much. This summary is also useful if you have never played in leagues or tournaments and have only played in bars, where everybody seems to make up their own rules. Even in leagues and tournaments, there are sometimes rule variations that are not standard. The summary presented here is based on the official BCA World Standardized Rules. If you are unfamiliar with any terms used below, you might find the glossary useful.

Figure 1.5 illustrates the required features of 8-ball and 9-ball racks. In **8-ball**, all 15 balls are used, and in **9-ball** only the balls numbered 1–9 are used. In an 8-ball rack, the only requirements are that the 8-ball must be in the center, one corner ball must be a **solid** (balls 1–7), and the other corner ball must be a **stripe** (balls 9–15). The remaining balls should be distributed randomly (i.e., solids or stripes should not be clustered together), although this is not a requirement. In a 9-ball rack, the only requirements are that the 1-ball must be in front and the 9-ball must be in the center. The objective of 8-ball is to pocket all of one of the groups (solids or stripes) and then pocket the 8-ball. In 9-ball, the objective is to pocket the 9-ball with the restriction that the lowest numbered ball on the table must always be struck first.

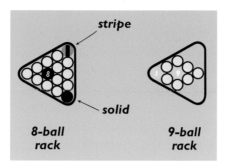

Figure 1.5 Proper 8-ball and 9-ball racks

The general rules that apply to both 8-ball and 9-ball include the following:

1. On the **break**, the first shot of the game, the cue ball must be played from behind the head string (i.e., in "the kitchen"). If an object ball is pocketed on the break, you get to continue with your turn, unless you **scratch** (i.e., you pocket the cue ball) on the break.

2. For a **legal shot**, the cue ball must contact a legal object ball first (see the specifics for 8-ball and 9-ball that follow); then, if an object ball is not pocketed, a ball (the cue ball or any object ball) must contact a cushion. If the first object ball contacted by the cue ball is frozen to a cushion and nothing is pocketed, a ball must still hit a cushion after the frozen ball leaves the cushion.

3. The following conditions result in a **foul**:

   a. The cue tip hits the cue ball more than once.

   b. The cue ball is pushed by the cue stick (i.e., the cue tip remains in contact with the cue ball much longer than with a normal-impact stroke). There is an exception to this rule if the cue ball is touching (i.e., frozen to) an object ball. In this case, it is legal to hit the cue ball with a normal stroke, even though the cue stick will push the cue ball.

   c. Something other than the cue tip (hand, clothing, cue stick, mechanical bridge, etc.) touches or moves any ball. The only ball contact allowed during a shot is a single hit of the cue tip onto the cue ball during stroke impact. Note: in some leagues and tournaments, only "cue ball fouls" are penalized. In this case, if you accidentally touch or move a ball other than the cue ball, there is no penalty. However, your opponent has the option to return any improperly moved balls back to their original locations.

d. Neither foot is in contact with the floor during cue ball impact.

e. The cue ball is jumped illegally. This occurs when the cue ball is struck far below center to lift it off the table surface with a miscue stick assist (e.g., to clear an obstacle ball). A **legal jump shot** requires that the cue ball be struck downward with an elevated cue, so the cue ball bounces off the slate (see Section 7.10, starting on page 240).

f. The cue ball or any object ball is driven (jumped) off the table, coming to rest off the playing surface (e.g., on the floor). Object balls driven off are not returned to the table and are considered pocketed (except the 8-ball or 9-ball per the specific rules that follow). *Note:* in some leagues and tournaments, object balls driven off the table (except the 8-ball in the game of 8-ball) must be **spotted** (returned to the table). To spot a ball, you place it on the foot spot if no other balls are in the way. If other balls occupy the foot space, you place the ball as close as possible directly behind the foot spot.

4. You relinquish control of the table (i.e., you end your turn) when you fail to pocket an object ball on a legal shot, commit a foul, or scratch.

5. A scratch, foul, or illegal shot results in **ball-in-hand**, in which your opponent can place the cue ball anywhere on the table in preparation for the next shot. The only exception to this is the break (see the 8-ball and 9-ball differences that follow).

Additional rules specific to the game of 8-ball include the following:

6. If you scratch on the break, your opponent can place the cue ball anywhere behind the head string (i.e., in the kitchen); and in executing the next shot, the cue ball must cross the head string before contacting any object ball.

7. If the 8-ball is pocketed on the break, the breaker (or the opponent, in the event of a scratch) has the option to re-rack and break again or to have the 8-ball spotted. *Note:* in some leagues

and tournaments, you win the game if you pocket the 8-ball on the break and do not scratch, and you lose the game if you pocket the 8-ball and scratch. This rule modification is appropriate on coin-operated tables where all pocketed balls are captured.

8. The table is considered **open** after the break, even if balls are pocketed on the break. In other words, solids or stripes are not yet chosen or designated. A group (solids or stripes) is assigned to a player only when he or she legally pockets a called ball in the group without a scratch or foul. When the table is open, any ball except the 8-ball may be struck by the cue ball first in making a legal called shot (e.g., you can hit a solid first to pocket a called stripe when the table is open).

9. Once the groups (solids or stripes) have been assigned (i.e., when the table is no longer open), the cue ball must contact a ball in the assigned group first.

10. A pocketed ball must be **called**, by designating the ball and intended pocket (e.g., "2-ball in the corner pocket"), unless it is totally obvious. The manner by which the ball reaches the pocket is of no consequence, provided the shot is legal. In other words, you do not need to specify rail contact, caroms, etc.

11. If an object ball other than the intended (called) ball is pocketed, it remains pocketed, regardless of whether the called ball is pocketed. However, if the object ball being called is not pocketed in the called pocket, you release control of the table. Note: in some leagues and tournaments, object balls pocketed by accident when the called ball is not pocketed are spotted. However, this rule modification cannot be enforced on coin-operated tables that capture all pocketed balls.

12. Normally, when you make a legal shot, your turn continues. An exception is when you declare "**safety**" or "in and safe" before executing the shot. Whether or not you pocket an object ball, you return control of the table to your opponent after the shot. The term "safety" is used because this practice is generally used to leave the cue ball in a difficult position for your opponent, which is safe for you (see Chapter 5).

13. You win the game when you pocket all of the balls in your assigned group and then pocket the 8-ball without scratching or committing a foul.

14. You lose the game if you do any of the following:
    a. foul or scratch when pocketing the 8-ball (except on the break). Note: in some leagues and tournaments, a scratch or foul in a failed attempt to pocket the 8-ball also results in a loss;
    b. drive (jump) the 8-ball off the table at any time;
    c. pocket the 8-ball before pocketing all of the balls in your group;
    d. pocket the 8-ball in the wrong (noncalled) pocket.

Additional rules specific to the game of 9-ball include:

15. If you scratch on the break, your opponent gets ball-in-hand.
16. On the first shot after the break, the player at the table (the breaker, if a ball was pocketed; otherwise the opponent) has the option to **push out**, where the cue ball can be hit anywhere, with or without contact with object balls or rails. The opponent then has the option of shooting next or returning control to the push-out player. The purpose for the push-out is to give the player some choice about whether to face the somewhat random postbreak table.
17. You win the game when you pocket the 9-ball, at any time, even on the break, provided the lowest numbered ball on the table is contacted first. Note: in some leagues and tournaments, pocketing the 9-ball on the break does not result in victory. Instead, the 9-ball is spotted and the game continues.
18. No balls need to be called. In slang terms, "**trash**" (making a ball by accident) counts. Note: in some leagues and tournaments, the 9-ball must be called, and spotted if it is pocketed without being called.
19. If the 9-ball is driven (jumped) off the table, it is spotted.
20. If you scratch or commit a foul when you pocket the 9-ball, it is spotted.

The rules summary presented above is far from complete, but it covers most of the situations that come up in normal play. The complete rules, which are much more lengthy and tedious, occupy twenty-eight pages in the BCA Official Rules Book!

Everybody seems to have strong opinions about rules variations, so I thought I would throw in my own two-cents worth. I strongly believe and profess that everybody should *always* use the BCA World

Standardized Rules outlined above, as written, without any modifications or special cases. In the future, I would personally like to see measures added to prevent felt damage (marks, scuffs, divots, tears, etc.). Currently, it is not illegal to forcibly drive a ball into the slate (e.g., with a poorly executed jump shot or with an aggressive massé shot), or to drive the cue tip into the felt (e.g., with an aggressive or poorly executed draw shot or a power break with a downward follow-through). These actions can cause permanent damage to the felt, which should not be allowed. In my opinion, there should be penalties (e.g., ball-in-hand) to discourage people from attempting such shots. I feel this way because I own my own table and my felt has suffered damage (permanent scuffs and marks) resulting from shots that are currently legal. I am sure that most table owners and billiards establishments would agree with me that we should discourage or even disallow shots that can cause equipment damage. Despite my rantings, I still respect the rules and encourage their use as written. Also, I would not want to totally disallow jump and massé shots, because they add excitement to the game, especially for TV audiences.

Section 1.04 *Using the book*

This book contains numerous figures that help illustrate basic concepts and principles and show practical examples. **Figure 1.6** shows two example shots that illustrate the graphical conventions used throughout the book. Cue ball motion is always shown with a solid arrow. Object-ball motion is always shown with a dashed arrow. English (see Chapter 4) and stroke speed are illustrated graphically. For the shot on the left, the cue ball is struck with no English (center hit) with a fast stroke. For the shot on the right, the cue ball is struck with bottom-right English with a medium-speed stroke. I don't think it is useful to try to define stroke speed in quantitative terms (e.g., in terms of cue-ball travel distance). Speed control requires intuition that can only come through practice and experience. Over time, you will develop a sense for how slow or fast you need to stroke the ball to achieve the desired ball-travel distances. I use the qualitative terms "slow," "medium," and "fast" just to help provide relative comparisons between different shots. When English is critical to the action of a shot, a curved arrow is usually shown at the place where the English creates an effect. In the right-hand shot, the right (counterclockwise) spin on the cue ball alters the cue ball's path off the end rail. When a shot involves multiple object balls (e.g., the right-hand shot), the object balls are numbered and colored; otherwise, the single object ball is shown black to distinguish it from the white cue ball (e.g., the left-hand shot).

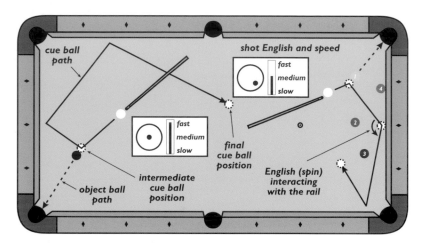

Figure 1.6 Example of terminology and symbols used in illustrations

One of the most valuable features of the book is the use of boxed principles to summarize important techniques and concepts. **Figure 1.7** shows the format used for these. The principles, like figures, are numbered within a chapter (e.g., **Principle 3.2** is the second principle appearing in Chapter 3). Following the number is a title, and below that is a concise statement of the principle. Finally, below that is a collection of concise bullet statements that provide more information including cross-references. A simple principle appeared above (**Principle 1.1** on page 3) and many more appear throughout the book.

> Principle x.y **Principle title** 
>
> *Concise statement of the principle.*
>
> • Bullets provide clarifications, cross-references to additional information, and exceptions.
> • Clip art images to the right of a principle are visual markers related to the principle (e.g., a chart showing a trend).

Figure 1.7 Format for principle boxes

Figure 1.8 shows clip-art markers that are used throughout the book to reference supplemental resources available on the book website, located at:

www.engr.colostate.edu/pool

The supplemental information includes video clips and technical background that directly support the information being presented. To get the most out of the book, you should view the information on the website when you come across the markers (especially the video clips). The **normal video** icon, labeled "NV," indicates that a standard video clip is available for viewing. The **high-speed video** icon, labeled "HSV," indicates that a slow motion, high-frame-rate video clip is available for viewing. The **technical proof** icon, labeled "TP," indicates that analytical background and mathematical formulas are available for reference. The technical proofs will probably be of interest only to readers with engineering or physics backgrounds (i.e., "geeks"); but even if you do not have a technical bent, you might want to take a look at one of two of them for kicks ("whoohoo!")

Note: A CD-ROM can be purchased on the book website for quick access to all of the supplemental resources.

normal video

high-speed video

technical proof

Figure 1.8 Supplemental clip-art markers used throughout the book

The glossary and index are other tools that can help you get the most out of the book. Refer to them anytime you do not fully understand a term or concept, or when you want to find additional information.

I hope you enjoy and learn from the remainder of the book. Good luck with your game! Pool is cool!

Chapter 2
Fundamentals

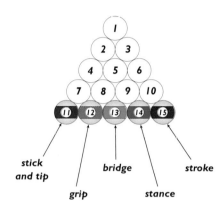

In this chapter you will learn and reinforce the fundamentals of pool-stroke mechanics. This is an important topic because if you cannot routinely stroke the cue stick straight and make solid contact with the cue ball, you will not have much success. If you do not learn how to hold and swing the stick straight and comfortably, and do not maintain a solid, stable, comfortable, and still stance, most of the information in this book will be of little use. You need to practice these fundamentals until they are second nature. Please spend most of your effort on the fundamentals, and not on the more advanced stuff later in the book (see **Principle 2.1**). When practicing, concentrate on short and easy shots, improving your ability to make the shots and control post-shot position with confidence. Do not work on long and difficult shots until you have completely mastered the "short game." Even experienced players can often benefit by improving the fundamentals of their game (e.g., ensuring their stance and stroke are solid). If you have access to a video camera, nothing is better than being able to see yourself shoot (from several different angles) to help diagnose potential problems with your fundamentals.

Principle 2.1 **The "short game"**

Very few pool games can be won by making advanced or difficult shots, but many games can be lost by not having strong fundamentals and the ability to make easy shots.

• Just like in golf, the "short game" is critical.

If you are not new to the game of pool, you might find this chapter a little boring because it deals with very basic fundamentals. However, you should try to have patience and read through it anyway to make sure you have not developed any bad habits. Also, try to keep in mind that if you don't have solid fundamentals, you won't be able to take full advantage of all of the cool tools and techniques presented throughout the book.

Section 2.01   *Cue stick and tip*

To shoot consistently and make good contact with the cue ball, the cue stick must be straight and the cue tip must be in good condition. In addition to being straight, the cue stick should also be as stiff as possible and have a weight that is comfortable for you. A cue stick that is flexible (not stiff) will tend to flex and deflect when the tip contacts the cue ball. This can cause significant deflection of the cue ball path and increase the chances for a **miscue**, where the tip loses firm contact with the cue ball during impact (see NV 2.1 and HSV 2.1). As with baseball-bat or golf-club selection, there is no optimal choice for the weight, and individual preferences will vary; but be aware that lighter sticks will usually be less stiff and stable, resulting in a less certain stroke.

The most important thing about the cue stick is the cue-tip condition (see **Principle 2.2**). If the tip is not shaped, textured, and chalked properly, the likelihood of miscues increases. When you miscue, the cue ball does not travel in the cue stick aiming-line direction. Instead, it bounces off to the side (see NV 2.1 and HSV 2.1). **Figure 2.1** shows a cue-tip shape that is considered good. The tip's curvature should be roughly the curvature of a nickel. As illustrated in **Figure 2.2a**, this results in good tip-ball contact for a wide range of ball contact points.

A flatter tip does not provide enough of a contact surface when the ball is hit off-center (see **Figure 2.2b**).

Principle 2.2 **Treat your cue tip well**

The cue stick tip must be shaped, textured, and chalked to ensure solid contact with the cue ball.

- Use a shaping tool (see **Figure 2.3**) or rough grit sandpaper to form the shape, and a scuff or roughening tool to create a good texture. The texture helps the tip accept and retain chalk.
- The tip shape should be rounded to the approximate curvature of a nickel (see **Figure 2.1**), or as curved as a dime if you plan to use significant English often.
- Make sure the entire tip contact area is chalked, especially on the outer portion where contact will occur with shots requiring English (see Chapter 4).
- Make sure you do not have an excessive amount of chalk. If there appears to be a lot of chalk on the tip, tap or bounce the stick to remove the excess.

normal video

NV 2.1 – Miscue due to off-center hit with no chalk

high-speed video

HSV 2.1– Miscue due to off-center hit with no chalk

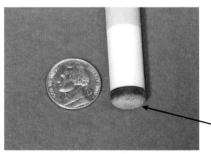

a good curvature for the tip is roughly the curvature of a nickel

Figure 2.1 Ideal cue-tip shape

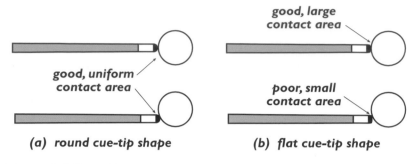

(a) round cue-tip shape   **(b) flat cue-tip shape**

Figure 2.2 The effect of cue-tip shape on ball contact

Figure 2.3 shows examples of some commercially available tools used to shape and roughen the tip surface. Roughening is important to help soften the tip surface and help the tip retain **chalk**, which dramatically increases the friction between the tip and the ball (see TP 2.1). You should get in the habit of chalking the entire cue-tip surface before every shot, especially for shots requiring English or power, to ensure the best possible contact.

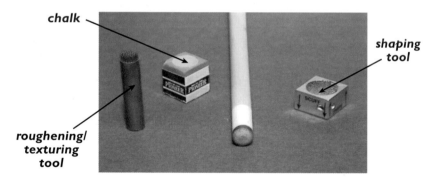

Figure 2.3 Cue-tip preparation tools

technical proof   TP 2.1 – Minimum cue-tip friction required for no-slip horizontal impact

Section 2.02 *Grip*

The **grip** refers to the hold between the stroking hand and the butt of the cue. For a right-handed person, the grip is established with the right hand. There is no optimal grip, and specific preferences will differ from person to person, but you should try to stick to the "best practices" summarized in **Principle 2.3**.

Principle 2.3 **Grip "best practices"**

A good grip should generally comply with the following list of "best practices":

- The grip should be comfortable and relaxed—not too firm and rigid (see **Principle 2.4**), but not too loose. For shots requiring significant force (e.g., a power break), the grip should be more firm than normal but not rigid.
- There should be a natural pivot point (e.g., the index finger or middle finger) during the stroking motion (see NV 2.2).
- The hand should be closed in front and open in back (see **Figure 2.4**).
- The wrist should be fairly relaxed and hang straight down at the bottom of the stroke (see **Figure 2.4**).
- The butt of the cue stick should be held at a point where the forearm will be close to vertical during the stroking motion (see **Figure 2.4**).

Principle 2.4 **Death grip**

Do not hold the cue stick too firmly or rigidly.

- This is a common mistake made by inexperienced and careless players.
- See the list of best practices in **Principle 2.3**.

**the wrist
is relaxed
and
straight**

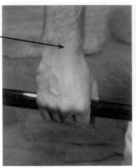

**the grip
is relaxed
and open
in back**

Figure 2.4 Good grip

normal video

NV 2.2 – Close-up of the grip during a good stroke

Figure 2.5 shows several examples of poor grips. The grip should not be too tight, the forearm should not be off vertical (i.e., the grip should not be too far back or forward), and the wrist should not be bent.

a) too tight   *b) too far back*   *c) wrist bent*

Figure 2.5 Bad grips

As with everything else in this chapter, the "best practices" listed in **Principle 2.3** should be taken simply as recommendations, not absolute requirements. The list describes practices followed by most good players. Your personal style may deviate from these practices somewhat, and that is fine because the most important thing is that you are comfortable. However, you should try to limit your idiosyncrasies and stick with the recommended techniques whenever possible.

Section 2.03   *Bridge*

The **bridge** refers to the hand or device used to support the shaft end of the cue close to the tip. A **mechanical bridge**, also referred to simply as the bridge, is used when the cue ball is too far away to establish a comfortable **hand bridge** (see more details later in this section). **Figure 2.6** shows examples of each of the different types of hand bridges. The **open bridge** or V-bridge (see **Figure 2.6a**), where the shaft slides in a V-shape created by the thumb and the base of the index finger, is the easiest to learn and is recommended for basic shots (see **Principle 2.5**). The **closed bridge** (see **Figure 2.6b**), where the index finger wraps around and constrains the stick from lifting up, is more appropriate for shots requiring power and English. For hitting follow shots (see Chapter 4), the open and closed bridges can be **elevated** by cupping the hand (see **Figure 2.6c**). A fully elevated open bridge (see **Figure 2.6d**), where only your fingertips provide support, is required to shoot over an obstacle ball. Finally, when the cue ball is close to a **rail**, you must modify your bridge to accommodate the table as shown in **Figure 2.7**. Guide the stick on the rail cushion between two fingers (see **Figure 2.7b**) whenever possible. This bridge is stable and comfortable and keeps the cue stick as level (non-elevated) as possible.

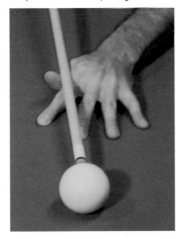

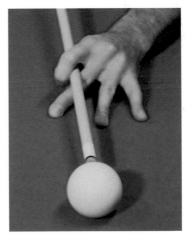

a) open (V-bridge)   *b) closed*

c) elevated (closed)

d) elevated (open V-bridge)

Figure 2.6 Various hand bridges

a) extended (open)   *b) two fingers over the stick*   *c) hand wrapped over the rail*

Figure 2.7 Various rail bridges

Principle 2.5 **Best bridge**

Use an open bridge when first learning to play, and for all shots not requiring power or English.

- The open bridge is the easiest to learn because it does not require much hand or finger dexterity.
- The open bridge provides the best visibility of the stick, for aiming and establishing the stroking direction.
- In general, an open bridge should not be used for shots requiring power or English. A closed bridge is better in these cases because it keeps the cue stick from lifting up during the stroke.

There are no optimal techniques for forming hand bridges, and specific preferences will differ from person to person. However, whatever technique you use, the bridge should be as stable and comfortable as possible. In general, you should try to stick to the "best practices" summarized in **Principle 2.6**.

Principle 2.6 **Bridge "best practices"**

A good bridge should generally comply with the following list of "best practices":

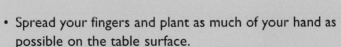

- Spread your fingers and plant as much of your hand as possible on the table surface.
- Make sure your hand and the cue stick are clean and dry. Use powder if necessary to help reduce friction. You can lightly sand the shaft with extremely fine grit sandpaper to improve the gliding action.
- Keep the bridge distance (the distance from the bridge to the cue tip) short for better accuracy. Increase the bridge distance only as necessary to avoid obstacle balls or to deliver more power, which requires a longer stroke.
- Use an open bridge for basic shots, for shots close to

the rail, and for elevated bridge shots required to reach over an obstacle ball or to execute massé or jump shots (see Chapter 7).
• Use a closed bridge for shots requiring power and English.

As shown in **Figure 2.8**, when using a mechanical bridge, rest it on the table and stabilize it with your bridge hand. Choose an elbow position resulting in the most comfortable, straight stroke. Many good players keep their elbow out to the side, flexing their whole arm during the stroke (see **Figure 2.8a** and NV 2.3). Another option is to keep the elbow down with the arm up, just flexing the elbow (see **Figure 2.8b** and NV 2.4). In any case, try to limit speed and spin when using the mechanical bridge to help reduce the possibility of a miscue (see **Principle 2.7**).

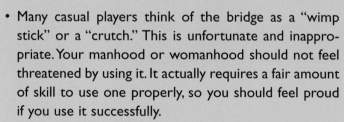

Principle 2.7 **Beware of the mechanical bridge**

Do not be afraid or embarrassed to use a mechanical bridge, but use it only when you cannot hit a shot comfortably and reliably without it.

• Many casual players think of the bridge as a "wimp stick" or a "crutch." This is unfortunate and inappropriate. Your manhood or womanhood should not feel threatened by using it. It actually requires a fair amount of skill to use one properly, so you should feel proud if you use it successfully.
• You can have much more control and stability with a hand bridge, especially for shots requiring English.

a) elbow down   **b) elbow out**

Figure 2.8 Mechanical-bridge technique

normal video

NV 2.3 – Mechanical-bridge stroke with elbow out

NV 2.4 – Mechanical-bridge stroke with elbow vertical

More advanced bridges and stances are discussed in Chapter 7 where massé and jump shots are presented. These shots require highly elevated and stable bridges that are not required for normal shots.

Section 2.04   *Stance*

Stance refers to your feet placement and body posture during a stroke. As with the bridge, stability and comfort are the most important factors. There is no optimal stance, and even professional players vary quite a bit when it comes to stance; however, you should try to stick to the "best practices" summarized in **Principle 2.8**.

Principle 2.8 **Stance "best practices"**

A good stance should generally comply with the following list of "best practices":

- Plant your feet far apart and far from your bridge-hand placement, for solid 3-point stability (see **Figure 2.9**). Most of your weight should be on your feet, fairly equally distributed.
- Some people find it comfortable to lock the knee of the back leg; otherwise, flex both knees a little, especially if you are tall. Some people even lock both knees. Again, comfort and stability are the keys.
- Before "addressing the ball," survey the shot and know exactly where you want to aim and how you want to execute the shot (see Chapter 3).
- Your dominant eye, entire arm (especially below the elbow), and the cue stick should all be in the same vertical plane during the entire stroke and follow-through (described more in the next section).
- Keep your head low and close to the stick to see the stick motion during the stroke.

Figure 2.9 shows an example of a good stance, per the best practices listed in **Principle 2.8**. Things that can go wrong with a stance are summarized in **Principle 2.9**.

relaxed and
straight grip
with the
arm vertical

head low
with the
eyes over
the cue
stick

feet spread
apart
supporting
the
weight
equally

three separated points of stable support

Figure 2.9 Good stance

Principle 2.9 **Stance "don'ts"**

Many things can go wrong with a stance, leading to poor or inconsistent play. Be aware of the following "don'ts":

WARNING
!

- Do not plant your feet close together. This reduces stability.
- Do not flex your knees too much. This can be tiring and less stable.
- Do not put too much weight on one foot. Again, this is less stable and more tiring.
- Do not stand too upright. This makes it more difficult to visualize your aiming line and to ensure that your cue stick is stroking along the aiming line.
- Do not lift your head, body, or cue stick during the shot or too early after the shot.

Section 2.05 *Stroke*

Stroke refers to the motion of your arm during a shot. Many things can go wrong with a stroke. In fact, problems with most players' games are usually related to their stroke mechanics. As with the other basics in this chapter, stroke technique is not an exact science; although some of the stroke necessities and recommendations are more important than some of the other basics. When working on your stroke, you should try to stick to the "best practices" summarized in **Principle 2.10**. Probably the most important things to remember are to move your arm only from the elbow down (see **Principle 2.11**), to keep the stroke level (see **Principle 2.12**), and to resist steering the stroke with "body English" during and after cue ball impact (see **Principle 2.13**). Stay particularly focused on keeping the stroke straight and following through.

Principle 2.10 **Stroke "best practices"**

A good stroke (see NV 2.5) should generally comply with the following list of "best practices":

- Keep your head and body still, even during your follow-through (see **Principle 2.11**).
- Keep the cue stick as level as possible (see **Principle 2.12**).
- During the stroke, keep your head low with your view over the cue stick, concentrating on moving the stick straight in the direction of your aiming line (see **Chapter 3**).
- Keep your stick straight during and after the stroke. Do not try to **"steer"** the stick during the follow-through (see **Principle 2.13**).
- Your stroking forearm should be close to vertical when the cue stick contacts the cue ball (see **Figure 2.9**). This results in natural, level (horizontal) motion of the cue stick. The elbow should point straight up and be close to your body.
- Do not go too fast on the back swing, and accelerate smoothly through the forward stroke.
- Take many practice strokes to ensure that your aim and anticipated cue-ball contact spot are appropriate for the shot you have already planned. Don't rethink your planning and second-guess at this stage. Also, gage the speed

and stroke length you will use for the shot during the practice strokes.

- During the final stroke, concentrate only on maintaining the aiming line and aim point, and keeping the stick moving straight during the stroke and follow-through.
- Move your eye gaze between the contact point on the cue ball and the aiming line, and use your peripheral vision to make sure the cue stick remains in the aiming plane. On the final stroke, concentrate your gaze toward the object ball along the aiming line to help reinforce a straight follow-through. For shots requiring significant power or English, you should concentrate your final gaze on the cue ball because any amount of error with your cue-ball contact point can cause you to miss the shot.
- See more recommendations listed in **Principle 2.14**.

normal video

NV 2.5 – A good stroke

Principle 2.11 **Don't move anything**

During your stroke and follow-through, keep everything still, especially your head and your body. The only thing you should move is your stroking arm from the elbow down.

- Failing to do this is the probable cause of most problems for people having difficulty with their game, especially inexperienced players.
- It is important to remain still, even during the follow-through.
- Your arm should swing like a pendulum from the elbow down. During the follow through, after contact with the cue ball, lower your elbow some to keep the cue stick moving level. This is particularly important with draw and follow shots (see Chapter 4) where a straight, driving follow-through is key.

Principle 2.12 **Level stroke**

If the cue stick is not level when it strikes the cue ball, the cue ball path will curve unless the cue ball is struck dead center.

- English curve causes this effect (see **Principle 4.10** on page 101).
- Sometimes you must elevate your cue stick to avoid obstacle balls or because the cue ball is close to a rail (see Section 2.03, starting on page 21).
- This effect can be used intentionally for massé shots (see Section 7.07, starting on page 231).

Principle 2.13 **Stroke "steer"**

Do not steer your follow-through (see NV 2.6).

- To help ensure a straight follow through, try to freeze and stay down after a shot, like you are posing for a photograph. Resist the tendency to lift up and watch where the balls are going. Also resist the urge to use **body English** in an attempt to telekinetically alter the paths of the balls. This does not work.
- If you do not follow through straight, unintentional aim adjustment, and English effects can result (see Chapter 4).

NV 2.6 – Steering follow-through

normal video

Principle 2.14 summarizes some more points to keep in mind concerning the stroke. These points are subtler than those presented in **Principle 2.10**, but they are still important.

Principle 2.14 **Additional stroke "best practices"**

Keep the following points in mind when executing your stroke:

- As shown in **Figure 2.10**, the cue-stick, the cue ball, your aiming target, and your dominant eye should all be aligned in the same vertical plane, called the **stroking plane**, during the entire stroke. Your entire arm should also remain in a vertical plane.
- When the cue ball is close to a rail, the tendency is to elevate the cue stick more than necessary. Try to limit cue-stick elevation. Use a rail bridge, with the stick sliding directly on the rail cushion (see **Figure 2.7** on page 22) to help keep the stick as low and level as possible.
- Make sure you have enough clearance between the stick and the rail, so your follow-through motion will not result in unintentional stick-rail contact during the stroke (especially behind your grip). Also make sure that, when your grip is above or outside of the rail, you will have enough clearance between your hand and the rail through the entire stroke.
- If the object ball is close to the cue ball, you might need to elevate your cue stick and shorten your follow-through to prevent a double hit of the cue ball, which would be a foul (see **Section 1.03** starting on page 6).

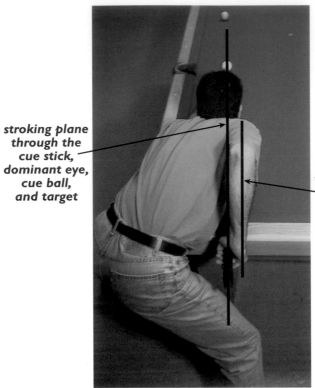

stroking plane
through the
cue stick,
dominant eye,
cue ball,
and target

the entire arm
is in a
vertical plane
aligned with
the stroking
plane

Figure 2.10 Stroking-plane alignment

Chapter 3
Executing Basic Shots

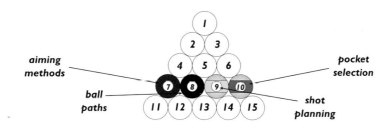

In this chapter, you will learn and reinforce the fundamentals of how to plan, aim, and execute basic shots. It is important to have strong fundamentals in this area because aiming accurately and predicting where the cue ball and object ball will go are important aspects of the game.

Section 3.01   *Introduction*

Figure 3.1 illustrates important terms related to aiming a basic shot. The cue stick is stroked in the direction of the **aiming line**, which results in the cue ball striking the object ball so it will head toward the desired target. The location of the cue ball when it strikes the object ball is illustrated by the dotted "**ghost ball**." After impact, the object ball will leave along the **impact line** (see **Principle 3.1**), also called the **line of action,** and the cue ball will leave along the **tangent line**. The angle between the aiming line and the impact line is called the **cut angle**. When the cut angle for a shot is not 0° (i.e., when the shot is not straight-in), the shot is called a **cut shot**. Everything else being the same, the larger the cut angle, the more difficult the shot will be (see more details later in this chapter). **Figure 3.2** illustrates various cut angles along with their qualitative levels of difficulty.

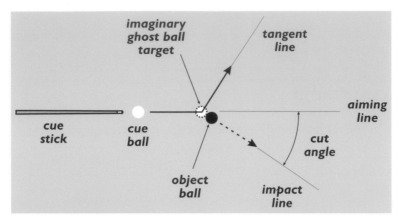

Figure 3.1 Basic shot terminology

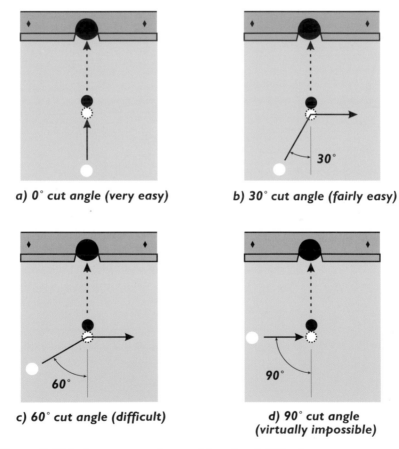

a) 0° cut angle (very easy)   *b) 30° cut angle (fairly easy)*

c) 60° cut angle (difficult)   *d) 90° cut angle (virtually impossible)*

Figure 3.2 Various cut angles and levels of difficulty

Section 3.02 *Aiming methods*

Principle 3.1 describes and **Figure 3.3** illustrates one of the most basic concepts in pool. To aim a shot, align your sight with the object ball and the desired target to determine the required contact point and impact line. Then aim by aligning your sight with the cue ball and the center of the imaginary ghost ball (see **Figure 3.3**). At impact, the center of the cue ball must be on the line of action (impact line) that goes through the center of the object ball. The aiming line does not pass through the **contact point** between the cue ball and object ball. Instead, to create the desired contact point, you must target the **aiming point** at the center of the ghost ball.

Principle 3.1 **Ghost-ball aiming**

*When the cue ball hits an object ball, the object ball will move in the direction of the impact line, which is the line between the ball centers at impact. The line of action should point towards your desired target. You must aim the cue ball at the ghost ball center, not the contact point (see **Figure 3.3**).*

- Inexperienced players often undercut cut shots (see **Principle 3.2**).
- The object ball path will diverge slightly from the impact line due to throw effects (see **Section 4.05**, starting on page 105) or cue ball English (see **Principle 4.11**, on page 102).

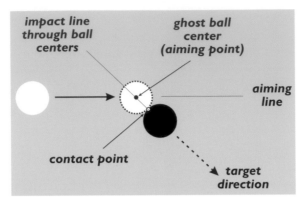

Figure 3.3 Aiming line and contact point

As summarized in **Principle 3.2**, cut shots are often missed because they are not cut enough. An inexperienced player is often tempted to aim at the required contact point instead of the imaginary ghost-ball center (see **Figure 3.3** and **Figure 3.4**). As shown in **Figure 3.4**, this results in a different actual contact point. The end result is that the actual cut angle is too small and the shot is missed. You must aim at the imaginary ghost-ball center, not the desired contact point (see **Principle 3.1**).

Principle 3.2 **Cut shots are often undercut**

If you aim at the desired contact point and not the imaginary ghost-ball target, a cut shot will not be cut enough (see Figure 3.4).

- Aiming at the required impact point creates a different actual contact point and impact line, resulting in a smaller actual cut angle (see **Figure 3.4**).
- Cut shots are often undercut due to the throwing effect of the cut angle (see **Section 4.05**, starting on page 105).

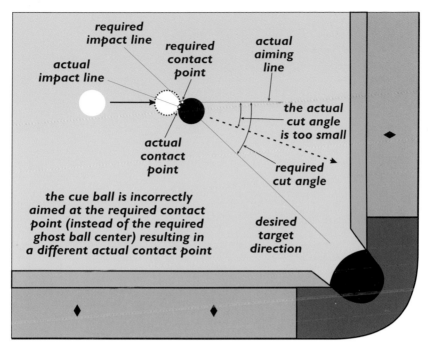

Figure 3.4 Undercutting a cut shot

You can practice the ghost-ball technique and develop your visualization and aiming skills by having someone place a spare ball at the desired impact location while you are aiming your shot. **Figure 3.5** shows an example shot and **Figure 3.6** shows how it can be practiced with an actual ghost ball. When your aim is established, have the person remove the ghost ball, and try to imagine the ghost ball in its place along with the resulting contact point (see NV 3.1). The practice object ball in **Figure 3.6** has a target circle that can be used to help line up and visualize the required contact point in relation to the required ghost-ball location. Do this several times (placing the ball and taking it away) with different cut angles and directions to help develop your ghost-ball perception abilities. The balls used in **Figure 3.6** are Elephant Practice Balls (see *www.elephantballs.com* for more information).

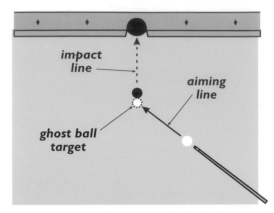

Figure 3.5 Shot illustrating the ghost ball aiming method

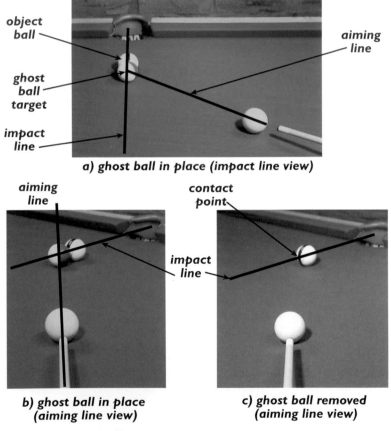

a) ghost ball in place (impact line view)

b) ghost ball in place
(aiming line view)

c) ghost ball removed
(aiming line view)

Figure 3.6 Ghost-ball aiming method

NV 3.1 – Practicing contact point and ghost-ball visualization

Figure 3.7, **Figure 3.8**, and NV 3.2 show how you can use the cue stick to help visualize the impact and tangent lines for a cut shot. Placing the cue stick over the object ball in the direction of your target defines the impact line. The tangent line will be perpendicular to this line. The cue stick can also help you visualize the ghost-ball target location for the cue ball. Now that you know the required location for the ghost-ball target, you can again use the cue stick to help visualize the appropriate aiming line for your stroke. **Figure 3.9** illustrates how this is done. The tip of the cue stick is placed on the felt at the center of the imaginary ghost-ball target, and the cue stick is pivoted about this point until it is in-line with the cue ball. This defines the aiming line (see NV 3.2).

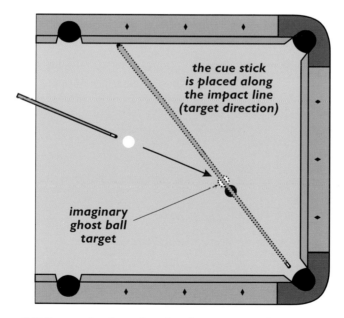

Figure 3.7 Example shot showing how to use the cue stick to help you aim

the cue stick is aligned along the required impact line

Figure 3.8 Using the cue stick to help visualize the impact line

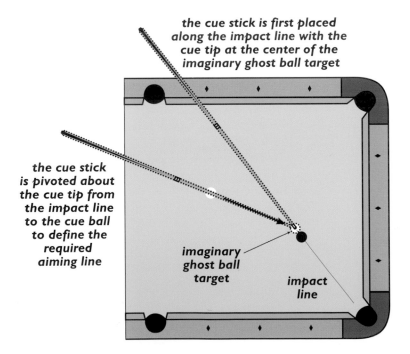

the cue stick is first placed along the impact line with the cue tip at the center of the imaginary ghost ball target

the cue stick is pivoted about the cue tip from the impact line to the cue ball to define the required aiming line

imaginary ghost ball target

impact line

Figure 3.9 Using the cue stick to help visualize the aiming line

normal video

NV 3.2 – Using the cue stick to help visualize the impact and aiming lines

When addressing the ball (no "Excuse me, Mr. Ball" is necessary) and taking your stance (see **Section 2.04**, starting on page 25), an upright look helps you visualize the ghost ball and see the angle before dropping your eye level to the final stance (see NV 3.3). Start your stance in an upright position, with the cue stick aligned with the aiming line and your head in the aiming plane, and gradually lower your upper body and head into the stance, keeping your head and gaze in the aiming plane. It helps to move your eyes up and down, between the ghost-ball target and the cue stick, to maintain the correct aiming plane. Align your dominant (aiming) eye with the cue stick along the aiming line and keep your head low and close to the stick during your stroke. Ideally, your chin should be close to touching the cue stick.

normal video

NV 3.3 – Addressing the ball and taking your stance

As you develop your aiming skills and experience-based intuition, you will learn to "see the angles" and might not need to try to visualize the impact line and ghost ball target, but it will still help to methodically line up and aim a shot, using your intuition as a reinforcement.

Section 3.03   *Cue ball path—the 90° rule*

A skill very important for executing basic (and more complex) shots is the ability to predict where the cue ball will go after impact with an object ball. **Figure 3.10** and **Principle 3.3** summarize one of the most important principles of pool related to this—the **90° rule**. It states that when the cue ball strikes an object ball with no topspin or bottom spin, the two balls will always separate at 90°. In other words, the tangent line will be perpendicular to the impact line. This is true regardless of the cut angle (see **Figure 3.10** and NV 3.4).

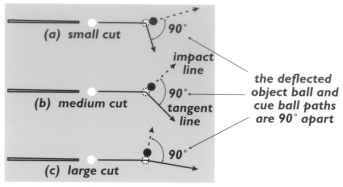

Figure 3.10 90° rule

Principle 3.3 **90° rule**

*With a stun shot where there is no topspin or bottom spin, after impact the cue ball will depart along the tangent line, which is perpendicular (at a right angle) to the impact line. In other words, the cue-ball and object-ball paths, after impact, will be 90° apart (see **Figure 3.10** and NV 3.4).*

- The cue-ball path will exactly coincide with the tangent line only when the cue ball hits the object ball with no topspin (due to follow or normal roll) or bottom spin (draw). **Figure 3.11** shows the type of shots where the 90° rule applies.
- Topspin (e.g., roll) results in angles less than 90°; bottom spin results in angles more than 90° (see **Chapter 4** for more information).
- Sidespin has practically no effect.
- The distance the cue ball travels after impact depends on the cut angle (see **Principle 3.4**).
- Even when the cue ball has top or bottom spin, it will still leave initially along the tangent line before curving due to the spin (see **Section 4.07**, starting on page 115).
- If the cue ball is rolling naturally, a more useful rule is the 30° rule (see the next section).

normal video

NV 3.4 — 90° rule with various entering angles

technical proof

TP 3.1 — 90° rule

The 90° rule applies exactly only for a **stun shot**, where the cue ball is sliding without topspin or bottom spin upon impact with the object ball. **Chapter 4**, (specifically **Section 4.01**, starting on page 80) provides details on spin and English effects, including a description of how and why the cue ball skids and develops normal forward roll (topspin) over time and distance. **Figure 3.11** illustrates some of the cases where the 90° rule applies. For shot *a* in **Figure 3.11** (the top-left shot), the cue ball is close to the object ball, so a center ball hit (or slightly below center) at almost any speed (except very slow) is acceptable because the cue ball will not have time or distance to develop forward roll. For shot *b* (the top-right shot), faster speed is used to ensure that the cue ball does not develop forward roll over the medium cue-ball distance. In shot *c* (the bottom-left shot), draw (bottom spin) is used instead of speed to counteract the effects of forward roll. In shot *d* (the bottom-right shot), both speed and draw are required to offset the forward roll that would normally develop over the larger distance. If you are confused by these examples now, have patience and hopefully the concepts will become clearer in **Chapter 4**.

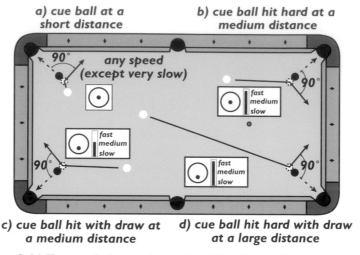

a) cue ball at a short distance

b) cue ball hit hard at a medium distance

c) cue ball hit with draw at a medium distance

d) cue ball hit hard with draw at a large distance

Figure 3.11 Types of shots where the 90° rule applies

Figure 3.12 shows a photograph of a hand shape that can be useful to help you visualize the 90° angle and the tangent-line direction. The index finger points in the direction of the target, along the required impact line, and the thumb indicates the direction of the resulting 90° tangent line. NV 3.5 shows some examples of how it can be used.

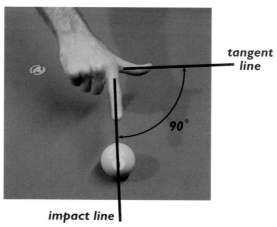

tangent line

90°

impact line

Figure 3.12 Using your hand to visualize the 90° rule impact and tangent lines

normal video

NV 3.5 – Using your hand to visualize the 90° rule impact and tangent lines

The distance the cue ball travels along the tangent line for a stun shot increases with cue ball speed and cut angle (see **Principle 3.4**). **Figure 3.13** shows a graph of object-ball and cue-ball speeds after the cue ball impacts the object ball (see TP 3.2). The speed values are reported as a percentage of the original cue ball speed. The graph shows how the ball speeds vary with cut angle. Notice that for small cut angles, the cue ball loses most of its speed because the speed is transferred to the object ball. At larger cut angles (for thin cut shots), the cue ball retains most of its speed and transfers very little to the object ball. The three vertical lines shown in **Figure 3.13** labeled a, b, and c represent three different cut shots that are illustrated in **Figure 3.14**. Shot a has a cut angle of 20°. According to the graph, at this cut angle the cue ball only retains about 35% of its original speed and the object ball acquires about 95% of the original cue ball speed. These numbers do not add to 100%, but don't fear—the results do not violate the laws of physics (see TP 3.2). The cut angle for shot b is 45°, and the cue ball and object ball both move at the same speed after impact. This is the only cut angle at which this is true. Shot c has a cut angle of 70° and the postimpact ball speed percentages are the opposite of those for shot a. The relative lengths of the arrows in **Figure 3.14** graphically illustrate the postimpact speeds for the three shots. When trying to gage the speed of a shot and predict how far each ball will travel, it is important to have an intuitive feel for the relationships between cue ball and object ball speeds after impact.

Principle 3.4 **Cut-angle speed**

For a stun shot, the speed of the cue ball after object impact increases with cut angle (see **Figure 3.13**).

- The speed also affects the shape of the cue ball path for non-stun shots (see **Section 4.07**, starting on page 115).
- Having an intuitive feel for this principle is important when using speed control for position play (see **Chapter 5**).

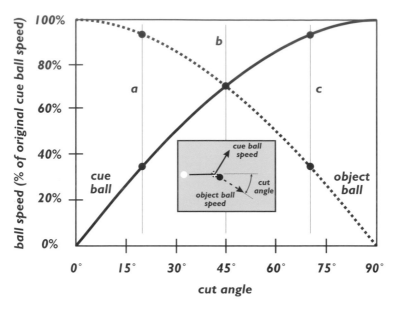

Figure 3.13 Object ball and cue ball speeds versus cut angle

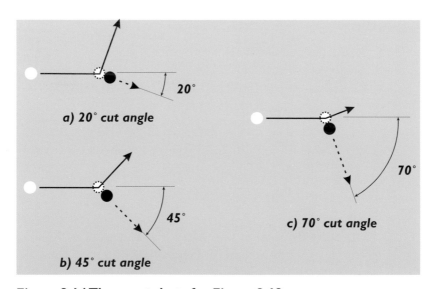

Figure 3.14 Three cut shots for Figure 3.13

technical proof

TP 3.2 – Ball speeds after impact

As pointed out in **Principle 3.3**, topspin and bottom spin deflect the cue ball motion away from the tangent line, and these effects must be taken into consideration. Even when a ball is rolling naturally, and not sliding across the felt, it has topspin that reduces the angle below 90°. These effects are described in detail in **Chapter 4**.

The one exception to the 90° rule is when the cue ball hits the object ball perfectly squarely, with no cut angle. In this case, the cue ball stops completely (i.e., it gets stunned into place), transferring all of its speed to the object ball. This is called a **stop shot** (see HSV 3.1 and HSV 3.2). An example is illustrated in **Figure 3.15** and executed in NV 3.6.

high-speed video

HSV 3.1 — Stop shot showing loss of bottom spin over distance

HSV 3.2 — Stop shot to prevent a scratch

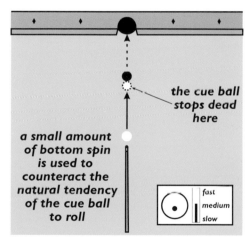

the cue ball stops dead here

a small amount of bottom spin is used to counteract the natural tendency of the cue ball to roll

fast
medium
slow

Figure 3.15 Stop shot example

normal video

NV 3.6 — Stop shot

The 90° rule is very useful for helping you prevent scratches, break up ball clusters, execute carom and billiard shots, and avoid obstacle balls. The scratch example is presented here; and the other examples, which are more advanced, are presented in **Chapter 7**. The 90° rule is also invaluable for planning the path of the cue ball, or any deflected ball, for position play. This topic is addressed in **Section 4.07** and **Chapter 5**.

Figure 3.16 and NV 3.7 show how the 90° rule can be used to help you prevent a scratch. If the object ball is pocketed with a firm stroke or slightly below center, such that the cue ball is sliding (and not rolling) when it contacts the object ball, the 90° rule predicts that the shot will definitely result in a scratch. To prevent the scratch, you need to make sure the cue ball does not hit the object ball with stun. If bottom spin (draw) is used, the cue ball can be directed along path A, avoiding the scratch. A slower stroke, resulting in natural ball roll, or a follow (topspin) shot, would result in path B, which also avoids the scratch. The effects of speed and spin on the cue ball path are presented in detail in **Section 4.07**.

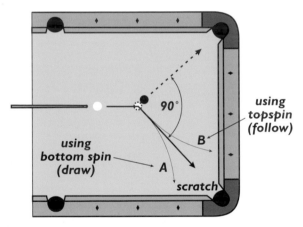

Figure 3.16 Using the 90° rule to check for and prevent a scratch

NV 3.7 – Using the 90° rule to check for and prevent a scratch

normal video

Section 3.04   *Cue ball path—the 30° rule*

As shown in the previous section, the tangent line and the 90° rule are useful for predicting the path of the cue ball when it strikes an object ball with no topspin or bottom spin (i.e., for stun shots). However, with many shots the cue ball is rolling (with topspin) by the time it strikes the object ball (see **Section 4.01**, starting on page 80). So, for many shots, the angle between the cue ball and the object ball will be less than 90°. Another useful rule for helping to predict the path of the cue ball when it is rolling is the **30° rule,** presented in **Principle 3.5** and **Figure 3.17**. It states that if the cue ball hits approximately half of the object ball (see **Figure 3.18**), the cue ball will deflect off at very close to 30° from its original path. Note that, unlike with the 90° rule, the 30° angle is measured between the original cue ball path and the deflected cue ball path. The deflected object-ball direction is not involved. With the 90° rule, the angle is measured between the deflected cue-ball and object-ball paths. An exact **half-ball hit**, where the center of the cue ball is aimed at the edge of the object ball, is illustrated in **Figure 3.18**.

Principle 3.5 **30° rule**

*When the cue ball hits an object ball with normal roll close to a half-ball hit (see **Figure 3.18**), the cue ball will deflect approximately 30° away from its initial aiming line (see **Figure 3.17**).*

- The 30° rule applies only when the cue ball is rolling without skidding at object-ball impact. **Figure 3.21** shows the type of shots where the 30° rule applies.
- The 30° rule is useful for planning carom and billiard shots (see **Section 7.02**, starting on page 205).
- There is a fairly large margin of error (see **Figure 3.19**). In other words, for a fairly large range of ball-hit fractions (see **Figure 3.20**), the cue ball path will still deflect by approximately 30°.
- The largest cue ball deflection (about 34°) occurs for an exact half-ball hit (see **Figure 3.19**).
- The 90° rule (see **Principle 3.3**, above) serves as another point of reference when shooting shots in between stun and normal roll.
- As with the 90° rule, the exact path of the cue ball depends on the speed of the shot (see **Section 4.07**, starting on page 115).

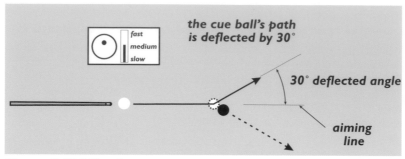

Figure 3.17 30° rule

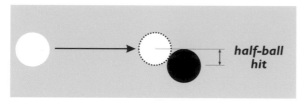

Figure 3.18 Half-ball hit

You might be asking yourself, "How often am I going to be shooting half-ball hits, and is the 30° rule so useful, after all?" Fortunately, as illustrated in **Figure 3.19**, the 30° rule applies over a wide range of ball-hit fractions (see TP 3.3). The center of the range is the half-ball hit, but the cue ball deflection is very close to 30° for ball-hit fractions as small as ¼ and as large as ¾. **Figure 3.20** illustrates the ball-hit-fraction range and corresponding cut angles, to convey the wide range of shots for which the 30° rule applies. With a quarter-ball hit (see **Figure 3.20a**), the center of the cue ball is aimed outside of the object ball edge, such that the projected cue ball path passes through ¼ of the object ball. With a half-ball hit (see **Figure 3.20b**), the center of the cue ball is aimed directly at the edge of the object ball such that the projected cue ball path passes through ½ of the object ball. With a three-quarter-ball hit (see **Figure 3.20c**), the center of the cue ball is aimed inside of the object-ball edge such that the projected cue ball path passes through ¾ of the object ball. These three cases cover a fairly large range of cut angles.

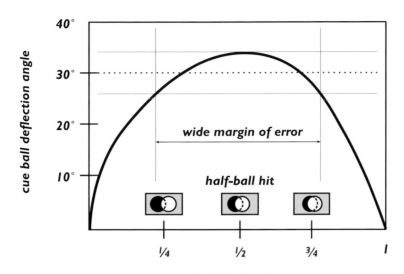

Figure 3.19 Large margin of error for 30° rule

TP 3.3 – 30° rule

technical proof

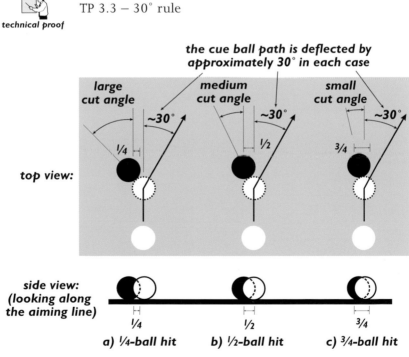

Figure 3.20 Various ball-hit fractions

Figure 3.21 illustrates some of the cases where the 30° rule applies. Remember, it applies only when the cue ball has developed complete forward roll by the time it reaches the object ball, and when the ball-hit fraction is in the approximate range ¼ to ¾. **Chapter 4**, (specifically **Section 4.01**, starting on page 80) provides details on spin and English effects, including a description of how and why the cue ball develops normal forward roll (topspin) over time and distance. For shot *a* in **Figure 3.21** (the top-left shot), the cue ball is close to the object ball, so follow (topspin) is required because the cue ball does not have enough distance and time to develop complete forward roll on its own. For shot *b* (the top-right shot), follow (topspin) is again required because the faster speed does not give the cue ball enough time to develop complete roll. In shot *c* (the bottom-left shot), because the cue ball is hit with slow speed, it will develop forward roll regardless of the English (except extreme draw). In shot *d* (the bottom-right shot), the large cue-ball distance provides enough time for roll to develop for most speeds and English (except fast draw shots). If you are confused by these examples now, have patience and hopefully the concepts will become clearer in **Chapter 4**.

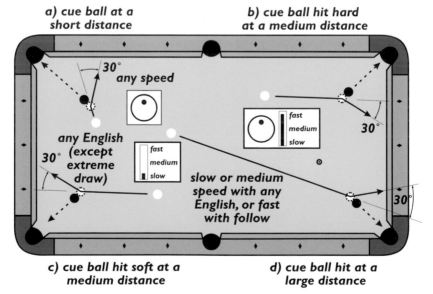

Figure 3.21 Types of shots where the 30° rule applies

To be able to apply the 30° rule effectively, you need to be able to visualize a 30° angle. **Figure 3.22** shows how to use you hand to help with this. For most people, if you form a relaxed but firm V-shape (peace sign or victory symbol) with your index and middle fingers, the angle between your fingers will be very close to 30°. **Figure 3.22**, NV 3.8, and NV 3.9 show how this hand V-shape is used in practice. If you point one of the fingers in the aiming-line direction, the other finger will indicate the direction the cue ball will travel after impact.

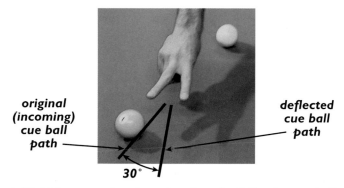

original (incoming) cue ball path

deflected cue ball path

30°

Figure 3.22 Using your hand to visualize the 30° rule cue-ball paths

normal video

NV 3.8 – Using your hand to visualize the 30° rule

When first trying to develop an intuition for the 30° angle, it might be helpful to use a 30°/60°/90° drafting triangle, which you can purchase at an art supply store (see **Figure 3.23**), or a template you can cut out of paper (refer to **Figure 3.24** for the proper proportions). Before making a shot, lay the triangle or template down on the table to help you learn to visualize the 30° angle, as shown in **Figure 3.23** and NV 3.9. **Figure 3.25** shows the example from NV 3.9 graphically. The point of the triangle should be placed at the center of the imaginary ghost-ball target, and one edge should be aligned with the original cue ball path (i.e., the aiming line). The remaining edge then shows the direction of the deflected cue ball path.

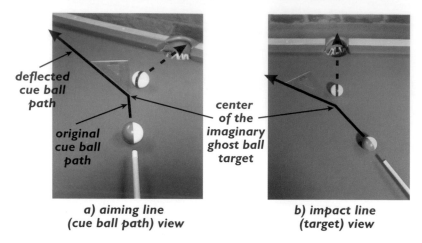

a) aiming line
(cue ball path) view

b) impact line
(target) view

Figure 3.23 Using a drafting triangle to visualize the 30° rule cue-ball path

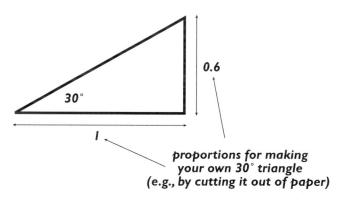

0.6

30°

1

proportions for making
your own 30° triangle
(e.g., by cutting it out of paper)

Figure 3.24 30° angle proportions

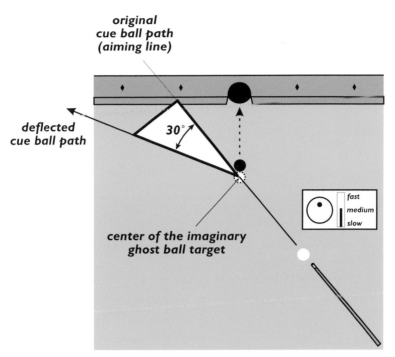

Figure 3.25 Example shot illustrating the 30° rule

    NV 3.9 – 30° rule example

As with the 90° rule, the 30° rule is very useful for helping you prevent scratches, break up ball clusters, execute carom and billiard shots, and avoid obstacle balls. The scratch example is presented here, and the other examples, which are more advanced, are presented in **Chapter 7**. The 30° rule is also invaluable for planning the path of the cue ball for position play. This topic is addressed in **Section 4.07** and **Chapter 5**.

Figure 3.26 and NV 3.10 show how the 30° rule can be used to prevent a scratch. If the object ball is pocketed with a slow stroke, so the cue ball is rolling when it contacts the object ball, the shot will definitely result in a scratch. If the ball is hit with more speed or with a partial stun stroke, the cue ball can be directed along path A or B instead, which avoids the scratch. The effects of speed and spin on the cue ball path are presented in detail in **Section 4.07**.

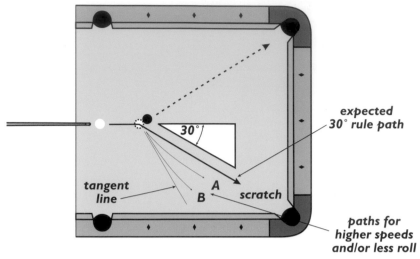

Figure 3.26 Using the 30° rule to check for and prevent a scratch

NV 3.10 – Using the 30° rule to check for and prevent a scratch

Both the 90° rule and the 30° rule can be used to plan carom and billiard shots, where you deflect the cue ball or an object ball off one object ball to pocket another. These shots can be difficult, but if you can accurately predict the angle at which a deflected ball will travel, carom and billiard shots can be useful weapons in your arsenal. **Section 7.02** covers how to plan and execute carom and billiard shots.

Section 3.05   *Basic shot planning*

If you are a good pool player, when you are deciding which ball to hit next, you are planning such that you can make a sequence of shots, not just the one ball you will pocket first. Doing this well requires good position control and strategy, which are described in detail in **Chapter 5**. If you are an inexperienced player and you are playing 8-ball, you will usually want to shoot at the ball that is easiest to pocket. **Principle 3.6** summarizes some points that can help in your shot-decision process. Sometimes, the best choice might not be obvious to an inexperienced player.

Principle 3.6 **The easiest and best shot**

The easiest—and usually the best—shot will be the one with the following attributes:

- The shot is short, the object ball is very close to a pocket, or the cue ball is close to the object ball (but not too close if there is a significant cut angle).
- The cut angle is small (i.e., the cue ball and object ball are lined up fairly well with the target pocket). It is difficult to visualize a shot when the cut angle is large, and cut shots suffer from some unfortunate side effects (see **Section 4.05**, starting on page 105).
- If you are shooting at a side pocket and the angle to the pocket is small (see **Section 3.06**, starting on page 60).
- No English is required to execute the shot. There are many pitfalls associated with using English (see **Chapter 4**).
- The shot can be made without excessive speed (see **Principle 3.7**). The effective target size of a pocket decreases with increased speed (see **Section 3.06**).

Figure 3.27 illustrates various example shots with different levels of difficulty, based on the attributes in **Principle 3.6**. Shot *a* (the top-left shot) is the easiest, because both balls are close to the pocket, and because the shot is lined up perfectly, straight into the pocket. Shot *b* (the top-right shot) is a little more difficult because the cue ball is farther from the object ball and there is a cut angle, but the object ball is still close to the pocket. Shot *c* (the bottom-left shot) is even more difficult because the cue ball is far from the object ball, and the object ball is far from the pocket, with a cut angle involved. Shot *d* is the most difficult, even though the cue ball is close to the object ball and the object ball is close to the pocket. The problem is the cut angle and the angle to the pocket are quite large. Being aware of the things that make a shot difficult can make you better at shot selection. Additional concepts and principles that can help you in selecting a shot, assessing its difficulty, and deciding the best place to aim are presented in Section 3.06 and **Chapter 5**.

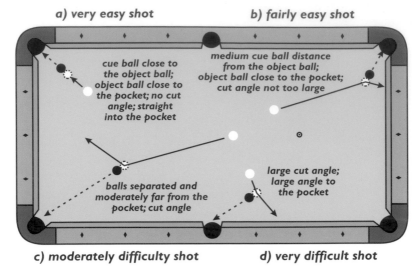

a) very easy shot   **b) fairly easy shot**

cue ball close to
the object ball;
object ball close to
the pocket; no cut
angle; straight
into the pocket

medium cue ball distance
from the object ball;
object ball close to the pocket;
cut angle not too large

balls separated and
moderately far from the
pocket; cut angle

large cut angle;
large angle to
the pocket

c) moderately difficulty shot   **d) very difficult shot**

Figure 3.27 Shot examples with various levels of difficulty

Once you have determined which ball you wish to pocket next, you should methodically follow a routine to ensure you take everything into consideration. It is important to make sure you have the shot completely planned before executing your stroke. You should not take your stance and start your practice strokes until you are completely sure about your shot. It is important that your mind be settled before the stroke so you can concentrate fully on executing the shot.

A recommended routine for planning and executing a shot follows (see NV 3.11):

1. **Choose the object ball and the target** based on **Principle 3.6** and, for more advanced play, the principles presented in **Chapter 5**.

2. **Determine exactly where you want the object ball to go** based on the information in Section 3.06 concerning effective target size and the pocket center.

3. Survey the shot and **visualize the target direction, aiming line, contact point, and ghost-ball target** (see Section 3.02, starting on page 35).

4. **Check for a possible scratch** using the 90° rule (see

Principle 3.3 on page 42) or the 30° rule (see **Principle 3.5** on page 49).

5. **Decide on any English** you might require to alter the cue ball path (see **Chapter 4** for more information), but avoid English when possible, because it makes the shot more difficult to control.

6. **Decide on the speed,** based on the desired cue ball position for the next shot. Always try to use as little speed as possible (see **Principle 3.7** and **Chapter 5**).

7. **Select a bridge** and take your stance, using the "best practices" presented in **Section 2.03**, starting on page 21, and **Section 2.04**, starting on page 25.

8. **Execute your stroke** using the best practices presented in **Section 2.05**, starting on page 27.

9. During the shot, be confident and remove any doubt or indecision from your mind. If you have already considered all of the shot elements above, you can now **dedicate all of your focus to executing the shot** to the best of your ability. ("Be the ball!")

normal video

NV 3.11 – Following the recommended routine for planning and executing a shot

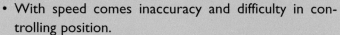

Principle 3.7 **Slow accuracy**

SLOW

Always use as little speed as possible to execute a shot.

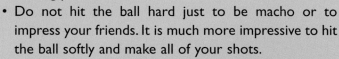

- With speed comes inaccuracy and difficulty in controlling position.
- Do not hit the ball hard just to be macho or to impress your friends. It is much more impressive to hit the ball softly and make all of your shots.
- A possible exception warranting extra speed is a break-up shot (see **Section 5.05**, starting on page 147).

Section 3.06 *Effective pocket size and center*

An important factor that might affect your decisions in shot planning is how the effective target size and center vary with different angles to the pocket. The remainder of this chapter presents an analysis of these issues. **Figure 3.28**, **Figure 3.29**, **Figure 3.30**, and **Figure 3.31** illustrate the basic terminology important for understanding shot difficulty. Important factors in determining the difficulty of a shot are the distance between the object ball and the pocket (see **Principle 3.8**) and the angle of the object-ball path from the pocket centerline. As illustrated in **Figure 3.28**, when the distance to the pocket is smaller, there is a much larger **margin of error**, which is a measure of how much the object-ball angle can vary from the target center and still enter the pocket. The **angle to the pocket**, as shown in **Figure 3.29**, is measured from the pocket centerline (straight-in) direction. As this angle gets larger, a shot becomes more difficult, because the effective size of the pocket gets smaller at larger angles. **Figure 3.29** also shows how the angle-to-pocket error is measured to define the margin of error.

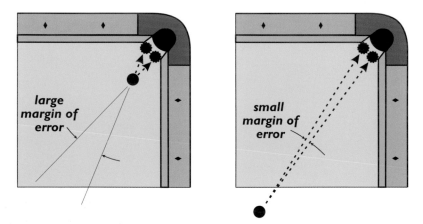

Figure 3.28 Margin of error of object-ball angle, based on distance to the pocket

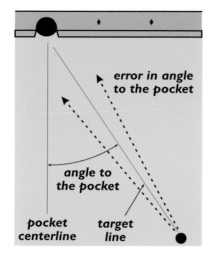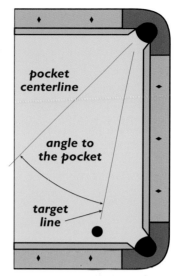

Figure 3.29 Angle to the pocket, and error in angle to the pocket

---

Principle 3.8 **Closer to the pocket is better**

*The margin of error decreases dramatically as the distance to the pocket increases (see **Figure 3.28**).*

• See TP 3.4 for the detailed analysis.

---

technical proof

TP 3.4 – Margin of error based on distance

Figure 3.30 illustrates two extreme object-ball target positions that result in pocketing the ball in a side pocket, for a given angle to the pocket. These positions define the effective **target size** and **target center** of the pocket. The target size is the distance between the two extreme target-position object-ball paths. The target center is the imaginary line between the two extreme position-target lines. The **offset** is the distance between the target center and the imaginary line through the pocket center. For a straight-in shot, where the angle to the pocket is 0°, the offset would be zero and the effective target center is the same as the pocket center.

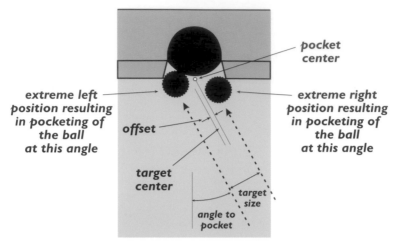

Figure 3.30 Effective target size and center for a side pocket

There are several differences between the side and corner pockets. As described in **Principle 3.9**, the most important difference is that the side pockets are bigger! However, with the corner pockets the object ball can deflect off the near rail and still enter the pocket. This increases the effective target size for the corner pocket at some angles, especially at slower speeds (see **Figure 3.31** and **Principle 3.10**).

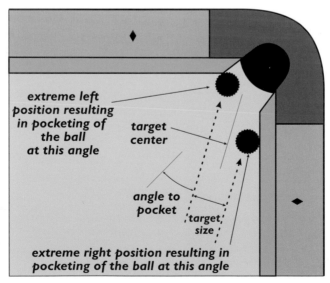

Figure 3.31 Effective target size and center for a corner pocket

Principle 3.9 **The side pockets are bigger**

The side pockets are bigger than the corner pockets.

- From point to point across the mouth of the pocket, a side-pocket opening (approximately 5 ½ inches) is larger than a corner-pocket opening (approximately 5 inches).
- The effective target size can be bigger for corner pockets for balls hit softly at shallow angles to the rail (see **Principle 3.10**).
- For straight-in shots that must be hit hard, the side pockets are "bigger" (see **Figure 3.39** on page 71).

Principle 3.10 **The corner pocket is sometimes "bigger" than the side pocket**

*The effective target size of the corner pocket for a slow hit is larger for shots adjacent to the rail than for straight-in shots (see **Figure 3.37** on page 69).*

- When the ball is hit harder, the ball is more prone to rattle out, especially if the near rail is glanced first (see **Principle 3.12**).

When shooting at a side pocket, care must be taken to avoid hitting the **near point** (see **Principle 3.11** and NV 3.12). As illustrated in **Figure 3.32** and **Figure 3.33**, this is particularly important for a higher speed shot. The near point must be avoided at high speed because contact with the point imparts significant sidespin to the ball, which causes the ball to deflect out of the pocket (see **Section 6.05**, starting on page 194 for more information). The sidespin is illustrated by the curved arrow in **Figure 3.32** and **Figure 3.33a**. In this case, the point imparts left (clockwise) spin on the ball.

Principle 3.11 **With a side pocket, avoid hitting the near point**

When aiming at a side pocket from an angle, adjust your aim away from the near point (see **Figure 3.32** *and* **Figure 3.33***).*

- Point contact causes rail-induced English (see **Section 6.05**) that causes the ball to rattle out of the pocket (see HSV 3.3).
- As illustrated in **Figure 3.30**, the target center is to the left of the pocket center, away from the near point.
- This advice is most important at higher speeds, but it should also be heeded at lower speeds.

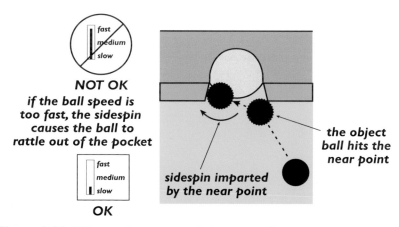

NOT OK
if the ball speed is too fast, the sidespin causes the ball to rattle out of the pocket

OK

the object ball hits the near point

sidespin imparted by the near point

Figure 3.32 Side-pocket near-point speed effect

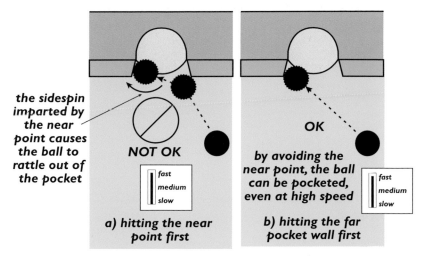

the sidespin imparted by the near point causes the ball to rattle out of the pocket

NOT OK

| fast |
| medium |
| slow |

a) hitting the near point first

OK

by avoiding the near point, the ball can be pocketed, even at high speed

| fast |
| medium |
| slow |

b) hitting the far pocket wall first

Figure 3.33 Avoiding side-pocket near-point for fast shots

normal video

NV 3.12 – Side-pocket near-point effects

high-speed video

HSV 3.3 – Side-pocket miss due to near-point deflection

HSV 3.4 – Side-pocket miss off far-pocket wall

HSV 3.5 – Side-pocket near miss due to wall rattle

HSV 3.6 – Side-pocket rattle out

When shooting at a corner pocket, care must be taken to avoid hitting the near rail or point (see **Principle 3.12**). As illustrated in **Figure 3.34** and **Figure 3.35**, this is particularly important for a higher speed shot. As with the side-pocket near-point effect described above, the rail imparts significant sidespin to the ball at higher speeds, which causes the ball to rattle out of the pocket.

Principle 3.12 **Corner-pocket rattle**

When shooting fast at a corner pocket, avoid hitting the near rail or point of the pocket (see **Figure 3.35***); otherwise, the ball will rattle out (see NV 3.13, NV 3.14, and HSV 3.8).*

- The rattle-out is due to rail-induced English (see **Section 7.06**).
- Rattle is of little or no concern when the ball is hit softly (see **Figure 3.34**). For soft shots, the effective pocket size is large because you can contact the rail far in front of the pocket (see NV 3.15).

Figure 3.34 Corner pocket-near rail speed effect

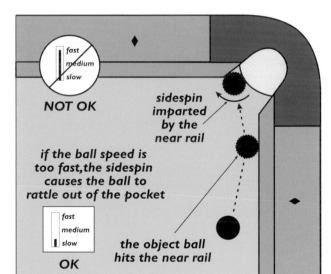

- 66 -

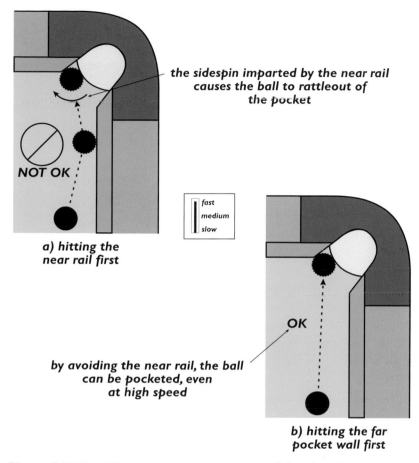

a) hitting the near rail first

the sidespin imparted by the near rail causes the ball to rattleout of the pocket

NOT OK

fast
medium
slow

by avoiding the near rail, the ball can be pocketed, even at high speed

OK

b) hitting the far pocket wall first

Figure 3.35 Avoiding corner-pocket near-rail for fast shots

Figure 3.36 illustrates a shot where knowledge of the corner-pocket near-rail speed effect (**Figure 3.34**) can be used to your advantage. To an inexperienced player, it might appear hopeless to pocket the solid in the corner pocket, because the obstacle stripe blocks the direct path to the pocket. However, by deflecting off the near rail with slow enough speed, the ball can be pocketed. If the speed were too high, the rail would impart significant sidespin to the ball, causing it to rattle out of the pocket (see **Principle 3.12**).

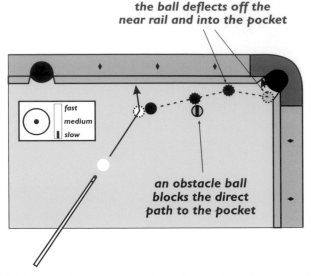

Figure 3.36 Example corner-pocket shot using slow speed off the near rail

normal video

NV 3.13 – Corner-pocket near-rail effects

NV 3.14 – Near-rail rattle

NV 3.15 – Large target size for shallow-angle rail shots

high-speed video

HSV 3.7 – Corner-pocket in, off near point

HSV 3.8 – Corner-pocket miss due to near-rail deflection

All of the principles and effects concerning pocket target information presented above can be summarized with a collection of graphs, generated from technical analyses (see TP 3.5–TP 3.12). **Figure 3.37** shows the results for the effective target size for slow shots into both side and corner pockets, as a function of the angle to the pocket. Notice that the side pocket has the largest effective target size at small angles to the pocket, but the size falls off dramatically as the angle from the center increases (see **Principle 3.13**). Notice that the corner-pocket effective target size is smaller than the side pocket for most pocket angles, but the corner pockets are more favorable at shallow angles to the rails (close to 40° from the pocket center). This effect is due to the ball's ability to go in after hitting the rail (see **Figure 3.34** and **Figure 3.36**), increasing the effective size of the pocket (see NV 3.15).

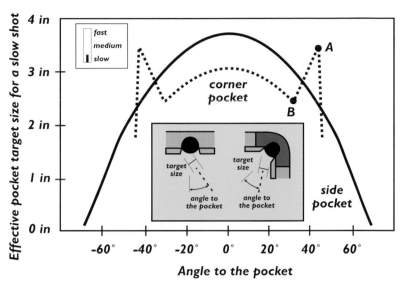

Figure 3.37 Effective pocket target sizes for a slow shot, based on the angle to the pocket

Principle 3.13 **Beware of large side-pocket angles**

*The side-pocket effective target size (and margin of error) decreases dramatically as the angle to the pocket increases (see **Figure 3.37**).*

- When the ball is hit harder, the effective size is even smaller (see **Figure 3.39**).

technical proof

TP 3.5 – Effective target sizes for slow shots into a side pocket at different angles

TP 3.6 – Effective target sizes for slow shots into a corner pocket at different angles

To help visualize some of the conclusions you can draw from **Figure 3.37**, **Figure 3.38** illustrates the shot directions for the two points labeled A and B on the corner pocket curve in **Figure 3.37**. Point A corresponds to an angle to the pocket of about 43°, and the effective pocket target size for that angle is about 3.4 inches. This is the largest effective pocket size compared to all other angles to the pocket; therefore, shots from that direction are the easiest to make in the corner pocket at slow speeds. Point B corresponds to an angle to the pocket of about 31° and the effective pocket target size for that angle is about 2.4 inches. This is much smaller (30% less) than the size for point A, so shots along the point B direction are much more (30% more) difficult to convert at slow speeds.

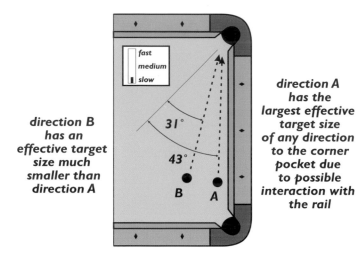

Figure 3.38 Example points from the graph in Figure 3.37

Figure 3.39 shows the results for the effective target size for fast shots into both side and corner pockets, as a function of the angle to the pocket. Notice that both pockets have the largest effective target size at small angles to the pocket. The size still falls off dramatically for the side pocket as the angle is increased. But the corner pocket effective size is still smaller for all angles to the pocket. This is because near-rail deflections result in missed shots at high speeds (see **Principle 3.12** on page 66). Also, by comparing **Figure 3.39** to **Figure 3.37**, you can see that the effective target size of a pocket is smaller at higher speeds (see **Principle 3.14**).

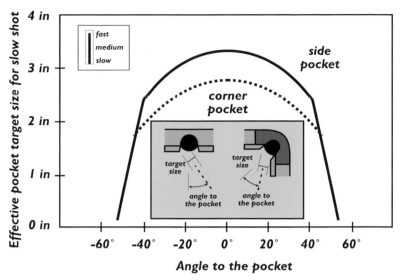

Figure 3.39 Effective pocket target sizes for a fast shot, based on the angle to the pocket

 technical proof

TP 3.7 – Effective target sizes for fast shots into a side pocket at different angles

TP 3.8 – Effective target sizes for fast shots into a corner pocket at different angles

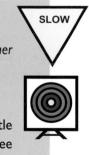

Principle 3.14 **Slower speed, bigger pockets**

*The effective target sizes of a pocket decrease at higher speeds (see **Figure 3.37** and **Figure 3.39**).*

- You must be more accurate for faster shots.
- When the ball is hit harder, it is more prone to rattle out, especially if the near rail is glanced first (see **Principle 3.11** and **Principle 3.12**).

The analyses used to create the plots above also quantify the target-center offsets that describe how far away from the pocket center you should aim. The detailed analyses and results can be found in TP 3.9. The most important conclusions are summarized in **Principle 3.15**.

TP 3.9 – Pocket-target center offsets, based on angle to the pocket

---

Principle 3.15 **Pocket center**

The center of the pocket is not always the best place to aim.

- You should aim at the geometric center of the pocket opening only for straight-in shots. For shots approaching the pocket at an angle, adjust your aim from the center towards the far-inside wall of the pocket (see **Figure 3.30** on page 62).
- Hitting the near rail or near point creates rail-induced English that can cause the ball to rattle out of the pocket, especially at high speed (see HSV 3.3 through HSV 3.8).
- Sometimes it is desirable to cheat the pocket (see **Principle 5.8** on page 137) when you have a straight-in shot but need deflection of the cue ball away from the impact line. English-induced throw can also be used to help cheat the aiming direction (see **Section 7.04**, starting on page 214).

Section 3.07   *Shot margins of error*

Using the concepts and graphs presented in the previous section, the allowable margin of error for different distances from the pocket can be predicted (see TP 3.10 and TP 3.11). **Figure 3.40** through **Figure 3.43** are plots of the results for side and corner pockets at slow and fast speeds. The **object-ball angle error** is a measure of the required shooting accuracy. For example, a margin of error of 3° implies that the object ball can be pocketed with an error in the target-line angle of as much as 3°. In the figures, if the object ball lies on or within one of the angle-error curves, then the object ball can be pocketed as long as the shot angle error is no more than the value reported. These plots combine the distance-to-the-pocket effects with the target-size effects into one illustration. All conclusions and results presented in the previous section can be seen graphically in these plots. The two shots (A and B) illustrated in **Figure 3.40** help illustrate the type of conclusions you can make. Neither shot has a cut angle, and both are the same distance from the pocket. However, the object-ball margins of error are quite different: 3° for shot A and 1.5° for shot B. Therefore, shot B would be twice as difficult as shot A to execute successfully.

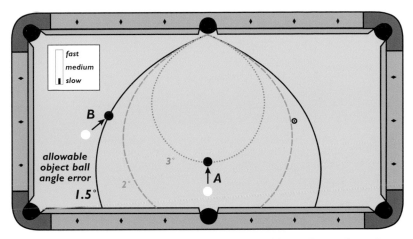

Figure 3.40 Side-pocket margin-of-error regions for a slow shot

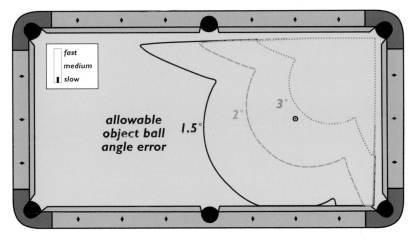

Figure 3.41 Corner-pocket margin-of-error regions for a slow shot

technical proof

TP 3.10 – Pocket margin-of-error regions for a slow shot

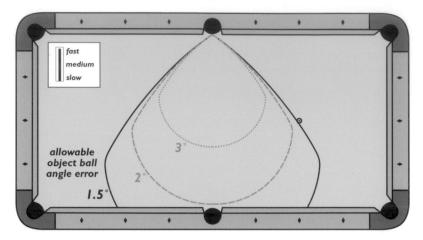

Figure 3.42 Side-pocket margin-of-error regions for a fast shot

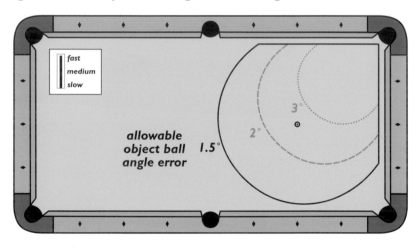

Figure 3.43 Corner-pocket margin-of-error regions for a fast shot

TP 3.11 – Pocket margin-of-error regions for a fast shot

technical proof

Figure 3.44 and **Figure 3.45** illustrate how the figures above can be useful in helping you understand shot selection. **Figure 3.44** shows two different object ball positions, both of which have the same cut angle and distance to the corner pocket. The question is which shot would be easier, assuming that either shot would create equally good position for the next shot. An inexperienced player might think each shot is equally easy (or difficult). However, as shown by the curves, shot A would be easier to execute because its margin of error is 2° versus 1.5° for shot B. That means shot A would be 33% easier than shot B.

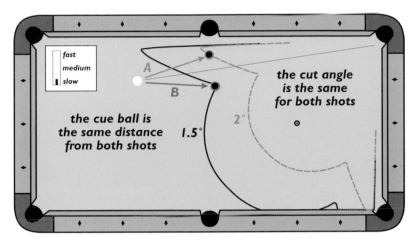

Figure 3.44 Choosing a shot based on the margins of error

Figure 3.45 shows an example where you need to decide between a corner- or side-pocket shot for a given object-ball location. Three different object-ball locations (A, B, and C) are shown. For each of these shots, the cut angle to the side pocket is the same as the cut angle to the corner pocket. Then how do you decide which pocket is easier to shoot at? With the margin-of-error regions shown, the answer is clear for each object-ball position. Position A is within the corner pocket region and outside of the side pocket region; therefore, the corner pocket is the clear best choice. Position B is within both regions and equally close to each region boundary; in this case, both pockets have the same level of difficulty, so you should pick the one that feels most comfortable. Position C is well within the side-pocket region and just outside of the corner-pocket region; therefore, the side pocket is the clear best choice.

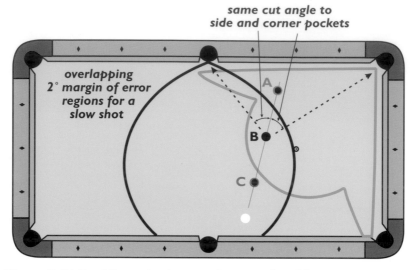

Figure 3.45 Deciding whether to shoot at the side or corner pocket

The margin-of-error region plots above concern **object-ball angle error**, which corresponds to how close the object-ball path needs to be to the target line. As **Figure 3.46** illustrates, the allowable **cue-ball angle error**, measured relative to the desired aiming line, needs to be even more accurate than that. Furthermore, a shot's difficulty increases as the distance between the object ball and the pocket increases, as the distance from the cue ball to the object ball increases (see **Principle 3.16**), and as the cut angle increases (see **Principle 3.17**). If all three measures increase together, the difficulty level increases and your margin of error decreases dramatically. A detailed analysis and plots showing the effects of cue ball distance, cut angle, and cut-angle error can be found in TP 3.12.

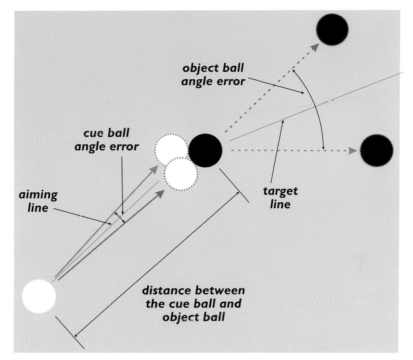

Figure 3.46 Cut-angle error and object-ball angle error

Principle 3.16 **Closer to the object ball is better**

The margin of error decreases dramatically as the distance between the cue ball and object ball increases (see TP 3.12).

- The margin of error also decreases with distance between the object ball and the target (see **Principle 3.8** on page 61).
- The margin of error also decreases with cut angle (see **Principle 3.17**).

Principle 3.17 **Smaller cut angle is much better**

The margin of error decreases dramatically as the cut angle increases (see TP 3.12).

- The margin of error also decreases with distance between the object ball and the target (see **Principle 3.8** on page 61).
- The margin of error also decreases with distance between the cue ball and object ball (see **Principle 3.16**).

technical proof

TP 3.12 – Object ball angle error, based on cut angle

Chapter 4
Spin and English

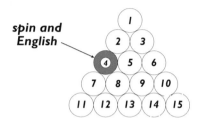

spin and
English

Welcome to the amazing and wonderful world of spin and English, where you hit the cue ball off-center to achieve desirable effects. If English is a new concept to you, you will marvel at the possibilities it creates. Learning and applying the principles in this chapter can help propel you to a new plateau of ability. However, as you learn, keep in mind that you should avoid English whenever possible. If you watch a truly great player when they are playing at the top of their game, it seems like all of their shots are easy. Well, that's true. A top-notch player is so good with fundamentals, speed control, and strategy, that they deliberately and skillfully leave themselves with an easy shot after every shot, rarely having to use significant English or other more advanced skills.

This chapter presents everything you need to know about spin and English, and the effects they have on aim, cue ball trajectory, and object ball motion. Before you proceed with this and later chapters, all of which cover increasingly more difficult concepts and techniques, it is important that you have practiced and are comfortable with all the materials and techniques presented in previous chapters. You need to be able to aim and stroke reliably, and to predict where the cue ball and object ball will go. Only after you have truly mastered the fundamentals can you advance your level of play to your highest potential.

Section 4.01   *Introduction*

Figure 4.1 illustrates the terminology used to describe spin and English. When you strike the cue ball exactly in the center, it will initially slide across the felt with no spin or rotation at all, creating what is called a **stun shot**. When the cue ball is struck above center, the result is called a **follow** or **topspin** shot. When the cue ball is struck below center, the result is called a **draw,** or **bottom spin,** or **backspin** shot. When the cue ball is struck to the left or right of center, the cue ball is given left or right sidespin called **English**. The term English can also be used to refer to any spin (left or right sidespin, topspin, or bottom spin) given to the cue ball, but usually it only refers to **sidespin**. Sometimes the term **vertical plane English** is used to describe follow and draw shots because they are created by moving the cue stick up or down (vertically), and the term **horizontal plane English** is used to refer to shots with sidespin English because they require moving the stick left or right (horizontally).

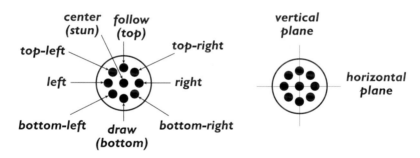

Figure 4.1 Types of English

Figure 4.2 and **Figure 4.3** illustrate the effects of vertical-plane and horizontal-plane English. Top English (follow) causes the cue ball to spin in the rolling direction. The spin can be faster than the normal topspin resulting from pure rolling. Bottom English (draw) causes the cue ball to slide across the felt with spin in a direction opposite from the normal rolling spin. **Left English** gives the cue ball clockwise (CW) spin and **right English** gives the cue ball counterclockwise (CCW) spin. The sidespin is retained and combines with the topspin that develops as the ball begins to roll.

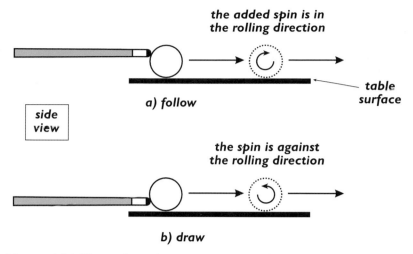

a) follow

the added spin is in
the rolling direction

side view

table surface

the spin is against
the rolling direction

b) draw

Figure 4.2 Effect of vertical-plane English (viewed from the side)

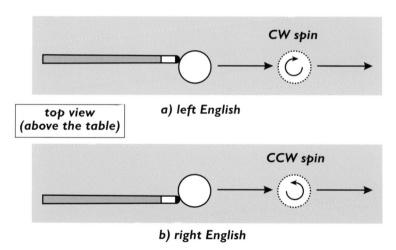

a) left English

top view
(above the table)

CW spin

b) right English

CCW spin

Figure 4.3 Effect of horizontal-plane English (viewed from above)

The biggest challenges in applying English are learning how far away from center to strike the ball and how hard to strike. In all cases, good tip preparation (see **Section 2.01**, starting on page 16) and straight follow-through are very important. Intuition for how far to hit the cue ball off-center and for the appropriate speed to use can come only with practice; but in general, the farther off-center and the faster you hit the ball, the more spin you impart. Commercially available practice balls (e.g., the Elephant Practice Ball shown in **Figure 4.4** [see more information at **www.elephantballs.com**]) can be useful in practicing your off-center adjustments, because they include a circle and target. After a shot, you can note the location of the chalk mark on the target to help you correlate the spot location to the shot reaction.

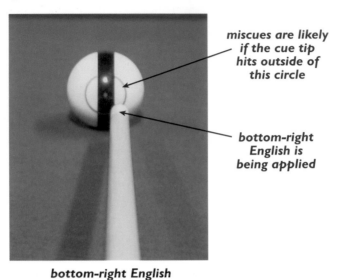

miscues are likely
if the cue tip
hits outside of
this circle

bottom-right
English is
being applied

bottom-right English

Figure 4.4 Elephant Practice Ball with an English circle

Throughout the book, the type of English being used for a particular example (e.g., bottom-right English, shown in **Figure 4.4**) is illustrated graphically as shown in **Figure 4.5**. In this case, the cue stick on the right is shown impacting the cue ball to the right of center, and the spin diagram on the left shows that, in addition to right English, bottom English (draw) is also being used.

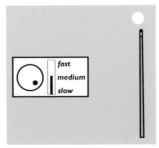

fast
medium
slow

Figure 4.5 Example of how English is illustrated

When using follow and draw, it is important to understand how the spin changes as the cue ball slides on the table cloth. The spin associated with follow and draw shots degrades as the cue ball travels. The harder you hit the shot, the longer the spin will persist, but most soft to medium shots with little or no English will eventually end up with pure **normal roll** where there is no longer any overrotation or **sliding** (aka slipping or skidding) between the cue ball and the cloth (see TP 4.1). When the cue ball hits a rail, the spin is altered (see **Section 6.05** and **Section 7.08**), but for now we will only consider cue ball motion before rail contact. **Figure 4.6** illustrates how vertical-plane spin is eventually transformed into normal roll for different types of vertical-plane-English shots (see **Principle 4.1**). With a center-ball hit (**Figure 4.6a**) the cue ball is initially sliding without rolling, but the sliding on the felt gradually builds up topspin to the point of normal roll. The increasing topspin is illustrated in the figure by the lengthening of the curved arrows. The speed of the cue ball slows as the cue ball slides. This is illustrated in the figure by the shortening of the straight arrows. Once the cue ball reaches normal roll, the roll persists until the ball slows to a stop. With a draw shot (**Figure 4.6b**) it takes a little longer for roll to develop; but eventually, all of the bottom spin is lost, creating stun, which then degrades to normal roll. With a follow shot (**Figure 4.6c**) the topspin degrades to normal roll; however, unlike with stun and draw, the speed actually increases, because the topspin is turning and sliding in the direction to create the normal roll. The draw shot takes the longest to reach normal roll because its spin first degrades to stun, and then to roll. **Figure 4.7** illustrates the forces in action to create the accelerating or slowing effects of the sliding. The forces from the cloth acting on the ball always oppose the direction of the sliding motion. Only when the ball is rolling naturally is there no sliding force.

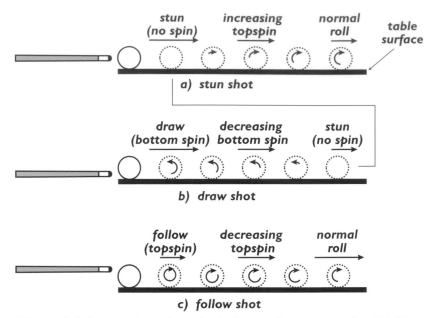

a) stun shot

b) draw shot

c) follow shot

Figure 4.6 Conversion of vertical-plane spin to normal roll (side view)

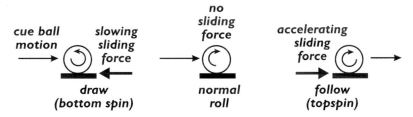

Figure 4.7 Sliding forces due to vertical-plane spin

Principle 4.1 **Normal roll**

*The cue ball gradually develops normal roll as it slides along the felt (see **Figure 4.6**).*

- This is true regardless of what type of vertical-plane English the ball has (draw, follow, or stun).
- Normal roll gives a ball the effects of a follow shot (see Section 4.03).

high-speed video HSV 3.1 – Stop shot showing loss of bottom spin over distance

technical proof TP 4.1 –Time and distance required to develop normal roll

When a ball is rolling naturally, it actually exhibits the effects of a follow shot (see Section 4.03), and you must be aware of this fact. Therefore, to hit a true stun or draw shot, you need to make sure that you hit the cue ball hard enough, and enough below center, so the cue ball will still have the desired spin by the time it reaches the object ball (see **Figure 4.6**). For longer shots, the only way to prevent follow effects is to hit the cue ball hard and below center.

As was illustrated in **Figure 4.6a**, if you use a center-ball hit, the cue ball slides at first, before it begins to roll. If you hit the cue ball at a certain height above center, it is possible to have the cue ball begin normal roll immediately. This could be important if you are trying to control the cue ball path with the aid of the 30° rule (see **Principle 3.5** on page 49). The technical name for the **normal-roll impact height** is the **center of percussion** (see TP 4.2). As illustrated in **Figure 4.8** and summarized in **Principle 4.2**, the height is 70% (i.e., ⁷⁄₁₀ of the ball diameter) above the table surface, which corresponds to 20% (i.e., ⅕ of the diameter) above the ball center. Cue-ball contact-heights below or above this point result in skidding or sliding before normal roll develops (see **Figure 4.6**).

normal roll

70%

Figure 4.8 Impact height for normal roll

technical proof TP 4.2 – Center of percussion of the cue ball

Principle 4.2 **Immediate cue ball roll**

*To have the cue ball roll immediately after impact, hit the ball above center at 7/10 of the ball's height above the table (see **Figure 4.8**).*

- If the cue ball is hit above or below this height, topspin, bottom spin, or stun is imparted and the cue ball over-rotates or slides some before rolling (see **Figure 4.6**).
- The technical term for the normal-roll impact height is the "center of percussion" (see TP 4.2).

Section 4.02   *Draw shot*

With a **draw shot**, the cue ball is struck below center to impart bottom spin. As illustrated in **Figure 4.9**, the effect of the bottom spin is to change the path of the cue ball after striking the object ball. Draw increases the angle between the final paths of the object ball and cue ball (i.e., the cue ball is "drawn" back). The harder the shot is hit, the longer the cue ball persists along the tangent line before curving; and the more bottom spin the ball has, the more it will curve (see more details in Section 4.07, starting on page 115). A draw shot is useful when you need to alter the path of the cue ball to avoid a scratch, achieve good position for the next shot, avoid hitting other balls, or purposely hit other balls. Scratch avoidance is described in this section and the other strategies are presented in **Chapter 5**.

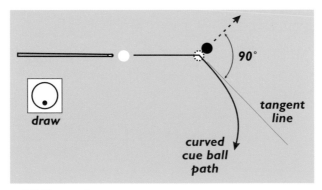

Figure 4.9 Draw shot

When there is very little or no bottom spin on the cue ball when it hits the object ball, the result is a **stun shot**. With a stun shot, the cue ball travels exactly along the tangent line 90° away from the object-ball path (see NV 4.1) as predicted by the 90° rule (see **Principle 3.3** on page 42).

normal video NV 4.1 – Stun shot

Figure 4.10 and NV 4.2 illustrate how a draw shot can be used to avoid a scratch. In this example, a stun shot resulting from a firm stroke or slight draw would cause the cue ball to travel straight along the tangent-line path into the pocket. (That's bad.) The draw causes the cue ball path to curve as shown instead, avoiding the scratch.

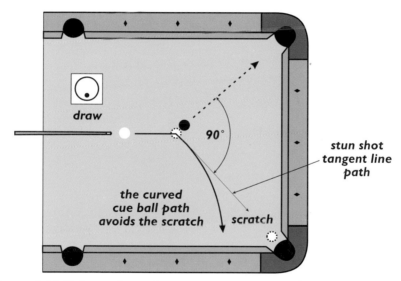

Figure 4.10 Using a draw shot to prevent a scratch

normal video NV 4.2 – Using a draw shot to prevent a scratch

Principle 4.3 summarizes the technique required for a good draw stroke. The most important attribute is follow-through. Many people try to elevate the stick and chop at the ball when shooting a draw shot.

This might be effective for short shots requiring little draw; however, in general, this is very poor technique. You should strive to keep the stick level and accelerate through the ball.

Principle 4.3 **Good draw**

A good draw shot with significant draw action is achieved with the following technique:

- Make sure the cue tip is in good condition (see **Section 2.01** on page 16).
- Keep the cue stick level during the entire stroke. Do not elevate the cue stick.
- Accelerate through the ball, and follow through straight and well past the cue ball starting location. Do not chop, jab, or poke at the ball. Accelerating through the ball keeps the cue tip in contact with the cue ball a little longer, allowing it to impart more spin.
- Hit the ball lower and softer (and level) rather than higher (but below center) and harder. This results in better control. Also, the slower speed might be required for position control for the next shot.
- An open hand bridge (see **Section 2.03** on page 21) can allow a better draw stroke because the cue stick can be stroked lower and more levelly.
- For longer shots, you need more spin or speed so some spin remains at object ball impact (see **Principle 4.1** on page 84).
- Draw shots are difficult to execute with a mechanical bridge or if the cue ball is close to a rail (mostly due to limitations on cue stick levelness and follow-through), so be cautious in these situations.

For a straight-on shot, where the cut angle is $0°$, the cue ball does not move at all along the tangent line. In this case, a draw shot will result in the cue ball coming straight back from the object ball, toward from where the cue ball was hit (see NV 4.3 and HSV 4.1). A special case of a straight-on draw shot is a **stop shot,** where the bottom spin wears off on the way to the object ball such that the cue ball has very little or no bottom spin at impact (see HSV 3.1 and **Figure 4.6b** on page 84). In this case, the cue ball comes to a complete stop after hitting the object ball (see NV 3.6 and HSV 3.2).

NV 4.3 – Straight-on draw shot

NV 3.6 – Stop shot

normal video

HSV 4.1 – Draw shot

HSV 3.1 – Stop shot showing loss of bottom spin over distance

high-speed video

HSV 3.2 – Stop shot to prevent a scratch

As summarized in **Principle 4.4**, a valuable application of draw is creating a slow stun shot that results in the least possible motion of the cue ball after impact with the object ball. This can be useful when you do not want the cue ball to move much after object-ball contact in preparation for the next shot (see NV 4.4). This type of shot is called a **kill shot**.

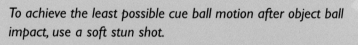

Principle 4.4 **Minimum cue ball motion**

To achieve the least possible cue ball motion after object ball impact, use a soft stun shot.

- With a stun shot, all of the cue ball speed in the direction of the impact line is lost.
- To achieve a soft stun, you must hit the cue ball very low and softly (but hard enough) so the skidding on the table cloth slows the ball and results in stun (see **Figure 4.6b**) at the point of impact with the object ball.

NV 4.4 – Using draw to minimize deflected motion of cue ball

normal video

Section 4.03   *Follow shot*

With a **follow shot**, the cue ball is struck above center to impart topspin. As illustrated in **Figure 4.11**, the effect of the topspin is to change the path of the cue ball after striking the object ball. Follow decreases the angle between the final paths of the object ball and cue ball. The harder the shot is hit, the longer the cue ball persists along the tangent line before curving; and the more topspin the ball has, the more it will curve (see more details in Section 4.07, starting on page 115). A follow shot is useful when you need to alter the path of the cue ball to avoid a scratch, achieve good position for the next shot, avoid hitting other balls, or purposely hit other balls. Scratch avoidance is described in this section, and the other strategies are presented in **Chapter 5**.

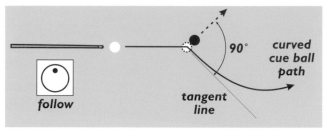

Figure 4.11 Follow shot

Figure 4.12 and NV 4.5 illustrate how a follow shot can be used to avoid a scratch. In this example, a stun shot, resulting from a firm stroke or slight draw, would cause the cue ball to travel straight along the tangent-line path into the pocket. (That's bad.) The follow causes the cue ball path to curve as shown instead, avoiding the scratch.

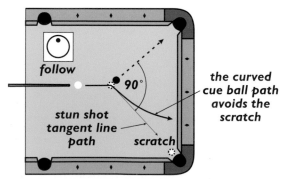

Figure 4.12 Using a follow shot to prevent a scratch

normal video
NV 4.5 – Using a follow shot to prevent a scratch

Principle 4.5 summarizes the technique required for a good follow stroke. As with the draw shot, the most important attribute is good follow-through. Also, try to keep the stick level, and accelerate through the ball.

Principle 4.5 **Good follow**

A good follow shot, with significant follow action, is achieved with the following technique:

- Make sure the cue tip is in good condition (see **Section 2.01** on page 16).
- Keep the cue stick level during the entire stroke.
- Accelerate through the ball, and follow through straight, well past the cue-ball starting location. Accelerating through the ball keeps the cue tip in contact with the cue ball a little longer, allowing it to impart more spin.
- For longer shots, you need more spin or speed, so some spin remains after sliding along the table cloth to the ball (see **Principle 4.1** on page 84).
- Follow shots can be difficult to execute with a mechanical bridge, so be cautious when not using a hand bridge.

For a straight-on shot, where the cut angle is 0°, the cue ball does not move at all along the tangent line. In this case, a follow shot will result in the cue ball following the object ball after impact (see NV 4.6).

A very useful shot that takes advantage of the follow effect, applied to an object ball illustrated in **Figure 4.13**. There is an obstacle ball (a stripe) in front of a pocket in which you hope to pocket an object ball (a solid). **Principle 4.6** summarizes the proper technique. This is a great shot because your opponent might not be thinking of it as a possibility; at the same time, you take away an easy shot (in slang terms, a "**duck**") from your opponent. Your opponent will no longer be able to use the ball as an automatic shot or opportunity to get position on another shot. This is good for you. The key to making this type of shot is to hit the object ball soft enough so it has time to develop normal roll. Inexperienced players will often think they need to hit the ball hard to "drive it through" the obstacle ball. This is exactly the wrong thing to do, because when you hit the object ball hard it has no time to develop normal roll. Instead, the object ball slides across the table cloth and hits the obstacle ball with no spin and comes to a complete stop after pocketing the obstacle ball.

normal video

NV 4.6 – Straight-on follow shot

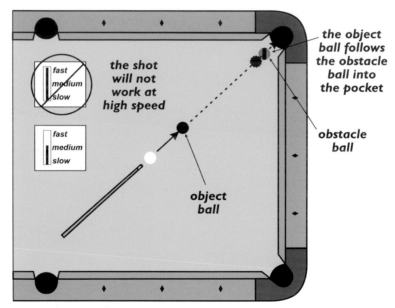

Figure 4.13 Following a ball through another

Principle 4.6 **Blocked pocket: no problem**

*To follow an obstacle ball into a pocket, hit the object ball soft enough to create normal roll (see **Figure 4.13** and NV 4.7).*

- This requires sufficient separation distance and a slow enough speed so the object ball will gain normal roll; otherwise, the object ball will slide and stop at impact.
- If the object ball is close to the obstacle ball, bottom spin on the cue ball can be used to impart a small amount of topspin to the object ball (see "English transfer" on page 105), to help it follow through the blocking ball.
- The object ball must hit the obstacle ball squarely (i.e., a direct hit) for the object ball to follow the obstacle ball into the pocket; otherwise, the object ball will be deflected along the obstacle-ball tangent line and not go in the pocket.
- These shots are much easier if the obstacle ball is deep in the pocket so the object ball will go in even if the obstacle ball is not hit perfectly squarely. It also helps if the cue ball is close to the object ball, and if the cut angle is small—so it is easier to hit the ball more accurately.

normal video

NV 4.7 – Following an obstacle ball into a pocket

high-speed video

HSV 4.2 – Following an obstacle ball into a pocket

An example where a follow shot might not have the desired effect is illustrated in **Figure 4.14**. When the cut angle is small, the cue ball loses most of its motion immediately at impact, then the topspin accelerates the ball forward. When the object ball is close to the rail and the cue ball hits the rail with significant topspin and slow forward speed, the cue ball retains the spin after rebounding off the rail, which causes the cue ball to accelerate to the rail again (see NV 4.8 and HSV 4.3). This only happens with follow shots when the object ball is close to the rail. As illustrated in **Figure 4.15**, when the object ball is farther from the rail the cue ball topspin gets converted to forward speed and normal roll (see **Figure 4.6c** on page 84). In that case, the ball rebounds off the rail as would be expected, returning toward the same end of the table from which the cue ball was hit (see NV 4.9).

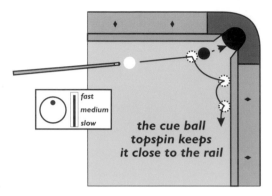

Figure 4.14 Rail-dribble follow shot

NV 4.8 – Rail-dribble follow shot

normal video

HSV 4.3 – Rail-dribble follow shot

high-speed video

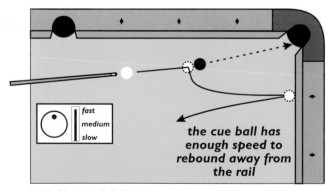

Figure 4.15 Normal follow shot into a rail

NV 4.9 – Normal follow shot into a rail

normal video

Section 4.04   *English (sidespin)*

Shots with horizontal-plane English (sidespin) are used to control the deflection of the cue ball after contacting a rail, either after object ball deflection or with a kick shot (see **Chapter 6**). This rail deflection is useful for position play when you are trying to control where the cue ball ends up for the next shot (see **Chapter 5**). Unlike with draw and follow, sidespin alone has no effect on the cue ball path until the cue ball contacts a rail.

The fundamentals of the effects of sidespin English are summarized in **Figure 4.16**. When the cue ball hits a rail with no English (**Figure 4.16a**) the rebounded path is not deflected at all. When the cue ball hits a rail with left English (**Figure 4.16b**), the cue ball deflects off the rail more to the left than it would otherwise (see NV 4.10). When the cue ball hits a rail with right English (**Figure 4.16c**), the cue ball deflects off the rail more to the right than it would otherwise (see NV 4.11). As illustrated by **Figure 4.17**, the deflection off the rail is caused by the sideways force the rail develops to oppose the direction of the cue ball spin (see HSV 6.10). Another way to understand it is that the cue ball tries to roll along the rail in the direction of the spin, while it is in contact with the rail. **Chapter 6** revisits these effects and applies them to kick and bank shots, where a complete understanding of English is crucial.

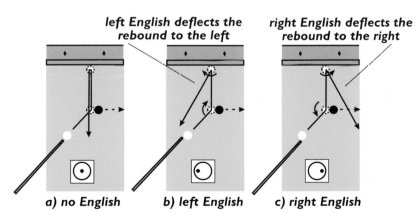

Figure 4.16 Sidespin deflection off a rail

NV 4.10 – Effect of left English
NV 4.11 – Effect of right English

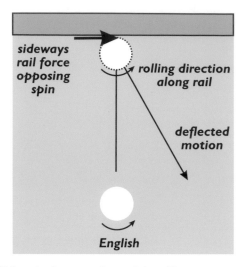

Figure 4.17 Sidespin interaction with rail

high-speed video

HSV 6.10 – Cue ball kicked straight into a rail with side English

Figure 4.18 and NV 4.12 show an example where English can be used to control cue ball position. The goal is to pocket the 1-ball in the top corner pocket and leave the cue ball in good position to pocket the 2-ball, then the 3-ball and 4-ball. This could represent a key sequence in a game of 9-ball. If the 1-ball were hit with no English, the cue ball might hit the 4-ball, leading to difficult-to-predict cue ball and 4-ball motion. That is why draw (bottom spin) is used. It widens the angle of the cue ball away from the 4-ball. If only draw were used, the cue ball might rebound off the end rail into the 3-ball, again leading to difficult-to-predict cue ball and 3-ball motion. That is why sidespin is used—in this case, right English. The right English flattens the rebound angle off the end rail sending the cue ball safely past the 3-ball, in good position to pocket the remainder of the balls. English can produce amazing results when it is used carefully and effectively.

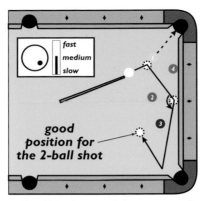

Figure 4.18 Using English for position control

NV 4.12 – Using English for position control

normal video

As **Principle 4.7** summarizes, English has virtually no effect on the path of the cue ball after object-ball impact and before any rail impact. If the cue ball has sidespin only, it will leave exactly along the tangent line after impact with the object ball. Only when the cue ball hits a rail does sidespin come into play. Sidespin can also alter the path of the object ball; and in some cases, this needs to be taken into consideration. This is called **throwing** and it is described more later in this section.

> ## Principle 4.7 **Tangent line and English independence**
>
>
>
> *Sidespin English has practically no effect on the motion of the cue ball after collision with an object ball (and before collision with a rail). The cue ball still leaves along the tangent line and curves only as a result of follow or draw.*
>
> - English has a strong effect on cue ball motion after rebound off a rail.
> - There is a small deviation from the tangent line path, due to throwing effects. When the object ball is thrown due to the English (see **Principle 4.11** on page 102), the object pushes back on the cue ball with an equal and opposite effect, causing the cue ball path to deflect slightly, but this effect can usually be neglected.

Unlike follow and draw, where the spin can wear off fairly quickly due to sliding on the felt (see **Figure 4.6** on page 84), sidespin English is more persistent (see **Principle 4.8**). This allows sidespin English shots to be hit more softly. This can greatly improve your accuracy, because a high-speed stroke is usually more difficult to control.

Principle 4.8 **English is persistent**

Even when the cue ball is hit softly with English, it takes a long distance for the sidespin to be completely lost.

- Some sidespin is lost fairly quickly (during initial sliding of the cue ball), but the remaining English decays slowly (as the cue ball rolls).

There are many pitfalls to be aware of when using sidespin English. The following factors that need to be considered when planning a shot:
- . cue ball deflection at higher speeds.
- cue ball curve, due to stick elevation.
- . object ball throw, due to the interaction of the spin with the object ball.
- rail rebound-angle effects.

The first three effects are described in detail below, and the last is covered in **Section 6.04**.

Because the cue ball is hit off-center for a shot with sidespin English, there will be a small sideways force acting on the cue ball away from the aiming line (see **Figure 4.19**). The sideways force is significant only for strong (high speed) strokes. The resulting effect is called **deflection,** or **squirt**, because the force causes the cue ball to veer off the expected path slightly (see **Figure 4.20**, NV 4.13, HSV 4.4, and HSV 4.5). The amount of deflection increases dramatically with shot speed. For slow shots, the deflection can be neglected; but for fast shots, you will miss the shot if you do not take deflection into consideration! For left English, the cue ball deflects to the right; and for right English, the cue ball deflects to the left. These effects are summarized in **Principle 4.9**.

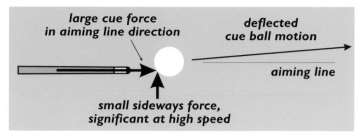

Figure 4.19 Cause of English deflection

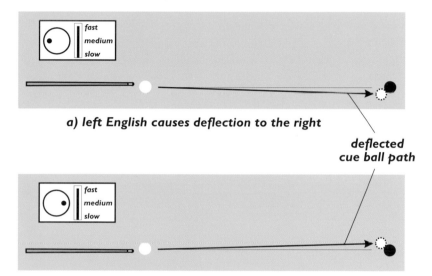

Figure 4.20 English deflection

Principle 4.9 **English deflection**

*A stroke with sidespin English results in deflection (aka squirt) of the cue ball away from the aiming line, in the direction opposite the English (see **Figure 4.20**).*

- Left English causes the cue ball to deflect to the right, and right English causes deflection to the left.
- This effect is more pronounced at higher speeds. Therefore, if a shot requiring sidespin English is not hit softly, you must aim crookedly to make the shot!

normal video

NV 4.13 – Squirt due to high-speed English

high-speed video

HSV 4.4 – Squirt due to high-speed English
HSV 4.5 – Squirt due to high speed English (close-up)

As summarized in **Principle 4.10**, whenever the cue stick is not level (i.e., it is elevated) when sidespin English is used, the cue ball path will curve away from the aiming-line direction (see **Figure 4.21** and NV 4.14). Normally, this effect will cause you to miss your shot, but sometimes (e.g., with massé shots, which are described in **Section 7.07**), the effect can work to your advantage.

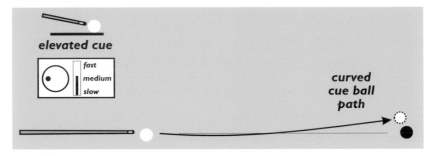

a) left English can cause curve to the left

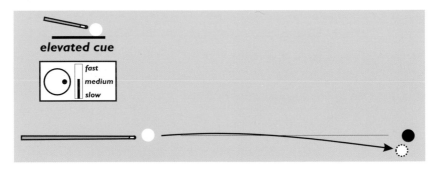

b) right English can cause curve to the right

Figure 4.21 English curve

Principle 4.10 **English curve**

*Elevating the cue stick when stroking a shot with sidespin English results in curving of the cue ball path in the direction of the English (see **Figure 4.21**).*

- Left English causes the cue ball to curve left, and right English causes curve to the right.
- For most shots, it is impossible to stroke the cue stick completely levelly because the stick must be held above the rails.
- You can use this effect to your advantage when trying to execute a massé shot (see **Section 7.07**).

NV 4.14 – English curve due to an elevated cue

normal video

Another complexity involved with using English is the effect the sidespin has on the object-ball motion. As illustrated in **Figure 4.22**, the sidespin creates a sideways friction-force on the object ball that **throws** (deflects) the object ball off the impact line (see TP 4.3). Left English throws the object ball to the right and right English throws the object ball to the left (see **Figure 4.23** and **Principle 4.11**). Surprisingly, the amount of throw increases dramatically at lower speeds (see **Principle 4.12**, HSV 4.6, and HSV 4.7), so you must be extremely careful when using English with soft shots, especially when the object ball is far from its target.

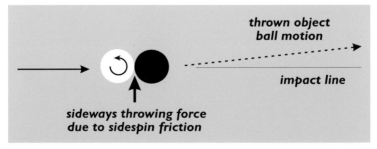

Figure 4.22 Throw action

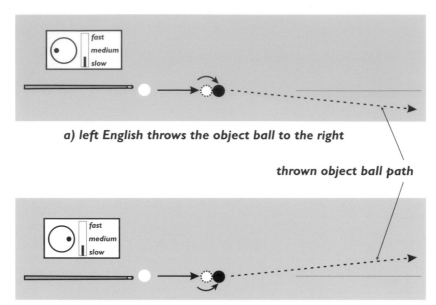

a) left English throws the object ball to the right

thrown object ball path

b) right English throws the object ball to the left

Figure 4.23 English throw

Principle 4.11 **English throw**

*If the cue ball hits an object ball with English, the object ball deflects from the impact line opposite the direction of the English (see **Figure 4.23**).*

- Left English throws the object ball to the right, and right English throws to the left.
- The amount of throw increases with more sidespin and slower ball speed (see **Principle 4.12**). This is because the sidespin sliding-force acts over a longer time during a slow collision.

Principle 4.12 **Slow throw**

The amount of English-induced object-ball throw increases with decreased cue ball speed (i.e., the softer you hit the cue ball, the more the object ball will be thrown).

- The throw is maximum for a direct hit with no cut angle.
- If the cue ball is far from the object ball and it is hit softly, much (possibly all) of the sidespin will wear off (be lost) during the rolling.
- A cut angle (without English) can also create object ball throw (see the next section).

high-speed video

HSV 4.6 – Object-ball throw at slow speed
HSV 4.7 – Object-ball throw at fast speed

technical proof

TP 4.3 – English-induced-throw effects

Normally, throw is something you worry about because it can cause you to miss a shot. However, there are some cases where throw can be used to your advantage. **Figure 4.24** illustrates one such example. The obstacle ball blocks the path the cue ball would need to take for a simple cut shot. Instead, the cue ball has to be aimed to miss the obstacle ball (the stripe) and right English must be used to throw the object ball (the solid) to the left, towards the pocket (see NV 4.15). The shot must be hit softly (but with enough English) because the amount of throw decreases significantly with speed. This shot is not that difficult, and it can be invaluable in a game if you need a little extra space for a shot. **Section 7.03** and **Section 7.04** present other opportunities where throw can be your friend.

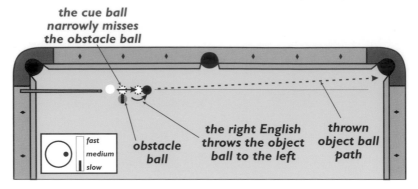

Figure 4.24 Using throw to make a partially blocked shot

NV 4.15 – Using throw to make a partially blocked shot

normal video

Figure 4.25 illustrates an interesting phenomenon involving English deflection and throw: the two effects tend to counteract each other. In fact, at certain speeds and for certain distances between the cue and object balls, the effects will exactly cancel each other. In the figure, the left English causes the cue ball to deflect to the right of the aiming line, and the throw deflects the object-ball motion to the right of the resulting impact line. The end result is that the object ball leaves along the original aiming line. Isn't it great when physics works in your favor? Faster speeds will result in more deflection and less throw, and slower speeds will result in less deflection and more throw.

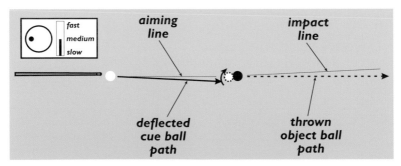

Figure 4.25 Deflection and throw cancellation

The throw effect due to English is sometimes referred to as **English-induced throw**, because other effects can also produce throw (e.g., collision-induced throw, presented in the next section). Another effect related to throw is **English transfer**. When a ball is thrown, the same friction force that creates the throw deflection also imparts a small amount of sidespin in the direction of the throw. If the cue ball has left English, the object ball will pick up a small amount of right spin; and if the cue ball has right English, the object ball will pick up a small amount of left spin (see the direction of English and the resulting throw force in **Figure 4.22** on page 101). This transferred spin can normally be neglected, but it can affect some types of shots (e.g., bank shots as described in **Chapter 6**).

Section 4.05   *Cut-shot effects*

In the previous section, we saw how English can throw the object ball off its expected impact-line path. Another source of throw is cut-shot friction. To distinguish this effect from English-induced throw, it is sometimes referred to as **collision-induced throw,** or **cut-induced throw**. Collision-induced throw and English-induced throw are really the same effect, both resulting from relative sideways friction between the cue ball and object ball (as shown in **Figure 4.22** on page 101).

As illustrated in **Figure 4.26**, when you hit a cut shot, the object ball is thrown in the direction of the cue ball motion. This is due to the friction between the cue ball and the object ball during impact. This throw must be accounted for when shooting cut shots (see **Figure 4.27** and **Principle 4.13**), especially longer shots where the margin of error is smaller.

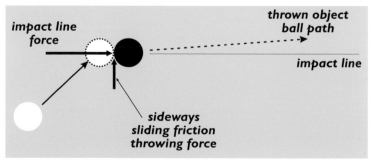

Figure 4.26 Cut shot throw

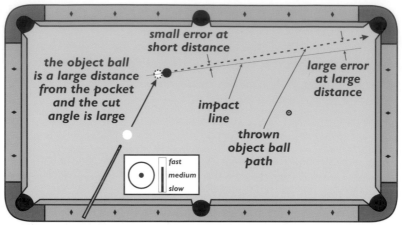

Figure 4.27 Example of overcutting a cut shot to compensate for throw

Principle 4.13 **You need to overcut cut shots**

*Cut shots usually must be overcut due to throwing of the object ball (see **Figure 4.27** and NV 4.16).*

- The amount of throw increases with cut angle (see TP 4.4) and distance from the pocket (see **Figure 4.27**).
- The amount of throw does not depend on the speed, because the sideways (sliding) force increases proportionally with the impact-line force.
- This is particularly important in rail-cut shots (see Section 4.06).
- The effect can be counteracted with outside English (see **Principle 4.14**).
- The amount of throw is even larger if the cue ball happens to be frozen to the object ball (see **Section 7.03**).

normal video

NV 4.16 – Overcutting a cut shot to compensate for throw

high-speed video

HSV 4.8 – Cut-shot throw at fast speed
HSV 4.9 – Cut-shot throw at slow speed

technical proof

TP 4.4 – Relationship between the amount of throw and cut angle

Cut-shot throw can be eliminated with what is called **outside English. Principle 4.14** describes this effect and **Figure 4.28** illustrates how it is used. In this case, left English is used to cut the ball to the right without throw. This works because the English counteracts the cut motion, so there is no sliding between the cue ball and the object ball during contact. Instead, the cue ball rolls on the object ball during impact. The English is called "outside" because the cue ball is hit on the side away from the object ball. In the case of **Figure 4.28**, the cue ball is hit on the left side of the object ball, on the left side of (outside) the cue ball path. The alternative is to adjust your cut-shot aim slightly and not use English (see **Figure 4.27**). This is probably the best option for most people. However, if you need to use English on a cut shot to achieve desired cue ball position for the next shot (see **Chapter 5**), you need to be aware of the throw effect. As **Figure 4.29** illustrates, the throw can be even more pronounced when **inside English** is used. In the case of **Figure 4.29**, the cue ball is hit on the same side as the object ball, on the right side of (inside) the cue ball path. As with any shot involving English, it takes practice to know how much English to use to achieve the desired effect. The effects of English and cut throw are very important in rail-cut shots presented in the next section.

Principle 4.14 **Eliminating cut throw**

*With cut shots, outside English can be used to minimize the effect of object-ball throw (see **Figure 4.28**).*

- Be very careful applying this principle, due to the difficulty in controlling shots with English (see **Principle 4.9** on page 99 and **Principle 4.10** on page 101).
- Be aware of the effect of English on cue ball motion after rail contact (see **Section 6.04** starting on page 186).

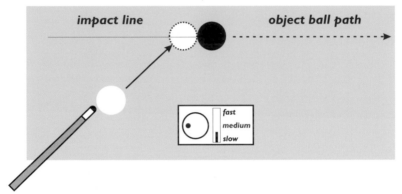

Figure 4.28 Using outside English to eliminate cut throw

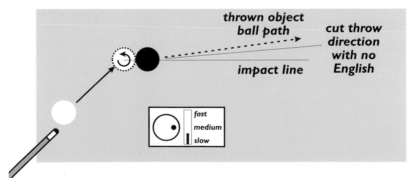

Figure 4.29 Increased throw with inside English

As with English transfer, described in the previous section, the cut throwing force also imparts a small amount of sidespin to the object ball. This is sometimes referred to as **collision-induced English,** or **cut-induced spin** (see **Principle 4.15**). As with English transfer, this effect is small and can usually be neglected. Bank shots are one exception, where cut-induced spin can affect a shot dramatically (see **Chapter 6**).

Principle 4.15 **Cut spin**

A cut shot (with or without English) can impart a small amount of sidespin to the object ball.

- This effect is very important when aiming bank shots (see **Section 6.06** starting on page 197).

Section 4.06   *Rail cut shots*

Figure 4.30 illustrates a **rail cut shot**, where the object ball is touching the rail and is pocketed in the corner pocket adjacent to the rail. This is a fairly common shot, because balls often come to rest against a rail in the rail grove. The figure shows the highest percentage way to make the shot, where you hit the rail first, just ahead of the object ball, with natural (running) English. When sidespin is in the rolling direction along the rail, the sidespin is referred to as **natural English,** or **running English**; and when the sidespin is opposite the rolling direction, the sidespin is referred to as **reverse English** (see **Section 6.05**). As summarized in **Principle 4.16**, the main reason for using natural English is that the sidespin helps kick the cue ball towards the object ball. Another reason is illustrated in **Figure 4.31**. Note that the cue ball compresses the rail and creates a rebound cut-shot on the object ball. As was presented in the previous section, this would result in collision-induced throw, away from the rail. Fortunately, the English-induced throw, resulting from the natural English, is in the opposite direction, allowing these effects to cancel.

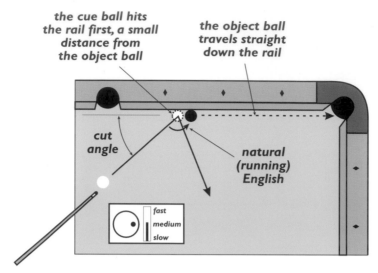

the cue ball hits the rail first, a small distance from the object ball

the object ball travels straight down the rail

cut angle

natural (running) English

fast
medium
slow

Figure 4.30 Rail cut shot (recommended method)

normal video

NV 4.17 – Rail cut shot with natural (running) English

high-speed video

HSV 4.10 – Rail cut shot with natural (running) English

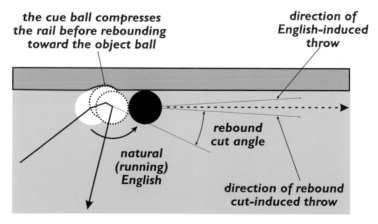

the cue ball compresses the rail before rebounding toward the object ball

direction of English-induced throw

natural (running) English

rebound cut angle

direction of rebound cut-induced throw

Figure 4.31 Rail–cut shot throw cancellation

Principle 4.16 **Rail cut shot**

*When cutting an object ball frozen (or close to frozen) on the rail, hit the rail first with natural (running) English (see **Figure 4.30**, NV 4.17, and HSV 4.10).*

- The natural (running) English helps kick the cue ball towards the object ball. This allows you to make rail cut shots with fairly large cut angles (even with cut angles close to 90°), which would be impossible if English were not used. For larger cut angles, you need to use more English.
- As illustrated in **Figure 4.31**, English-induced throw resulting from the natural English (see **Principle 4.11** starting on page 102) helps cancel the rebound cut-angle collision-induced throw (see **Principle 4.13**, on page 106).
- Make sure you do not hit the ball first. There is a fairly large margin of error if you hit the rail first, but practically no margin of error (i.e., you would almost always miss the shot) if you hit the ball first. Hitting the object first causes it to rebound off the rail.
- In general, you should hit no more than about ⅛ inch to ¼ inch ahead of the object ball. Aim closer to the object ball for shots with larger cut angles.
- If you need to elevate the cue stick (to avoid an obstacle ball or because the cue ball is frozen to a rail) or if a shot requires fast cue ball speed, you need to be aware of and correct for the effects of English deflection, curve, and throw (see Section 4.04 starting on page 95).

Figures 4.32–4.34 illustrate several things that can go wrong with rail cut shots. Some inexperienced players believe that the best approach for rail cut shots is to try to hit the rail and object ball at exactly the same time. This is appropriate advice for cut shots with small cut angles. It also works for short cut shots where the object ball is close to the target pocket, because there is a fairly large margin of error. However, as illustrated in **Figure 4.32**, the problem with hitting the object ball and rail at the same time is that the cut angle creates collision-induced throw that drives the object ball into the rail, causing it to rebound away from the rail slightly. This can be corrected using outside English (in this case, left English); but again, this is not the recommended approach. Hitting the rail first with natural English is a much better approach (see **Principle 4.16**). Your margin or error is much larger and you can easily make large cut-angle rail shots that are nearly impossible when trying to hit the ball and rail at the same time.

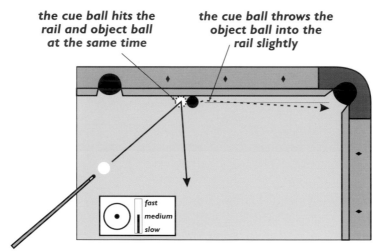

the cue ball hits the rail and object ball at the same time

the cue ball throws the object ball into the rail slightly

fast
medium
slow

Figure 4.32 Rail cut shot (common mistake)

Figure 4.33 shows what can happen if you hit the rail too early (i.e., the gap between the cue ball and object ball, during rail contact, is too large). The cue ball deflects too far off the rail and cuts the object ball into the rail, causing it to rebound away from the rail (see HSV 4.11 and HSV 4.12). In general, you should hit no more than about ⅛ inch to ¼ inch ahead of the object ball. The gap between the cue ball and object ball at rail impact should be smaller for shots with larger cut angles.

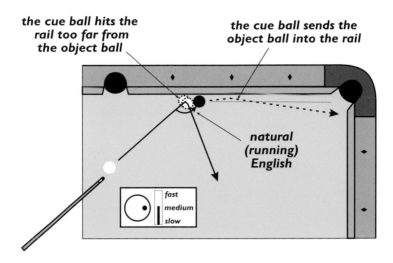

the cue ball hits the
rail too far from
the object ball

the cue ball sends the
object ball into the rail

natural
(running)
English

fast
medium
slow

close-up view:

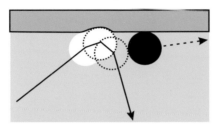

Figure 4.33 Rail cut shot (gap too large)

high-speed video

HSV 4.11 – Rail cut with running English, hitting the rail very early

HSV 4.12 – Rail cut with running English, hitting the rail early

Figure 4.34 shows what happens if the cue ball is hit too close to the object ball with significant speed. The cue ball compresses the rail significantly and hits the object ball before it has rebounded completely. The result is that the cue ball hits the object ball with a cut angle away from the rail, causing the object ball to leave the rail immediately (see HSV 4.13 through HSV 4.16). When you need to hit a cut shot hard, you need to hit the rail a little earlier than normal. Anytime you use sidespin English with a higher speed shot, you also must be aware of and adjust for English deflection (see **Principle 4.9** on page 99), which affects the cue ball's path to the rail. For the shot in **Figure 4.34**, the English deflection will be to the left, so the cue ball will hit the rail earlier automatically as a result of using the English at the higher speed. Isn't it nice when physics works in your favor?

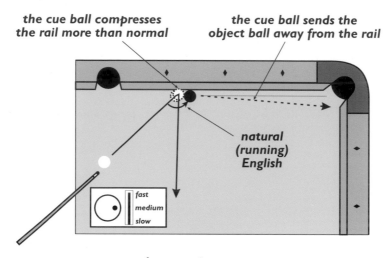

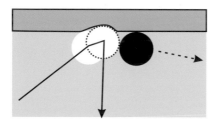

Figure 4.34 Rail cut shot (too fast)

high-speed video

HSV 4.13 – Rail cut with running English, hitting the rail late and too hard

HSV 4.14 – Rail cut with reverse English, with kiss away from the rail

HSV 4.15 – Rail cut, slightly away from the rail, exaggerating the effect of **Figure 4.34**

HSV 4.16 – Rail cut, slightly away from the rail, exaggerating the desired effects of **Figure 4.30**

Section 4.07 *Controlling the cue ball path*

Section 3.03 (starting on page 41) and **Section 3.04** (on page 48) presented the 90° and 30° rules, which are important for predicting the path of the cue ball after object-ball impact. Being able to predict cue ball motion is an important skill to have in trying to avoid a scratch, for planning break-up or avoidance shots, and for position play (see **Chapter 5**). This section provides more information by looking at the effects of cut angle, speed, and English on these rules. An understanding of these effects is critical to becoming a great player. Position play and strategy execution require that you have the ability to plan and predict where the cue ball will go after pocketing an object ball. **Chapter 5** presents various applications and examples of these principles.

Figure 4.35 and **Figure 4.36** illustrate the effects of cut angle on the path of the cue ball, for draw and follow shots at various cut angles. **Principle 4.17** summarizes the main conclusions that can be drawn from the figures. The amount of deviation away from the 90° tangent line increases with the amount of top or bottom spin, and the directness of impact. For small cut angles, the cue path deviates from the tangent-line path the most dramatically. In the extreme case of a straight-on shot with draw, the cue ball departs at an angle of 180° (see path d in **Figure 4.35**). A straight-on follow shot results in a depart angle of 0° (see path d in **Figure 4.36**).

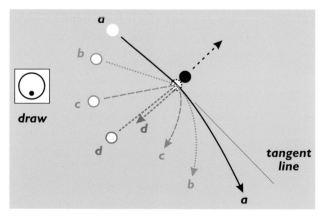

Figure 4.35 Effect of cut angle on draw shot

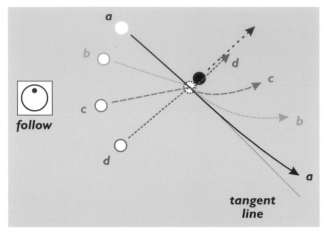

Figure 4.36 Effect of cut angle on follow shot

Principle 4.17 **90° rule cut-angle effects**

*The smaller the cut angle (i.e., the more squarely the cue ball hits the object ball), the more dramatic the effect top or bottom spin will be in moving the cue ball path away from the tangent-line direction (see **Principle 3.3** on page 42).*

- Even when the cue ball has top or bottom spin, it will still initially leave along the tangent line before curving due to the spin. However, for a small cut angle the curving begins almost immediately (see NV 4.18 and NV 4.19).
- With higher speed, the cue ball remains on the tangent line longer before deflecting (curving) due to draw or follow (see **Principle 4.18**).

normal video

NV 4.18 – Large cue-ball deviation from the tangent line, with follow and small cut angle

NV 4.19 – Large cue-ball deviation from the tangent line, with draw and small cut angle

The path of the cue ball after impact with the object ball also depends on the speed of the shot. **Figure 4.37** and **Figure 4.38** illustrate the effect for draw and follow shots at various speeds. **Principle**

4.18 summarizes the main conclusions that can be drawn from the figures. The harder a shot is hit, the longer the cue ball stays on the tangent-line path before deviating due to follow or draw (see NV 4.20 and NV 4.21). Only with a stun shot (no follow or draw) does the cue ball travel exactly along the tangent line, regardless of the speed.

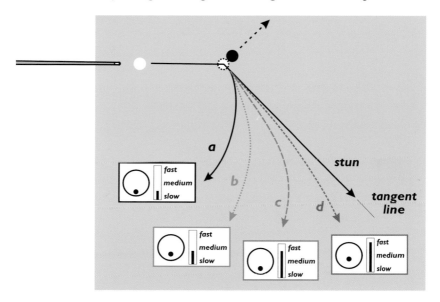

Figure 4.37 Effect of speed on draw-shot tangent line persistence

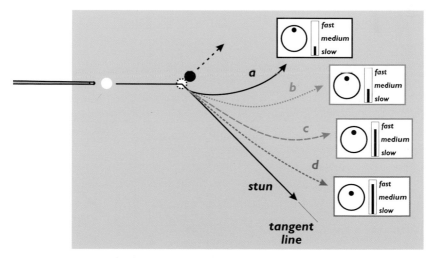

Figure 4.38 Effect of speed on follow-shot tangent-line persistence

Principle 4.18 **Cue-ball curve delay**

Even if a cue ball has draw or follow when striking an object ball, it will still leave initially along the tangent-line path before curving due to the spin.

- With higher speed, the path of the cue ball takes longer to deviate from the tangent-line path.
- Be careful when using draw or follow to help avoid an obstacle ball or a scratch, if the cue ball is close to the obstacle ball or pocket in the tangent-line path (see **Figure 4.39**).

normal video

NV 4.20 – Delay of follow, tangent-line deflection with higher speed

NV 4.21 – Delay of draw, tangent-line deflection with higher speed

Figure 4.39 illustrates an example shot where knowledge of the speed effect described above is important. An inexperienced player might think, "Hit it hard with follow, to avoid the scratch in the side pocket." This is terribly flawed thinking. The right thing to do is to hit the cue ball soft enough, with slight follow resulting in cue-ball roll, so the cue ball starts deflecting away from the tangent line as soon as possible (see NV 4.22). If you hit the shot hard, you will scratch in the side pocket, regardless of what type of English (top, bottom, or side) you put on the cue ball!

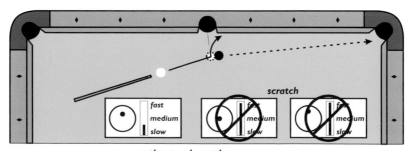

the speed must be slow enough to avoid the scratch

Figure 4.39 Avoiding a tangent-line scratch using slow speed

normal video

NV 4.22 — Avoiding a tangent-line scratch using slow-speed roll

Figure 4.40 shows another example where understanding the effects of speed and vertical-plane English (draw or follow) is important in predicting the path of the cue ball. The figure shows a cut shot close to a rail, but not adjacent to a side pocket as was shown in **Figure 4.39**. This is a very common shot when playing for position, where you always want to leave angles on shots (i.e., create cut shots) to help you position the cue ball for the next shot (see more details in **Chapter 5**). As you can see in **Figure 4.40** and NV 4.23, speed and vertical-plane English can give you a tremendous amount of control over the cue ball path. Because the cut angle is small, the effects of slow roll produce paths like *d*. For faster shots with vertical-plane English, the spin persists and gradually takes effect after rail contact, resulting in curved paths (see paths *a* and *c*). Path *b* shows the expected tangent-line motion and rail deflection that occurs when the cue ball has stun (no spin) at object ball impact.

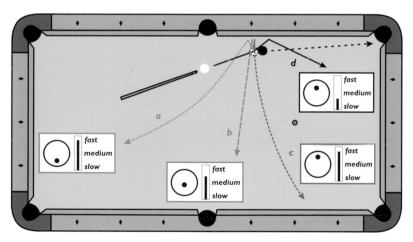

Figure 4.40 Cue-ball path control for a cut shot next to a rail

normal video

NV 4.23 — Cue-ball path control for a cut shot next to a rail

As with the 90° rule, the exact path of the cue ball predicted by the 30° rule also depends on the speed of the shot. **Figure 4.41** illustrates this effect. Again, the harder you hit the shot, the longer the cue ball persists along the tangent line before curving to the 30° heading (see NV 4.24).

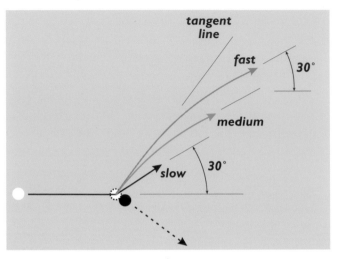

Figure 4.41 Effect of speed on 30° rule

normal video

NV 4.24 –30° rule speed effects

Section 4.08   *English examples and advice*

The principles presented in this chapter, if mastered, can give you tremendous control over the path of the cue ball and enable you to be a good position-control player. However, you should be very careful using sidespin English and should avoid it when possible (see **Principle 4.19**). As will be discussed in **Chapter 5**, speed control, draw, and follow are usually better options than sidespin English for position control. But sometimes, to avoid obstacle balls or to achieve desired cue ball position, you need to use sidespin English to execute a shot properly (e.g., see **Figure 4.18** on page 97).

Principle 4.19 **Beware of English**

Do not use sidespin English unless you must.

- The effects of English deflection, curve, and throw can be extremely difficult to control (see **Principle 4.9**, **Principle 4.10**, and **Principle 4.11** on pages 99–102). The longer and faster the shot is, the harder it is to control the cue ball trajectory.
- Speed control, in combination with follow or draw, is usually a better option than sidespin English (see **Section 5.02**).
- If you do need to use sidespin English, a softer stroke will minimize deflection, but be aware that a slower speed will result in more throw (see **Principle 4.12** on page 103). Also, keep your stick as level as possible during the stroke to minimize curving.
- The chances for a miscue increase dramatically when you use English. If you miscue, it is usually because you did not keep the cue stick level during your stroke, tried to hit the cue ball too far off center, or had poor tip contact (see **Section 2.01**, starting on page 16).

The following examples will illustrate just how useful English (draw, follow, or sidespin) can be when it is needed. **Figure 4.42** through **Figure 4.44** illustrate the same shot executed with different types of English. **Figure 4.42** shows various examples of English and corresponding ball paths for a slow-speed stroke. **Figure 4.43** and **Figure 4.44** show how the ball paths change with increasing stroke speed. With different combinations of English and speed, you can position the cue ball at practically any place on the table after pocketing the shot. The English and speed also give you a great deal of control over the path the cue ball takes to its final position (see NV 4.25).

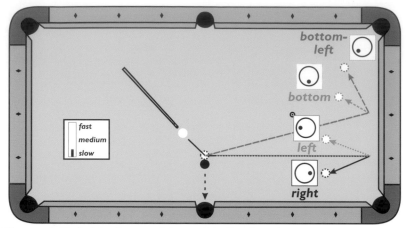

Figure 4.42 Achieving position with English (slow speed)

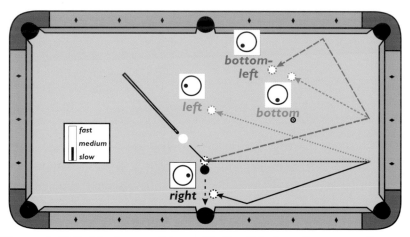

Figure 4.43 Achieving position with English (medium speed)

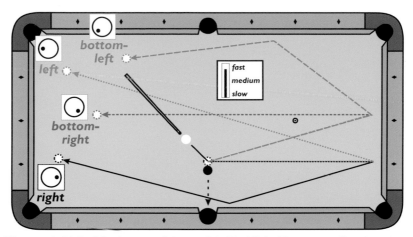

Figure 4.44 Achieving position with English (fast speed)

normal video

NV 4.25 – Positioning the cue ball at various spots on the table from an easy side-pocket shot

Chapter 5
Position Play and Strategy

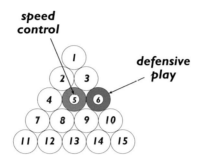

In this chapter, you will learn how to use speed, angles, and planning to control cue ball motion to your advantage. The ability to control cue ball position is what really separates the good players from the great ones. Position play, strategy, and safety play are very important, especially in the game of 9-ball.

Section 5.01   *Introduction*

As **Principle 5.1** summarizes, the "Holy Grail" of pool is the ability to run an entire table without having to use excessive speed or English—achieving perfect position on every shot. This is possible, but it requires excellent speed control and position planning. This chapter presents the fundamentals of these techniques and some examples of how to apply them strategically. The fundamentals of shot planning were presented in **Section 3.05**, starting on page 56. You might want to review that section again before proceeding with this chapter, which is more advanced.

Principle 5.1 **The "Holy Grail" of pool**

The "Holy Grail" of pool is the ability to hit every shot softly without English, to have the object ball go in, to leave the cue ball in a perfect position for the next shot, and to have this happen every shot.

- This requires excellent speed control, position planning, and strategy.

Often, the ball layout, your position, or your lack of skill, prevents you from achieving the "Holy Grail" of **Principle 5.1**. In those cases and in cases when you are presented with an impossible or difficult shot, you should strive for the next best thing to the "Holy Grail," which is the ability to play a perfect **safety**. The goal in this shot is to leave the cue ball in a place such that your opponent will have no chance to make a shot. Hopefully, this would result in a ball-in-hand for you, which would allow you to continue to pursue the "Holy Grail" of pool. Safety play is presented in detail in Section 5.06.

Section 5.02 *Position-play fundamentals*

Pool is all about where you can leave the cue ball in preparation for making the next shot. If you can play good position, you will win consistently. In fact, this is the skill that really separates professional players from casual or league players. A good position player will dominate a player with great shot-making skills but poor position-play skills. The most useful and common techniques for controlling cue ball position include:

- speed control.
- leaving angles.
- using draw and follow.
- using sidespin English and rail interaction.
- using rail-first shots.
- cheating a pocket.

Each of these techniques is described below with practical examples.

Using **speed control** with no English is always preferable to using English because it is easier to execute and control, and is safe from miscue and other pitfalls associated with English (see **Principle 5.2**). Speed control implies that you do not use any spin or English and hit the cue ball in the center, with just the right amount of speed, so that after you make an object ball, the cue ball rolls to a location desirable for making the next object ball.

Principle 5.2 **Ideal position control**

Whenever possible, hit the cue ball in the center with just enough speed to achieve position for the next shot.

- Draw, follow, and sidespin English are more difficult to control. English suffers from many pitfalls (see **Section 4.04**, starting on page 95).
- It is very important to be familiar with the 90° and 30° rules (see **Section 3.03**, starting on page 41, and **Section 3.04**, starting on page 48) and the effects of speed (see **Section 4.07**, starting on page 115) to be able to predict the cue ball path.
- Good speed control is critical (see **Principle 5.3**).

Principle 5.3 **Speed is key**

To be a great pool player you must have excellent speed control and be able to predict ball-travel distances.

- Intuition and feel for how much speed to use can come only with extensive practice and experience.
- Because every table is different, you will need to experiment on each table before playing to help calibrate yourself for the table conditions.

A necessary skill for effective speed control is the ability to **leave an angle** on a shot (see **Principle 5.4**). This is where you try to leave the cue ball in a position such that you have a cut shot, rather than a straight-in shot, on the next ball, so speed control can be used again to create position on the following shot. **Figure 5.1** shows an example of a two-shot sequence where the cut angle is favorable. The 1-ball can be pocketed with a soft, center stroke, leaving perfect position for the 2-ball on the next shot. **Figure 5.2** shows an example where you are faced with a more difficult position-control situation. After pocketing the 1-ball, the cue ball will travel up-table (to the left in the figure), away from the 2-ball. You must be careful not to scratch in the bottom-left corner pocket and make sure the cue ball has enough speed to make it back down-table to get position on the 2-ball. You also must be careful not to get too close to the 2-ball, which can make the shot on the 2-ball more difficult, if not impossible. Finally, you must be careful not to scratch in the bottom-right corner pocket. If you do not get good position on the 2-ball for a straight-in or small cut shot you will be forced to attempt a bank shot or safety, which is not ideal.

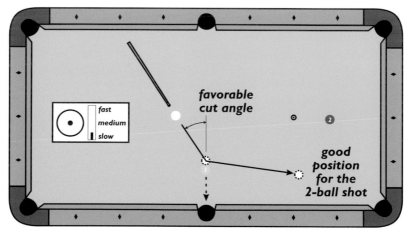

Figure 5.1 Favorable angle for position control

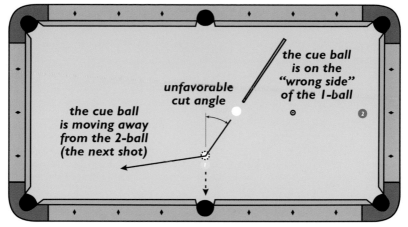

Figure 5.2 Unfavorable angle for position control

Principle 5.4 **Leave angles on shots**

For effective position play, you need to leave yourself with favorable cut angles to enable easy positioning for follow-on shots.

- **Figure 5.1** shows an example of a favorable cut angle for pocketing the 1-ball and setting up for the 2-ball. **Figure 5.2** shows an unfavorable angle.
- To leave angles and create position on successive shots, you usually need to think three balls ahead (see **Principle 5.5**).

Figure 5.3 shows an example where speed control, used with angles, is all that is needed to easily execute a three-shot sequence. The 1-ball is pocketed with a soft, center stroke, resulting in good position for the 2-ball with a favorable cut angle. The 2-ball is pocketed with a slightly harder stroke so the cue ball kicks off the foot rail, resulting in good position on the 3-ball. No shot in the sequence requires English or excessive speed, which should always be your goal. As summarized in **Principle 5.5**, the key to good position play is thinking three balls ahead. **Figure 5.3** and NV 5.1 provide a good example of this principle. When planning the 1-ball shot you need to think ahead to the 2-ball and 3-ball so you will know how much speed to use to result in a good angle for the 2-ball shot, enabling easy position for the 3-ball. Again, because this shot sequence is planned well, each shot can be hit softly with no English, resulting in three short-distance, easy shots. This is good.

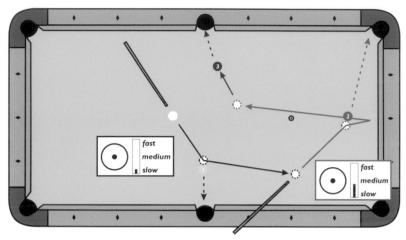

Figure 5.3 Speed- and angle-control example

NV 5.1 – Using speed and angle control to pocket a three-ball sequence

normal video

Principle 5.5 **Always think three balls ahead**

For effective position play, plan three balls ahead to know what angle to create for the next shot.

• **Figure 5.3** and **Figure 5.4** provide good examples of this principle.

Figure 5.4 and NV 5.2 show another sequence where using speed control and leaving angles can result in three relatively easy shots. The 1-ball shot requires medium-fast speed, because the cut angle is small, and the cue ball leaves along the tangent line much slower than it approaches the object ball. For the 2-ball shot, because the shot speed is relatively slow, the cue ball will be rolling naturally by the time it arrives at the 2-ball. Therefore, a center-ball hit is appropriate. The cue ball roll (topspin) results in the deflected path into the rail, providing an easy shot on the 3-ball.

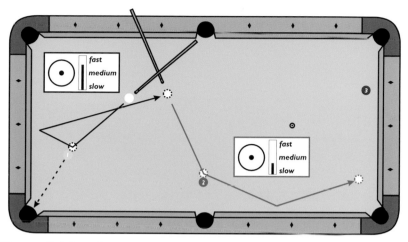

Figure 5.4 Another speed- and angle-control example

normal video

NV 5.2 – Using speed and angle control to pocket another three-ball sequence

When speed control alone is not satisfactory to achieve the desired cue ball position, **draw**, **follow**, and **English** can be added to help. **Section 4.07** (starting on page 115) and **Section 4.08** (starting on page 120) present using draw and follow to control the cue ball path and using sidespin English to alter the path of the cue ball after it strikes a rail. In general, draw and follow are better alternatives than sidespin English (see **Principle 5.6**). Furthermore, when you have a choice (e.g., with ball-in-hand), follow is better than draw because it is much easier to control. With follow, you can often rely only on normal roll and speed control. With draw, you need to try to impart exactly the correct amount of bottom spin—which degrades at different rates depending upon shot speed and the condition of the table cloth, and is therefore difficult to control.

Principle 5.6 **Follow and draw are often better than sidespin English**

When speed control alone is not sufficient for cue ball control, use follow or draw. Do not rely on sidespin English and rail interaction, unless speed control and draw or follow are too limiting.

WARNING
!

- Sidespin English suffers from many pitfalls (see **Section 4.04**, starting on page 95).
- You must be aware of speed and spin effects, and how they relate to the 90° and 30° rules (see **Section 4.07**, starting on page 115).
- Follow, or just normal roll, is easier to control than draw, because there are fewer variables to control.

Figure 5.5 and NV 5.3 illustrate an example where speed control alone is not sufficient for good position control. To leave position on the 2-ball after making the 1-ball, bottom-right English is required. The bottom spin pulls the cue-ball path back from the 1-ball tangent line, to avoid impact with the 4-ball. The right English flattens the angle of the cue ball off the foot rail, enabling the cue ball to avoid hitting the 3-ball. Appropriate speed on the 1-ball shot results in good position for the 2-ball. In the figure, the cue ball position after the 1-ball shot results in a straight-in shot on the 2-ball. Then, a slow draw shot on the 2-ball stops the cue ball in place after impact, leaving an easy shot on the 3-ball and then the 4-ball. The English on the 1-ball shot results in a very easy run of the four balls. If English is not used on the 1-ball shot, the cue ball will hit other balls, and the probability for making all four balls will be low.

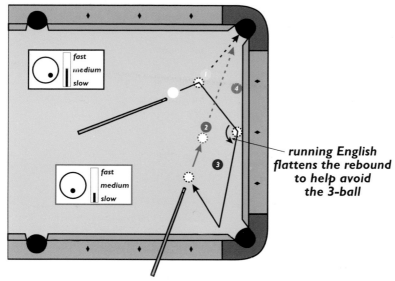

Figure 5.5 Example using draw and side English

normal video

NV 5.3 – Using side English to help run a four-shot sequence

Another application for English in position play is using reverse English to help "kill" the cue ball on a cut shot with rail contact. As shown in **Figure 5.6**, the numerous obstacle "stripes" present a challenging position-control problem in pocketing the last solid and setting up for a reasonable shot on the 8-ball. Bottom English must be used to direct the postimpact cue ball motion in a safe direction. If follow or a normal roll shot were used, the cue ball would hit the upper stripe, making it difficult to predict where the cue ball would end up. Also, if just bottom English were used, the cue ball would most likely travel too far up-table (to the left, in the figure) after rail impact, leaving a difficult shot on the 8-ball. Running English would make the situation even worse. Reverse English, because it decreases (shortens) the rebound angle off the rail and slows the cue ball after rail contact, offers a good solution that leads to a fairly easy shot on the 8-ball (see NV 5.4).

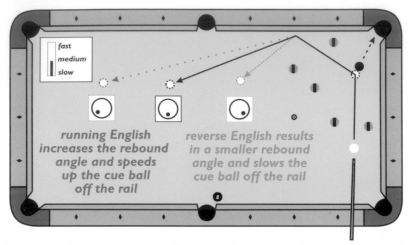

Figure 5.6 Using reverse English to kill the cue-ball motion off a rail

normal video

NV 5.4 – Using reverse English to kill the cue-ball motion off a rail

Another technique that can be useful in position play is hitting the rail first, in shots where the object ball is close to a pocket. **Figure 5.7** and NV 5.5 show an example of a **rail-first shot**. If the 1-ball were hit directly, it would be very difficult to achieve good position for the 2-ball. Extreme draw could be used to bring the cue ball up-table (to the left, in the figure), but it would be difficult to control the amount of draw, and there would be a lot of uncertainty in where the cue ball would end up. By glancing off the rail first, the 1-ball is still pocketed easily, and the cue ball then follows a natural path, leaving good position for the 2-ball shot. No English or excessive speed is required, although the rail does induce natural English, which lengthens the rebound off the bottom rail (on the right, in the figure).

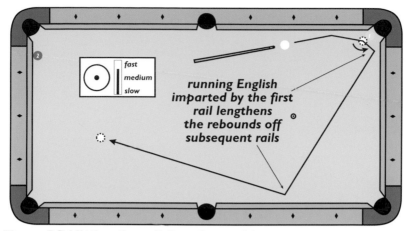

Figure 5.7 Hitting the rail first, for position

 NV 5.5 – Hitting the rail first, for position

normal video

Another case where a rail-first shot is useful is when there is an obstacle ball preventing a straight-in shot. In the example shown in **Figure 5.8**, there is an obstacle ball between the cue ball and the 1-ball, preventing a straight shot at the 1-ball. In this case, we have little choice but to hit the rail first (see NV 5.6). An alternative would be to kick the cue ball off the bottom rail to pocket the 1-ball, but this is a more difficult shot, and it might not result in good position for the 2-ball shot.

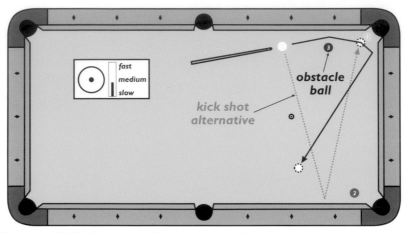

Figure 5.8 Hitting the rail first, to avoid an obstacle ball

normal video

NV 5.6 – Hitting the rail first to avoid an obstacle ball

Principle 5.7 **Hitting the rail first**

*Sometimes it is prudent or necessary to deflect the cue ball off a rail, to achieve good position (see **Figure 5.7**) or to avoid an obstacle ball (see **Figure 5.8**).*

* This is a type of a kick shot (see more details in **Section 6.03**).

A final technique that can be used to help with position control is called "**cheating the pocket**." This technique comes into play when you are faced with a straight-in shot, but you want the cue ball to travel off the line to the pocket, after pocketing the ball. **Figure 5.9** and NV 5.7 illustrate an example of how this is done. The cue ball is perfectly lined up to hit the 1-ball straight into the side pocket. However, if the 1-ball is hit straight in, the cue ball will remain on the line going through the side pockets. To get the cue ball closer to the 2-ball for an easier next shot, you can cheat the pocket. In other words, you hit the 1-ball at an angle away from the center of the pocket. The 1-ball still goes in, but now, with a draw stroke, you can position the cue ball closer to the 2-ball for an easy next shot. In this example, draw is a better option than follow because the 3-ball is in the way.

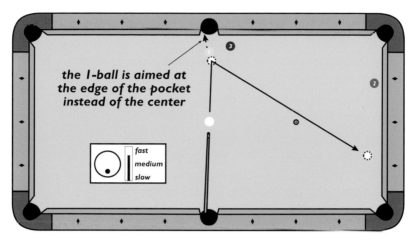

Figure 5.9 Cheating the pocket to achieve position

NV 5.7 – Cheating a pocket

normal video

Principle 5.8 **Cheating a pocket**

You can aim away from the center of a pocket to help achieve desired cue ball position for the next shot (see **Figure 5.9**).

- The amount you can cheat a pocket is much larger when the object ball is closer to the pocket because the effective target size is much larger (see **Section 3.06**, starting on page 60).

Section 5.03 *The makable region*

The previous section presented various techniques that can be used to achieve good position from one shot to the next. Often, there are many places you can leave the cue ball that would be considered good positions. So how do you choose the best place to try to leave the cue ball? Some placements will result in easier shots than others; but in deciding where to leave the cue ball, you must consider more than just the position for the next shot. You must also consider the difficulty in reaching each possible position and choose a shot that will not be too difficult—ideally, with a large margin of error. **Figure 5.10** shows an example where these ideas are important. The figure shows the end of an 8-ball game where you are shooting solids and have only one more ball to pocket before attempting the 8-ball. Obviously, you want to pocket the ball in the top-left corner pocket and leave the cue ball in a position from which you can easily pocket the 8-ball. **Figure 5.11** illustrates what I call the **makable region**. The shaded region shows all the places from where the 8-ball can be pocketed in the bottom-right corner pocket (without using kick or bank shots, which are described in **Chapter 6**). Therefore, after pocketing the ball in the top-left corner pocket, you need to make sure the cue ball ends up somewhere in the makable region, so the 8-ball can be pocketed. But where is the best place to target within the makable region?

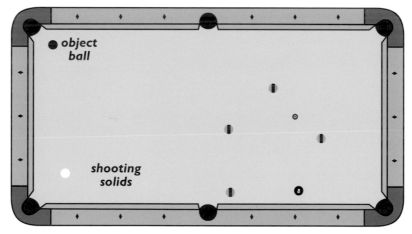

Figure 5.10 Example shot with several position-play alternatives

Figure 5.12, **Figure 5.13**, and **Figure 5.14** illustrate various shots that will pocket the last solid and leave the cue ball in the makable region. **Figure 5.12** shows an example of extremely poor shot selection. First, because the cue ball bounces off two rails, it is difficult to

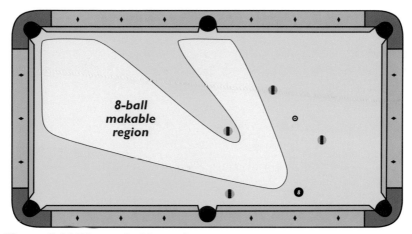

Figure 5.11 The makable region

control the speed and the rebound angles of the shot. Second, because the cue ball path leaves the makable region twice (and can leave it again if the shot speed is too fast), you risk leaving the cue ball in a place where you cannot pocket the 8-ball (see **Principle 5.9**). Finally, even if you leave the cue ball in the exact position shown, you still have a fairly difficult cut shot to win the game.

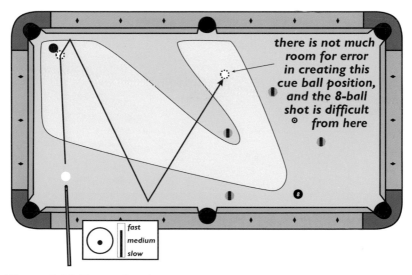

Figure 5.12 Example of poor position and a difficult shot

Principle 5.9 **Stay in the makable region**

SCHOOL ZONE

When playing for position for the next shot, try to have the cue ball remain, during its entire motion, in the makable region for the next shot.

• If the cue ball leaves and enters the makable region (e.g., see **Figure 5.12**), you risk leaving yourself with an unmakable shot if your speed control is not precise.

Figure 5.13 shows another example of poor shot selection. Again, the cue ball leaves the makable region and speed control is critical. Left English is also being used, which increases the difficulty factor and introduces all the potential pitfalls that come with using English (see **Chapter 4**). With this shot, there is also a chance of scratching in the side pocket or hitting one of the stripes, which can lead to unpredictable results. If this shot is executed perfectly, the cue ball is left in a great place to pocket the 8-ball with ease; however, there is too much risk involved.

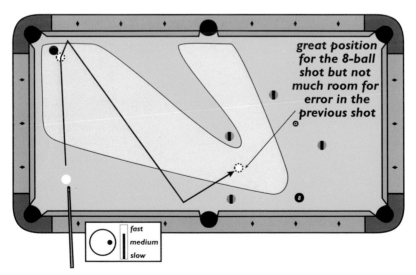

Figure 5.13 Example of great position from a risky and difficult shot

Figure 5.14 shows the best shot for this example. The cue ball is hit softly with no English, making the shot very easy to control. Also, the cue ball never leaves the makable region, even if there is a large error in the speed or angle of the shot. The large circle in the figure illustrates the margin of error. The actual margin or error is even larger than the circle implies because as long as the cue ball is left anywhere in the shaded region (even outside of the circle shown), you can still pocket the 8-ball. If you leave the cue ball within the circle shown, the shot on the 8-ball is not as easy as the shot resulting from executing the **Figure 5.13** shot perfectly; but again, the risk level is too high with the **Figure 5.13** shot. **Principle 5.10** summarizes the results of this example.

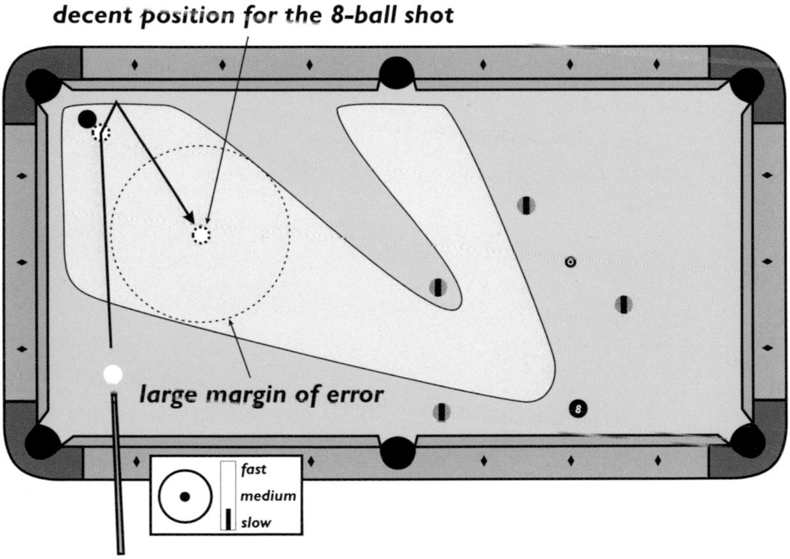

Figure 5.14 Example of good position from a safe and easy shot

Principle 5.10 **The best spot in the makable region**

*When playing for position for the next shot, try to aim for a safe portion of the makable region, where there is a large margin of error (see **Figure 5.14**).*

- Do not always play for the easiest follow-on shot (see **Figure 5.13**).
- Try not to leave the makable region during the shot (see **Principle 5.9**).
- See **Section 3.05** (starting on page 56) for information on how to assess shot difficulty from different regions within the makable region.

When trying to position the cue ball for a shot, be aware that when the cue ball is close to or against a rail, the difficulty of the shot increases dramatically (see **Figure 5.15**). As summarized in **Principle 5.11**, because the rail partially hides the cue ball, and because the cue stick needs to be elevated, several disadvantages arise.

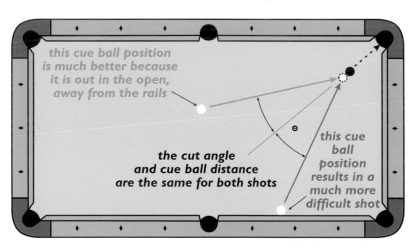

Figure 5.15 Keep the cue ball away from the rail

Principle 5.11 **Keep the cue ball away from the rail**

*Everything else being the same, when the cue ball is close to or against a rail, the shot is much more difficult than if the cue ball were away from the rail (see **Figure 5.15**).*

- You have to elevate the cue stick to provide solid contact with the cue ball; this makes it more difficult to aim and can lead to English curve (see **Principle 4.10** on page 101).
- You have to use an elevated, extended-rail hand bridge, which is not as stable as a normal hand bridge (see **Section 2.03**, starting on page 21).
- You do not have as many choices for English, because you do not have full access to the cue ball.
- The cue ball will have normal roll or follow, unless you elevate the cue stick and use a firm downward draw stroke, which is difficult to execute consistently.

Section 5.04   *Ball groupings*

In the game of 8-ball, one basic strategy that can help in planning how to run a table is looking for and exploiting **ball groupings**. A ball grouping is a set of two or more balls of the same type (stripes or solid), in the same general area of the table, that can be easily pocketed in sequence with high-percentage shots. Looking for ball groupings allows you to divide a run of many balls into separate runs of smaller numbers of balls. **Figure 5.16** shows an example table layout where this technique can be applied. The solids player has all seven balls remaining, but by dividing the balls into groupings, running the table can seem a lot more manageable. Instead of thinking, "I have to pocket all seven balls," you can think, "All I have to do is pocket the grouping of four balls at the tail end of the table, being sure to leave angle on the last ball to get up-table, and then pocket the grouping of three balls at the head end of the table."

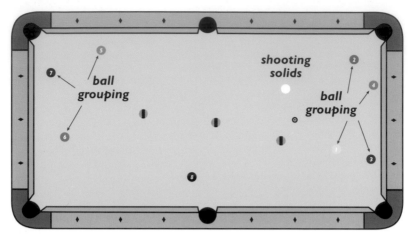

Figure 5.16 Example table layout with ball groupings

Figure 5.17 illustrates how the first cluster can be easily pocketed. The 1-ball is pocketed with a stop shot. A soft center-hit is used on the 2-ball shot, to set up for a soft shot on the 3-ball, to set up for the 4-ball. Note how an angle is left for the 4-ball shot to make it easier to get up-table for the second ball grouping, as illustrated in **Figure 5.18**. Top-left English is used to achieve the cue-ball trajectory shown. With the resulting cue ball position, **Figure 5.19** illustrates how the second grouping of balls can be pocketed. The 5-ball, 6-ball, and 7-ball are all easily pocketed with soft to medium speed shots, each leading to good position for the subsequent shot. Note how an angle is left on the 7-ball to help achieve good position on the 8-ball, for an easy victory.

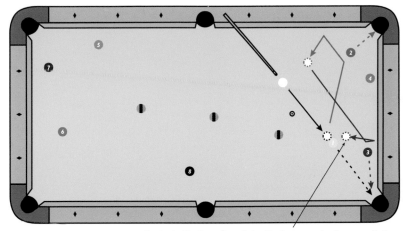

*an angle is left for the 4-ball shot to help send the
cue ball up-table for the second grouping*

Figure 5.17 Pocketing the first grouping of balls

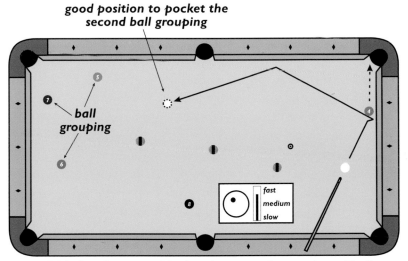

*good position to pocket the
second ball grouping*

*ball
grouping*

Figure 5.18 Getting up-table for the second grouping of balls

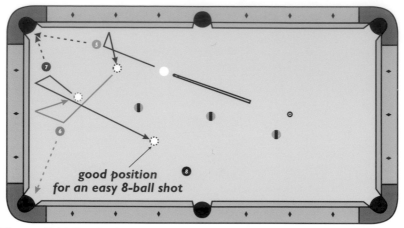

Figure 5.19 Pocketing the second grouping of balls

One huge advantage of shooting within a ball grouping is that your margin of error can often be quite large. The reason for this is that the makable regions for all of the balls (see the previous section) often overlap and cover a large area of the table, within and around the grouping. Therefore, you can leave the cue ball almost anywhere within the grouping and still be able to make a good shot. **Figure 5.20** illustrates a good example for a grouping of three balls, assuming you are playing 8-ball. The makable regions for the three balls cover much of the table. This makes it easy to approach the grouping with the cue ball, because you will have a shot from almost any position. The best direction from which to approach the ball grouping is illustrated in the figure. With this approach, the cue ball remains in the areas of makable-region overlap, giving you more options for your first shot. Also, regardless of how poor your speed control is, you are guaranteed to have a shot, because the cue ball will never be outside of a makable region. As **Principle 5.12** summarizes, the best place to aim when approaching a ball grouping is the center of the region of overlap of makable regions. Two recommended cue-ball target positions are illustrated in the figure.

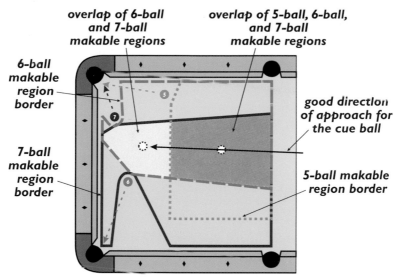

overlap of 6-ball and 7-ball makable regions

overlap of 5-ball, 6-ball, and 7-ball makable regions

6-ball makable region border

7-ball makable region border

good direction of approach for the cue ball

5-ball makable region border

Figure 5.20 Overlap of makable regions in a ball grouping

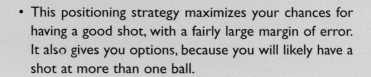

Principle 5.12 **Aim for makable-region overlaps**

*When approaching a ball grouping, aim for the center of the area of overlap of makable regions (see **Figure 5.20**).*

- This positioning strategy maximizes your chances for having a good shot, with a fairly large margin of error. It also gives you options, because you will likely have a shot at more than one ball.

Section 5.05   *Break-up and avoidance shots*

When attempting to "run the table" (i.e., make the entire sequence of balls necessary to win the game), there will be times when you need to break up balls that are tied up and cannot be made easily. These are called **break-up shots**. At other times, you will want to avoid hitting balls that are in favorable locations (e.g., balls set up for easy shots, or balls blocking shots for your opponent). These are called **avoidance shots**. The methods for cue-ball path control presented in **Section 4.07** (starting on page 115) are invaluable in these situations.

Figure 5.21 shows a table layout that presents an ideal opportunity for a break-up shot. An inexperienced player might think, "The 2-ball is a 'duck' in the pocket, and the cue ball is so close, I should definitely pocket that ball first." An experienced player would instead think, "I want to win the game by pocketing the four remaining solids and then the 8-ball. To do this, I need to break up the 3-ball and 4-ball. Neither ball can be pocketed easily, if at all, in their current positions. Also, the 2-ball is a good insurance policy in case I need an easy shot to get me out of trouble later, helping me achieve position for another shot. Therefore, I will leave the 2-ball there, pocket the 1-ball first, and break up the 3-ball and 4-ball in the process." In a shot like this, the 2-ball is called an **insurance ball** because it can be pocketed fairly easily from almost any spot on the table, in case you lose control of the cue ball on a previous shot.

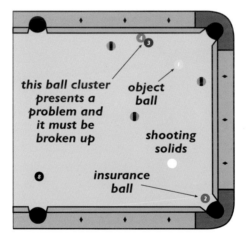

Figure 5.21 Example break-up opportunity

Figure 5.22 illustrates how the 90° rule is used to plan the break-up shot. Bottom English and medium to fast speed are used to ensure that the cue ball has no spin when it contacts the 1-ball. When the cue ball hits an object ball with no vertical-plane spin (i.e., a stun shot), the cue ball and object-ball paths separate at 90° (see **Section 3.03**, starting on page 41). In this example, the cue ball will deflect off the 1-ball and hit the 3-ball fairly squarely, causing the 3-ball and 4-ball to separate and rebound off the rail. A possible end result of the shot is shown in **Figure 5.23**. The 3-ball and 4-ball are no longer tied up. More importantly, the remaining balls can now be pocketed with ease, resulting in a victory. As illustrated in **Figure 5.24**, the 3-ball is made first, then the 2-ball. After pocketing the 2-ball, the cue ball can be left in good position for a straight-in shot on the 4 ball, resulting in an easy shot on the 8-ball.

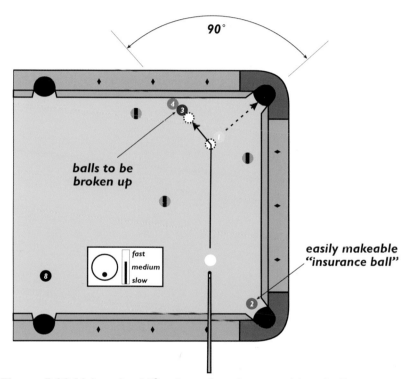

Figure 5.22 Using the 90° rule to break up problem balls

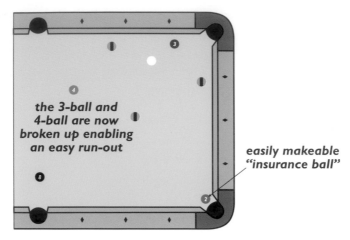

Figure 5.23 Possible table layout after a break-up shot

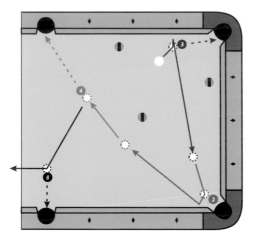

Figure 5.24 Running the table after a break-up shot

With a break-up shot, the goal is to purposely drive the cue ball into object balls. With avoidance shots, the goal is to purposely avoid hitting certain balls. In the game of 8-ball, the balls you want to avoid could be your own (stripes or solids), if they already happen to be in good places (e.g., close to a pocket, or blocking shots for your opponent). The balls to avoid could also be your opponent's balls if they happen to be in a bad place for your opponent (e.g., tied up in a cluster). Also, sometimes you just want to avoid hitting balls so the cue ball can end up in good position for your next shot. **Figure 5.25** shows a table layout where an avoidance shot is appropriate, assuming you are shooting solids. The two stripes are tied up, and you would like to leave them that way so if you do not run the table, your opponent will be faced with a difficult shot. You also need to avoid the stripes to reliably control the position of the cue ball.

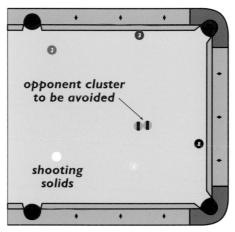

Figure 5.25 Example table layout requiring an avoidance shot

Figure 5.26 shows how the 30° rule (see **Section 3.04**, starting on page 48) can be used to plan the path of the cue ball, assuming the 1-ball will be pocketed first. Note that the 90° rule would predict that the cue ball would deflect directly into the tied-up stripes. But remember, the 90° rule only applies exactly in the case of a stun stroke. In this shot, the cue ball will be rolling when it hits the 1-ball. The roll is ensured by the use of a slight follow stroke. After hitting the 1-ball, the cue ball's path is deflected approximately 30°, resulting in good position for the 2-ball, after rebound off the end rail. **Figure 5.27** shows how the remainder of the table can be run easily, resulting in victory.

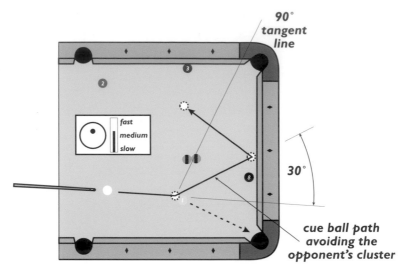

Figure 5.26 Using the 30° rule to plan an avoidance shot

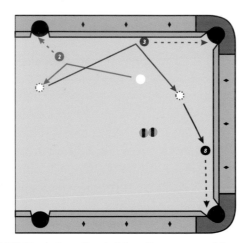

Figure 5.27 Running the table after an avoidance shot

Section 5.06   *Safeties and defensive play*

This section presents what are probably the most important topics for advanced pool play in this book: safeties and defensive play. A **safety** is a legal shot where you deliberately miss, with the goal of leaving the cue ball in a difficult position for your opponent. Hopefully, after a safety, your opponent will not even be able to execute a legal shot (e.g., hitting a legal object ball first) resulting in ball-in-hand for your next shot (see **Section 1.03**, starting on page 6). When a good player has ball-in-hand, he or she will often be able to run the table. Defensive play is a technique you use when you are not confident you will make a particular shot. The goal of a **defensive shot** is to leave the cue ball in a place that would be unfavorable for your opponent if you miss the shot—and hopefully, favorable for you if you happen to make the shot. "Favorable" for you could mean you can make another shot or have a chance to execute a good safety shot. "Unfavorable" for your opponent means he or she will not be able to easily make a shot or to play a safety where the cue ball ends up; and hopefully, your opponent's shot could result in a ball-in-hand for you.

Often the biggest hurdle for beginner or intermediate players with safety and defensive play is becoming comfortable with the idea of not playing an offensive shot. Sometimes it is better to skillfully miss a shot rather than to attempt to make a risky and difficult shot. Some people consider safety and defensive play to be wimpy or even belligerent. That's ridiculous (see **Principle 5.13**)! Safeties and defensive play are very important aspects of the game of pool. These types of shots require thoughtful strategy and much skill, and good safety play is often what separates a great player from a good player. If you find yourself playing an inexperienced opponent (e.g., in a bar) who does not appreciate the skill involved with playing safeties and defense, try to disguise your safeties as "missed shot," adding a dramatic sigh or expletive for effect when you "miss" the shot. If they are not smart enough to realize the importance of defense and safeties in pool, they are also probably not smart enough to realize that you are being deceptive.

Principle 5.13 **Defense and safeties are OK**

If you are not absolutely confident about making a shot, plan the shot defensively or play a safety.

- Playing a defensive shot or a safety is skillful, not shameful.
- A safety is much better (i.e., increases you chances for victory) than a shot of desperation.

One of the most basic principles concerning defensive play in the game of 8-ball is summarized in **Principle 5.14**. If you are not totally confident that you will make a shot, try to hit it at speed slow enough so that if you miss, you will leave your ball blocking the pocket. Also, as was shown in **Section 3.06** (starting on page 60), you have a better chance of making most shots when they are hit softly, due to the larger effective size of the pocket. **Figure 5.28** shows an example where a slow defensive shot is appropriate. A stripe is blocking the path to the 2-ball, so the best shot is to cut the 1-ball in the bottom-corner pocket. However, when a cut angle is large your margin of error is fairly small (see **Principle 3.17** on page 78). Therefore, as illustrated in **Figure 5.29**, you should hit the 1-ball just hard enough to get the 1-ball to and into the pocket. This is referred to as using **pocket speed**. That way, if you miss, the corner pocket will be blocked. Draw is used on the 1-ball shot to help avoid incidental ball collisions, and to achieve good position for the 2-ball shot. If you make the 1-ball, the position is good for pocketing the 2-ball and for getting position on the 8-ball to win the game. If you happen to miss the 1-ball, the corner pocket will be blocked, and your opponent will be faced with a difficult shot. This is a perfect shot because if you make it you will easily win the game, and if you miss it your opponent faces a difficult situation. That's what defensive play is all about. This type of shot is also called a **two-way shot** because there are two favorable ways the shot can work out. You should always look for these opportunities because a two-way shot can be a win-win situation (see more later in this section).

Principle 5.14 **Blocked pocket from soft defensive miss**

In the game of 8-ball, hit shots softly when possible, so if you miss a shot you leave your object ball close to or blocking the target pocket.

- Sometimes, blocking a pocket can be more damaging to your opponent than making the shot (see **Figure 5.29**).
- If you cannot block a pocket easily with a missed shot, at least try to ensure that the final cue ball position will still be difficult for your opponent.

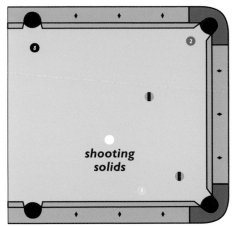

Figure 5.28 Example shot where you should block the pocket if you miss

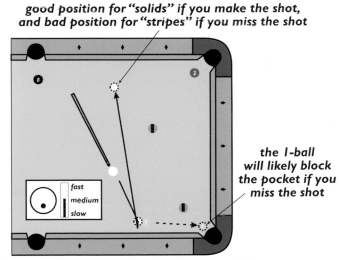

Figure 5.29 Missed shot, leading to blocked pocket

Safeties are used most often when you are faced with a difficult or impossible shot. Safeties can also be used when you are faced with a makable shot but you have an opportunity to leave your opponent in an extremely difficult situation. In either case, the goal for executing a safety is to get ball-in-hand in the event that your opponent cannot execute a legal shot (i.e., hitting a legal object ball first without a foul) after you play your safety shot. A good player with ball-in-hand can usually win the game, unless the ball layout on the table is extremely poor (e.g., if several sets of balls are tightly clustered or touching). As **Principle 5.15** summarizes, the best offensive shot you can make might sometimes be a defensive safety shot.

Principle 5.15 **The best offense is a good defense**

A well-played safety can result in ball-in-hand. Therefore, this seemingly defensive shot can result in a great opportunity for offense.

- A well-planned safety is usually a better choice than a risky attempt at a difficult shot.
- A good player can often run the table to win the game when presented with ball-in-hand.

Figure 5.30 shows an ideal opportunity for a safety in a game of 9-ball. You could attempt the 1-ball-2-ball combination in the side pocket, which is tempting, because the balls are so close together and so close to the pocket. However, combination shots are often more difficult than they seem (see **Section 7.01**). No other shot on the 1-ball is really possible without significant risk. The safety shot illustrated in **Figure 5.31**, called a **position safety**, is a much better alternative. It is fairly easy to execute, and more importantly, it is very effective. In this example you make no attempt to pocket a ball. Instead, you send the 1-ball up-table (to the left, in the figure) and try to have it come to rest as close as possible to the head rail. At the same time, bottom English is used to help send the cue ball down-table, so that it comes to rest as close as possible to the foot rail. **Figure 5.32** shows the ideal ball layout after the shot. Having the 1-ball close to the rail limits shot possibilities for your opponent, and having the cue ball close to a rail forces your opponent to elevate the cue stick and hit the cue ball above center, which reduces accuracy. The cue ball placement also takes advantage of the 5-ball, 6-ball, and 9-ball, which serve as obstacle balls for your opponent, making it more difficult for him or her to shoot for the 1-ball. Chances are, your opponent will not be able to even make contact with the 1-ball on the next shot. This will give you ball-in-hand, providing a good opportunity to make several shots and a chance to run the table for a victory.

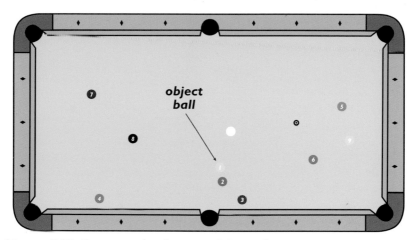

Figure 5.30 Opportunity for a position safety

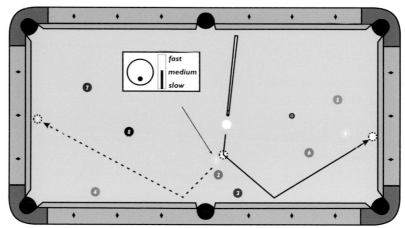

Figure 5.31 Executing a position safety

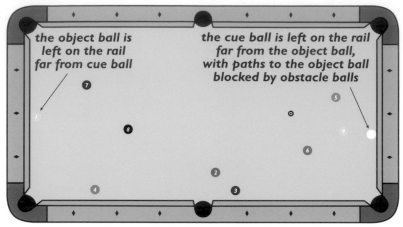

the object ball is left on the rail far from cue ball

the cue ball is left on the rail far from the object ball, with paths to the object ball blocked by obstacle balls

Figure 5.32 End result of a position safety

Figure 5.33 shows an example ball layout representing an excellent safety opportunity in a game of 8-ball. You are shooting solids. The only open, non-rail shot is a rail cut-shot on the 5-ball, in the upper-right corner pocket, but this is a difficult shot. You could also attempt a 1-ball-3-ball combination shot, or a kick shot at the 4-ball, but these shots are also difficult. Instead, because the 1-ball and 2-ball are so close together and so close to the cue ball, you have an excellent opportunity for a **frozen-ball safety**. **Figure 5.34** and NV 5.8 illustrate how to execute the shot. The 1-ball is hit rather squarely, with slight draw. The result is that the cue ball nearly comes to a stop and drifts a little toward the 2-ball. **Figure 5.35** shows the final ball layout. Ideally, the cue ball ends up frozen to (touching) the 2-ball. This **snookers** your opponent by blocking all straight paths to his or her balls. With the layout shown in the figure, it would be very difficult for your opponent to make contact with either stripe on the next shot. This would result in ball-in-hand, which would give you a good opportunity to pocket the remaining solids and win the game.

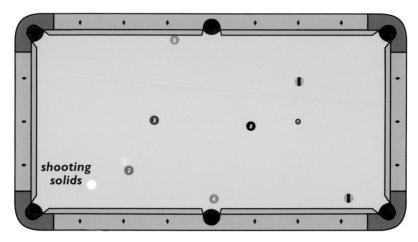

Figure 5.33 Opportunity for a frozen-ball safety

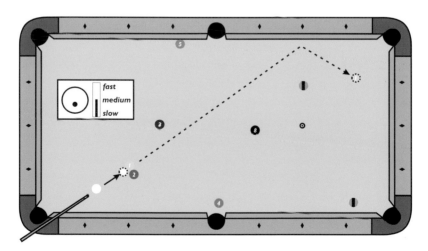

Figure 5.34 Executing a frozen-ball safety

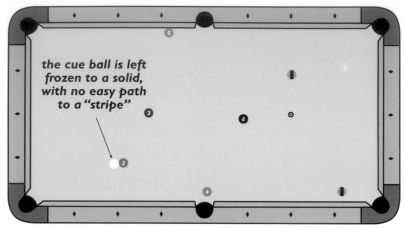

Figure 5.35 End result of a frozen-ball safety

normal video

NV 5.8 – Freeze the cue ball on an object ball, for a safety

Sometimes, when you are faced with a difficult shot, you can play a **two-way shot**. This is where you attempt a shot while playing for a safety, in case you miss the shot. This strategy is related to the blocked-pocket defense described in **Principle 5.14** (on page 154), but here your added goal (besides trying to make the shot) is to leave the cue ball in a very difficult place for your opponent. Hopefully, if you miss the shot, the strategy will result in ball-in-hand for you on the next shot. **Figure 5.36** shows an example opportunity for a two-way shot in a game of 9-ball. There are no easy shots available. About the only reasonable attempts are a 1-ball-4-ball combination in the bottom side pocket, or a 1-ball bank shot into the top-left corner pocket. However, these are difficult shots, so you want to have a defensive (or offensive-safety) mindset. **Figure 5.37** illustrates a good approach: attempt the 1-ball bank, while leaving the cue ball in a good place for you and a bad place for your opponent. With the final placement shown in **Figure 5.38**, you would have an easy shot on the 2-ball and a good chance to run the table, if you pocket the 1-ball. If you miss the 1-ball, your opponent would be faced with an extremely difficult shot on the 1-ball that would probably result in ball-in-hand for you (unless your opponent is very good at executing a jump shot as described in

Section 7.10). With ball-in-hand, you could then smile, or even taunt your opponent—if a friend—saying, "It's *too bad* I missed that shot."

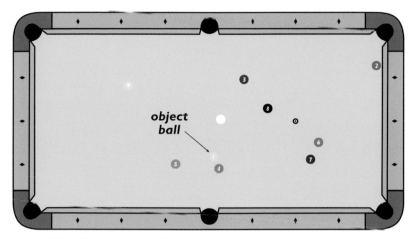

Figure 5.36 Opportunity for a two-way shot

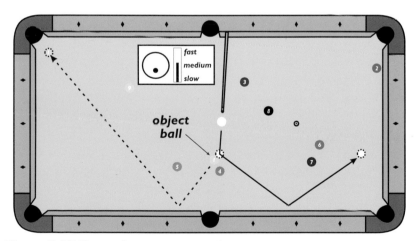

Figure 5.37 Executing a two-way shot

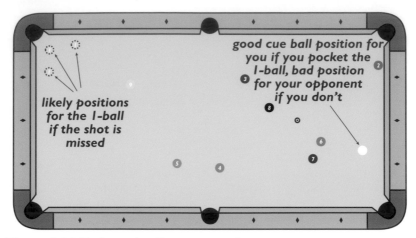

Figure 5.38 End result of a two-way shot

In the game of 8-ball, there is a special safety shot called **in-and-safe** (see the 8-ball rules in **Section 1.03**, starting on page 6). This is where you make a legal shot, and then turn over table control to your opponent, provided you declare your intention (by stating "in-and-safe" or "safety") before the shot. **Figure 5.39** illustrates an opportunity where playing an in-and-safe is an option. With the layout shown, assuming you are shooting solids, you might not feel totally confident to run the table. Fortunately, by playing an in-and-safe with the easy shot illustrated in **Figure 5.40**, you can create a good chance to win the game. As shown in **Figure 5.41**, the cue ball position left for your opponent would put him or her in a difficult situation, because it is very unlikely he or she would be able to execute a legal shot on a stripe. This would result in ball-in-hand for you. With ball-in-hand, it would be fairly straightforward to run the three remaining solids and pocket the 8-ball for the win. **Figure 5.42** shows an example of how you could run the table to pocket the remaining solids and win the game.

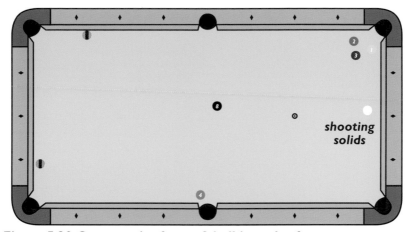

Figure 5.39 Opportunity for an 8-ball in-and-safe

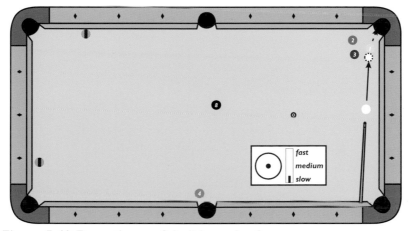

Figure 5.40 Executing an 8-ball in-and-safe

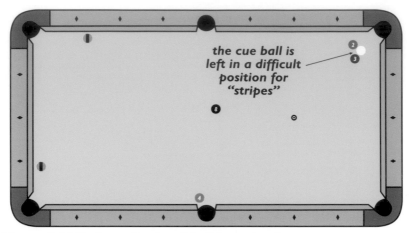

Figure 5.41 End result of an 8-ball in-and-safe

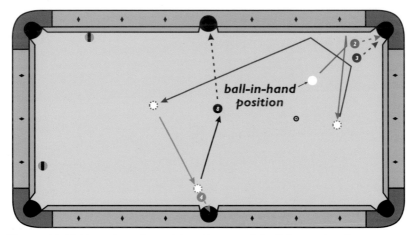

Figure 5.42 Running the table after an 8-ball in-and-safe

Once you are comfortable with the ideas of safeties and defensive play, the next step is to remain aware of possible safety and defensive-play opportunities while you are playing. Many players have tunnel vision, or stubbornness, that prevents them from seeing possible safety and defensive plays. They just want to make a shot, no matter how difficult or risky it might be. As **Principle 5.16** summarizes, always keep your eyes open for possible safety opportunities.

Principle 5.16 **Always look for safeties**

*Always try to be aware of, and actively look for, safety oppor-
tunities.*

- Refer to this section for what types of safety shots to
  look for (including position safeties, frozen-ball
  safeties, two-way shots, or in-and-safe shots).

There is nothing better than a well-executed safety. Inexperienced players that have yet to "see the light" might not agree; but if they fall victim to
safeties enough, they will learn to appreciate the skill and to bravely join the
ranks of winning players. The ball-in-hand reward is extremely valuable;
and for a good player it will usually lead to victory. When presented with
ball-in-hand, choose your first shot carefully, because it is the one time you
can guarantee where the cue ball will be, in preparation for a shot.
Principle 5.17 summarizes the opportunities to look for and exploit when
you have ball-in-hand. Don't just take an obvious shot. Think several shots
ahead, and look for the critical shot that will be necessary to win the game.

Principle 5.17 **Things you can do with ball-in-hand**

*With ball-in-hand, look for the opportunities listed, involving
shots that might be critical to winning a game.*

- If playing 8-ball, locate the object ball for which it will
  be hardest to achieve position, and consider making
  this shot first.
- If balls are clustered together, consider a break-up
  shot (see **Section 5.05** starting on page 147).
- If the table layout is very problematic (e.g., with several clusters and poorly positioned balls), consider making a ball, and then setting up for a safety shot. Consider
  some of the shot types presented in this section.
- If there are no problem balls, run the table using fundamental position-play techniques (see **Section 5.02**,
  starting on page 126).

Because safeties can be so great, there is the danger that your opponent will execute a great safety shot against you. If this happens, and you have no reasonable chance of contacting a legal object ball, you should accept that your opponent will get ball-in-hand. What, then, can you do in these situations? **Figure 5.43** illustrates a 9-ball example of this dilemma. You have no reasonable chance to make contact with the 3-ball. In this case, the best thing to do is to leave your opponent with a difficult ball layout. **Figure 5.44** illustrates a possible solution. Because you are hitting the 7-ball first, and not the 3-ball, your opponent will have ball-in-hand on the next shot; but there was no reasonable way to prevent ball-in-hand anyway. However, by freezing the 7-ball against the 3-ball, you have prevented your opponent from having an easy shot on the 3-ball. **Figure 5.45** shows the final ball layout. If, instead, you had tried to make contact with the 3-ball first, by attempting a wild multiple-rail kick shot, your opponent would still have ball-in-hand and have a good chance to run the table and win the game. Now, because you have purposefully (and deviously) changed the ball layout, your opponent might be forced to attempt another safety shot. This is a better alternative than losing the game.

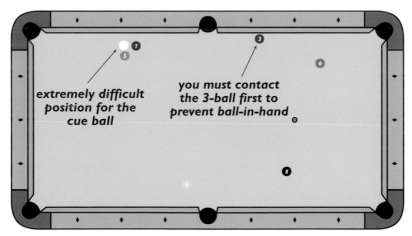

Figure 5.43 Example ball layout after a well-executed safety

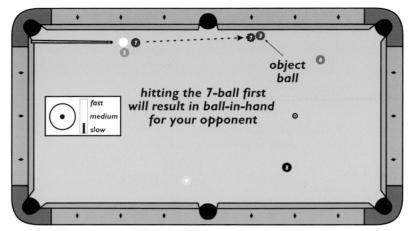

Figure 5.44 Possible reply to a well-executed safety

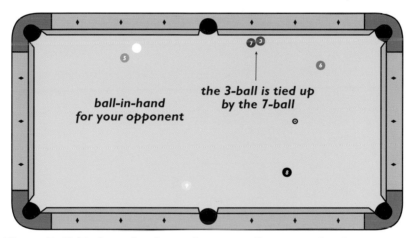

Figure 5.45 End result of a reply to a well-executed safety

I want to end this chapter with what may be the most important advice in this entire book: *Learn from your mistakes!!!* (see **Principle 5.18**) Top players in most sports contemplate every missed shot or error to learn from their mistakes. The goal of this is to not repeat the same mistake in the future. Tiger Woods, the golf legend, is an excellent example of this. The next time you see him on TV, observe how intense he is after a missed shot. I think his intensity and his desire to improve are among his best skills.

Principle 5.18 **Learn from your mistakes**

Use every mistake as a learning experience to improve your game. Immediately after a missed shot, try to figure out what caused the miss, so you can prevent it from reoccurring in the future.

- Possible explanations for missing a shot include:
    - poor stroke or follow-through
    - insufficient cut angle to account for cut throw
    - failure to account for English deflection, curve, or throw
    - poor shot selection based on your level of ability.

Chapter 6
Bank and Kick Shots

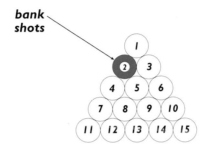

This chapter presents everything you ever wanted or needed to know about executing bank shots and kick shots, where you bounce balls off rail cushions to your advantage. If you have the ability to make a wide variety of bank and kick shots, you will be able to get out of many difficult situations and win many more games.

Section 6.01   *Introduction*

Figure 6.1 illustrates **bank shot** terminology. The cue ball strikes the object ball, with or without a cut angle, and drives the object ball to the rail. The **approach angle** (aka angle of approach, angle of incidence, or entering angle) is the angle the object-ball path forms with the perpendicular to the rail. The angle is small for balls hit more directly at the rail, and large for balls striking at a glancing angle. In the figure, the approach angle is about 40°. The **rebound angle** (aka angle of rebound, angle of reflection, or leaving angle) is the angle at which the object ball leaves after striking the rail. The approach and rebound angles are measured relative to the position the ball is in when it is in contact with the rail, in the **rail grove**. The rail grove is the imaginary line adjacent to the rail, locating the center of the banked ball when it is in contact with the rail. The rail grove is the line upon which a ball rolls when it travels down a rail (e.g., with a rail cut shot). Sometimes, the rail grove is visible on tables as a result of excessive use.

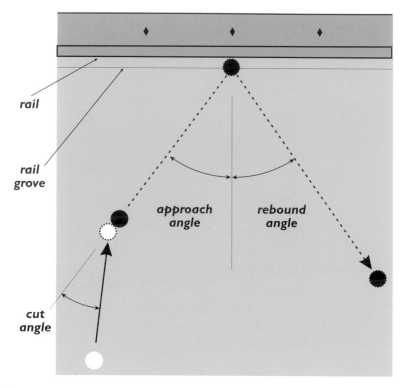

Figure 6.1 Bank-shot terminology

When the cue ball is banked off the rail before contacting the object ball (see **Figure 6.2**), the shot is called a **kick shot**. These shots are sometimes the only way to pocket a ball, and can often be the only reply to a well executed safety. Fortunately, all of the methods used to aim normal bank shots can also be used to plan kick shots; although, with kick shots you have more control over the spin and English of the ball hitting the rail (the cue ball).

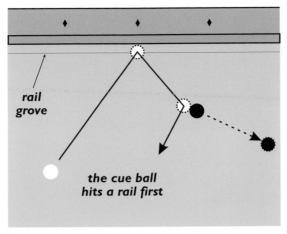

Figure 6.2 Kick shot

There are many different methods for aiming bank and kick shots. They are based on basic geometry principles. The most basic and practical methods are presented in Section 6.02 and Section 6.03, and they include the following:

- equal rail-distance bank shot
- equal extended-rail-distance bank shot
- parallel midpoint-line bank shot
- mirror-image kick shot
- equal separation-distance kick shot

Section 7.06 presents some additional, more complicated, methods useful in planning multiple-rail bank and kick shots.

Principle 6.1 summarizes the geometric assumption upon which all of the bank- and kick-shot aiming methods are based. It is the same principle that governs how rays of light reflect off mirrors: "The angle of incidence equals the angle of reflection." (If you had a high school physics class, maybe you vaguely remember this concept.) Unfortunately, this assumption is true for a pool ball bouncing off a rail only when the ball hits the rail with medium speed and no sidespin (see Section 6.04). However, the aiming methods for bank and kick shots that are based on the reflection principle are still useful because they provide good aiming references from which you can make adjustments derived from your experience-based intuition. Even if the required adjustments are not intuitively obvious to you, or you are not totally confident with your intuition, you can plan the adjustments based on the speed and spin principles presented in Section 6.04, Section 6.05, and Section 6.06.

Principle 6.1 **Bank-shot geometry**

*Generally, a bank-shot rebound angle (the angle of reflection) is the same as the approach angle (the angle of incidence) (**see Figure 6.1**).*

- This statement is not true at fast or slow speeds, or when the object ball is close to the rail (see **Section 6.04**), with English (see **Section 6.05**), or for cut shots (see **Section 6.06**).

As illustrated in **Figure 6.3**, if you could use a mirror to help you aim bank and kick shots, it would be very easy to visualize the ideal required aiming-direction. You would simply need to move the mirror along the rail (in the rail grove) until you could see the target pocket in the reflection. If you shot the object ball at the image in the mirror with medium speed, the object ball would bounce off the rail into the pocket (provided the mirror were removed during the shot). Unfortunately, using a mirror as an aiming aid is illegal, because you are not allowed to use any special equipment as an aiming aid. If you are using a mirror for practice, don't forget to have someone remove the mirror before you shoot (especially if you are superstitious, or if you borrowed a "special" mirror from your spouse).

mirror placed at the aiming point on the rail

the target pocket is visible in the mirror

a) overhead view

b) aiming line view

Figure 6.3 Aiming a bank shot with a mirror

Section 6.02   *Bank-shot aiming methods*

The most basic method for aiming bank shots is illustrated in **Figure 6.4**. It is called the **equal rail-distance method** and is based on **Principle 6.1**. To use the method, you move your rail-impact aim point along the bank rail until the distances shown in the figure are equal. The distances are measured along the bank rail or along the rail opposite from the bank rail, adjacent to the target pocket. As summarized in **Principle 6.2**, the distances that are equal are between the projected aiming-line point and the rail-impact aim point, and between the rail-impact aim point and the target point. Note that all of the points are defined along the rail groves, which is important when trying to measure distances accurately.

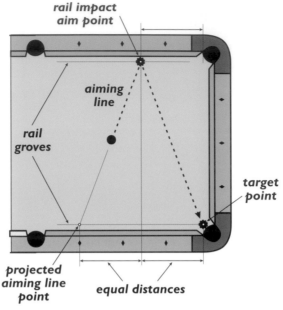

Figure 6.4 Equal rail-distance bank method

Principle 6.2 **Equal rail-distance bank method**

*To make a medium-speed bank shot with no English, the rail distances between the projected aiming-line point, rail-impact aim point, and target point must be equal (see **Figure 6.4** and NV 6.1).*

- This principle is a direct consequence of **Principle 6.1** on page 172.
- The distances are not equal at fast or slow speeds, or when the object ball is close to the rail (see **Section 6.04**), with English (see **Section 6.05**), or for cut shots (see **Section 6.06**).

NV 6.1 – Equal-distance bank method

To use the equal rail-distance method, first use your intuition to determine where you think the rail-impact aim point should be. This defines the estimated aiming line, which you can project to the bottom rail (e.g., using the cue stick) to define the projected aiming-line point. Then, check to see if the distance from the target point to the projected aiming-line point is twice the distance from the target point to the rail-impact aim point. As shown in **Figure 6.4**, the shorter distance can be easily measured along either rail or, as an alternative to measuring the distance from the target point to the rail-impact aim point, you could measure the distance from the rail-impact aim point to the projected aiming-line point. If the distances are not equal, you need to adjust your aim. As illustrated in **Figure 6.5**, if your first guess for the rail-impact aim point if too far to the right, the rail distances will not be equal and you will need to move your aim point to the left, to equalize the rail distances and the approach and rebound angles. **Figure 6.6** shows what happens if your guess is in error in the other direction. Again, you must move the aim point (in this case, to the right) until the rail distances are equal. This technique takes a little practice at first, but as you get better with aiming bank shots, your initial guess will be fairly close, and might require only a small adjustment to equalize the distances. NV 6.1 shows the equal rail-distance method being used in practice.

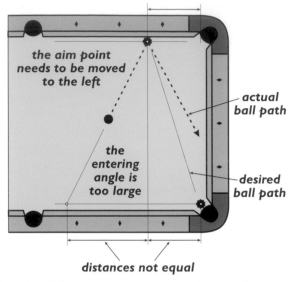

Figure 6.5 Equal rail-distance error—aim point too far to the right

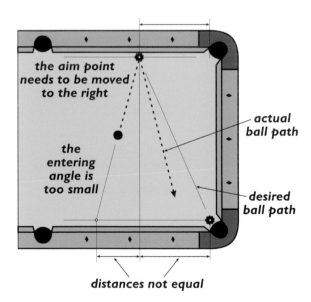

Figure 6.6 Equal rail-distance error—aim point too far to the left

With all banking methods, you need to be able to estimate distances along the rails. Fortunately, the billiard table manufacturers provide us with the diamonds to help. (The diamonds also look cool on the table.) The diamonds are equally spaced along each rail, with three between each pocket. In addition to the visible diamonds on the rails, you must also be aware of the diamond locations corresponding to the pockets. For a side pocket, the imaginary diamond is centered in the pocket in-line with the other diamonds. However, for a corner pocket there are two different imaginary diamond locations depending upon the rail along which you are measuring. **Figure 6.7** illustrates these locations. The corner-pocket diamonds are located in-line with the other diamonds, centered on the edge of the adjacent rail. When using the diamonds to accurately measure distance along a rail to a target point in the pocket, these locations are important.

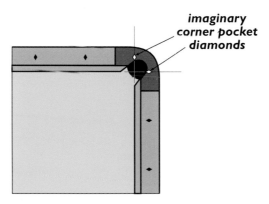

Figure 6.7 Corner pocket imaginary-diamond locations

Figure 6.8 illustrates how a typical corner-pocket target point is not exactly aligned with the imaginary diamond location. To aim the bank shot precisely, this misalignment would have an impact on how you measure the rail distances. To simplify things when first using a banking method to aim corner-pocket shots, you might just assume that your target point is aligned with the appropriate imaginary diamond. For example, in **Figure 6.8** the projected aiming-line point is exactly three diamonds away from the imaginary corner-pocket diamond. Therefore, you would predict the required rail-impact aim point to be one and a half diamonds from the target, and you would come fairly close to the desired target point. Measuring more accurately, the projected aiming-line point is actually a little less than three diamonds away from the target. Therefore, the rail-impact aim point should be a little less than one and a half diamonds from the projected aim point, as shown in the figure. With medium speed, the ball would rebound directly into the pocket center, as shown.

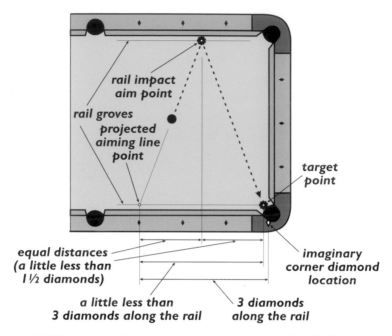

Figure 6.8 Using the diamonds to measure equal rail distances

Principle 6.3 summarizes and **Figure 6.9** illustrates a very important point concerning how to use the diamonds. They should be used for measurement purposes only, and not as aiming points. The target point, rail-impact aim point, and projected aiming-line point need to be located in the rail groves adjacent to the diamonds. When you aim your shot, you aim directly at the rail-impact point, not at the diamond adjacent to the point. **Figure 6.9** shows the path the ball takes if you aim directly at the diamond. The ball does not even come close to going into the pocket. The ball path resulting from aiming at the equal-distance rail-impact point shown is also not perfect—the ball does not enter the center of the pocket. This is because the center of the pocket is a little to the left of the imaginary corner-pocket diamond (see **Figure 6.8**). The rail-impact aim point would need to be moved a small amount to the left of the second diamond (but not near as far left as the diamond aiming line would suggest) to equalize the distances between the projected aiming-line point, the rail-impact aim point, and the pocket-center target point.

Principle 6.3 **Do not aim directly at the diamonds**

When lining up basic bank-shot geometry, use the diamonds to measure rail distances, but aim to and from points in the rail groves adjacent to the diamond locations (see Figure 6.9).

- In some multirail banking methods (e.g., the 5-System and Plus System sometimes used in three-cushion billiard games), you do aim directly at the diamonds (see TP 7.2 in **Section 7.06**).

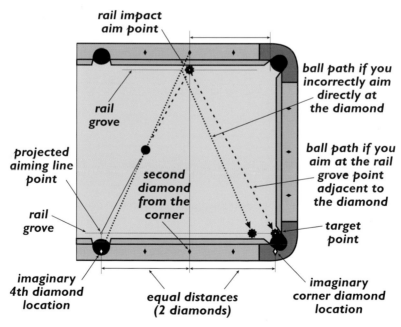

Figure 6.9 Aim at the rail-grove points, not the diamonds

The equal rail-distance method presented above can also be used for shots where your aiming-line direction, when projected back, extends beyond the table. **Figure 6.10** illustrates such a case. The method for this type of shot is really the same as the equal rail-distance method. But when you need to measure beyond the table, I call the technique the **equal extended-rail-distance bank method**. As before, you move your rail-impact aim point until the distances between the projected aiming-line point, rail-impact aim point, and target point are equal. NV 6.2 shows how the method is used in practice.

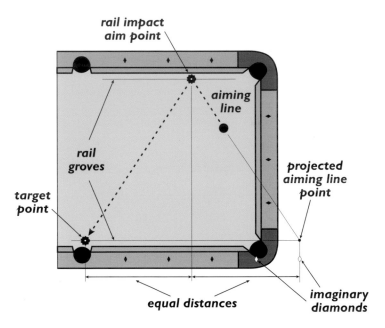

Figure 6.10 Equal extended-rail-distance bank method

NV 6.2 – Equal extended-rail-distance bank method

normal video

An alternative to the equal rail-distance method presented above is illustrated in **Figure 6.11** and summarized in **Principle 6.4**. It is called the **parallel midpoint-line bank method,** and it is also based on **Principle 6.1** on page 172 (see TP 6.1). It is conceptually a little more complicated than the equal rail-distance method, but it is straightforward and does not require trial and error with an initial guess and adjustments. To use the method, first imagine a line between the current object-ball position (point A) and the desired target-location (point B). Next, bisect this line (line AB) to find the midpoint. Then, imagine a line (e.g., by using the cue stick) through this midpoint, and the mirror image of the target ball on the other side of the table (point C). This line (line DC) is labeled as the "midpoint line" in the figure. It defines the direction at which the object ball needs to approach the rail from point A to rebound off the rail at the rail-impact point (point E) and be pocketed at point B (i.e., line AE is parallel to the midpoint line). The rail-impact aim point (point E) can be found by projecting the midpoint line to the rail adjacent to the target (point D). The aim point (point E) is directly across from point D and can be located using the diamonds. In this case, point D, and therefore point E, is a little more than one and a half diamonds from the corner pocket. This method involves more steps and requires that you visualize various lines and the midpoint of a line, but it can be a good alternative if you dislike the equal rail-distance method.

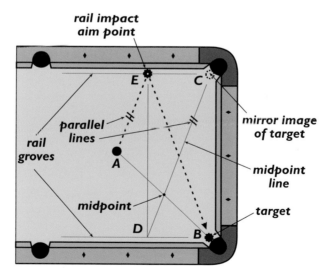

Figure 6.11 Parallel midpoint-line bank method

Principle 6.4 **Parallel midpoint-line bank method**

*To make a medium-speed bank shot with no English, the aiming line must be parallel to the line connecting the midpoint between the ball and the target, and the mirror image of the target (see **Figure 6.11** and NV 6.3).*

- This principle is a direct consequence of **Principle 6.1** on page 172 (see TP 6.1).
- The principle is not valid at fast or slow speeds, or when the object ball is close to the rail (see Section 6.04), with English (see Section 6.05), or for cut shots (see Section 6.06).

normal video

NV 6.3 – Parallel midpoint-line bank method example

technical proof

TP 6.1 – Parallel midpoint-line bank method geometry

Section 6.03   *Kick-shot aiming methods*

With a kick shot, the cue ball rebounds off a rail before striking the object ball. If the target ball is close to a pocket, as shown in **Figure 6.12**, the bank-shot methods presented in the previous section can be used to aim the shot, except that you plan the path of the cue ball instead of the object ball. The main difference is that you have more control over the English of the banking ball (the cue ball). The good news concerning this fact is that you do not need to worry about cut shot effects (see Section 6.06). However, you must be very careful not to put unintentional English on the cue ball (see Section 6.05).

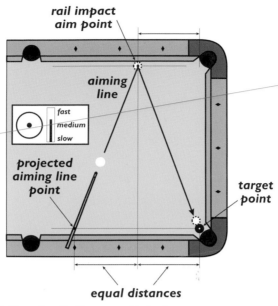

Figure 6.12 Equal rail-distance kick shot

For kick shots where the object ball is close to the banking rail or far from the target pocket, the following methods are more appropriate. The first method, called the **mirror-image kick-shot method**, is illustrated in **Figure 6.13** and summarized in **Principle 6.5**. To use the method, you simply visualize the mirror image of the object ball reflected about the rail grove, and aim at the imaginary mirror-image ball. The mirror-image ball can be difficult to visualize when the object ball is far from the rail; but when it is closer, the method is fairly easy to apply. When you get comfortable with and good at visualizing the mirror-image ball, you can even plan for the desired amount of cut angle you want between the cue ball and object ball, by aiming with the appropriate cut angle at the mirror-image ball. **Figure 6.14** illustrates how this is done. Notice that the direction of the cut angle is reversed in the mirror image. To make the object ball in the pocket, the cue ball strikes to the right of center of the object ball. In the mirror image, you need to aim to the left of center of the mirror-image with the same amount of cut angle.

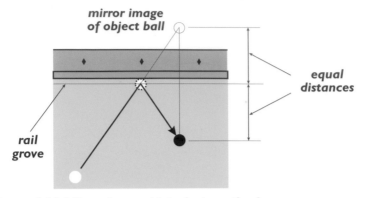

Figure 6.13 Mirror-image kick-shot method

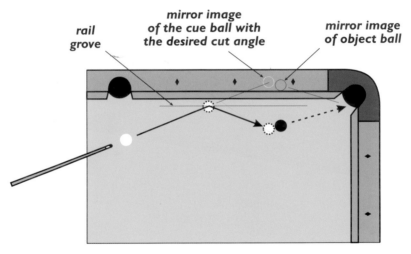

Figure 6.14 Mirror-image kick-shot with a cut angle

Principle 6.5 **Mirror-image kick-shot method**

*For a medium speed kick shot with no English, you can aim directly at the mirror image of the object ball reflected about the rail grove (see **Figure 6.13**, **Figure 6.14**, and NV 6.4).*

- This principle is a direct consequence of **Principle 6.1** on page 172 (see TP 6.2).
- You need to adjust your aim at fast or slow speeds (see Section 6.04) and when English is used (see Section 6.05).

normal video

NV 6.4 – Mirror-image kick-shot method

technical proof

TP 6.2 – Mirror-image kick-shot method geometry

Another method for aiming kick shots is illustrated in **Figure 6.15**. It is called the **equal separation-distance kick-shot method**. It is applied in very much the same way as the equal rail-distance bank-shot method presented in Section 6.02. First, you visualize where you want the cue ball to hit the object ball (position A). Next, you guess at an aiming line to define the rail-impact aim point (position B). Then, you imagine position C of the cue ball adjacent to position A. Next, you check the distances of positions A and C from the centerline through position B. If they are equal, the aim direction and rail-impact point B are correct. If the distances are unequal, you need to adjust your aim, just as with the equal rail-distance method, presented in Section 6.02. If you use your cue stick to visualize the aiming line with the tip at point B, it is easier to visualize the distances between the centerline and points A and C by keeping the cue stick along the aiming line, and by looking down the centerline (see NV 6.5). It is difficult to use the rail diamonds to help compare the distances with this method. However, you do not need to measure the distances but just be able to visualize whether or not they are equal.

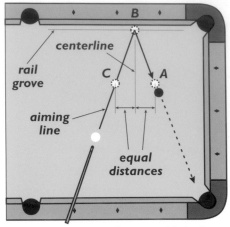

Figure 6.15 Equal separation-distance kick-shot method

NV 6.5 – Equal separation-distance kick-shot method

normal video

Section 6.04   *Speed effects*

The rebound angle for kick and bank shots will differ from the approach angle due to speed, spin, and cut-angle effects. It is important to be aware of all of these effects; otherwise, the bank aiming-methods presented in the previous two sections will not be of much use. All of these methods assume that the rebound angle is exactly equal to the approach angle. By understanding the principles presented in this section, Section 6.05, and Section 6.06, you will be able to make adjustments to the bank aiming-method results where appropriate. With these techniques, you will be able to confidently execute a wide variety of kick and bank shots.

The most fundamental factor affecting a kick or bank shot rebound angle is speed. As summarized by **Principle 6.6**, the rebound angle decreases when the speed increases (see **Figure 6.16**). This phenomenon is due to what I call **rail throwback**, which is caused by sideways compression of the rail (see **Figure 6.17** and HSV 6.1). The sideways compression results in sideways forces that oppose the ball's sideways motion, thereby reducing the rebound angle. The rebound angle is said to be "shortened."

Principle 6.6 **Rail throwback at high speed**

*With kick and bank shots, higher speed results in a smaller rebound angle (see **Figure 6.16** and NV 6.6).*

SPEED
LIMIT
##

- At slower speeds, the rebound angle increases (see **Principle 6.7**).
- The effect is most pronounced for medium-angle bank shots, especially where the approach angle is between about 20° and 50°. The largest throwback occurs at about 30°.
- When the object ball is closer to the rail to begin with, the rebound angle can be even smaller (see **Principle 6.8**).

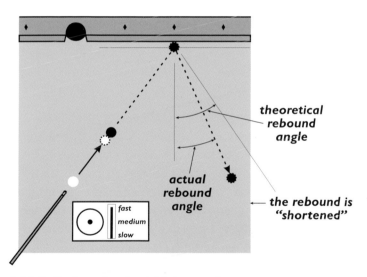

Figure 6.16 Rail throwback at high speed

NV 6.6 – Bank high-speed effect

normal video

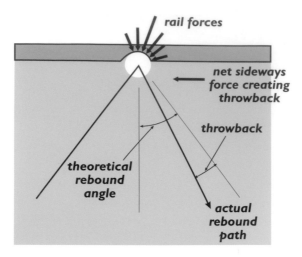

Figure 6.17 Rail deformation and throwback

 HSV 6.1 — Rail deformation during high-speed bank

high-speed video

Figure 6.18 shows an example where you can use the high-speed throwback effect to your advantage to execute a bank shot. Due to the stripes on the table the solid has no direct path to a pocket. The only option is to try to execute a bank shot or to play a safety. The stripe labeled as "obstacle ball" makes it impossible to execute an equal rail-distance bank shot where the rebound angle is the same as the approach angle. However, a possible solution is to shoot clear of the obstacle ball with enough speed so the rebound angle is smaller than the approach angle, as shown in the figure. The tough part is having a feel for how much speed to use. This intuition can come only with a great deal of practice and experience, but it does help to be aware of the facts presented in **Principle 6.6**.

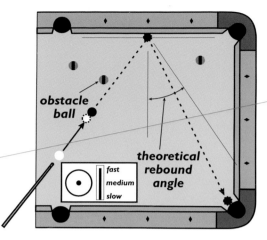

Figure 6.18 Using the bank high-speed effect to avoid an obstacle ball

As summarized by **Principle 6.7**, the rebound angle increases when the speed decreases (see **Figure 6.19**). The primary cause for this effect is topspin resulting from normal roll of the banking ball. When a ball bounces off a rail with topspin, the rebound path curves due to the angular momentum of the spin, effectively increasing the rebound angle. A secondary cause for the larger effective rebound angle is rail-rebound inefficiency (described by a technical factor called the coefficient of restitution, presented in TP 6.3). The banked ball loses some of its speed in the direction perpendicular to the rail, because the rail is not perfectly elastic (i.e., the rail does not rebound perfectly). This effect results in a larger rebound angle. The rebound angle is said to be "lengthened."

Principle 6.7 **Curved rebound path due to slow-speed roll**

*With kick and bank shots, lower speed results in a larger rebound angle (see **Figure 6.19** and NV 6.7).*

- At faster speeds, the rebound angle decreases (see **Principle 6.6**).
- The rebound path curves due to the topspin momentum of the banked ball due to normal roll. The rebound angle is also increased slightly due to rail rebound inefficiency (see TP 6.3).
- The effect is more pronounced for medium approach angles. The largest deflection occurs at about 45°, where the forward-roll direction is perpendicular to the rebound direction.
- When the object ball is close to the rail to begin with, there is not as much curve (see **Principle 6.8**).
- For kick shots, bottom spin can be used to help reduce this effect, and topspin can increase the effect (see HSV 6.2 through HSV 6.5).

SPEED LIMIT

##

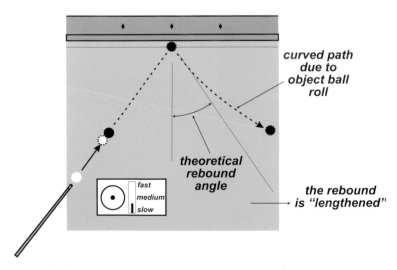

curved path due to object ball roll

theoretical rebound angle

fast
medium
slow

the rebound is "lengthened"

Figure 6.19 Curved rebound path due to slow-speed roll

normal video

NV 6.7 – Bank low-speed effect

high-speed video

HSV 6.2 – Cue ball kicked off a rail at an angle, with top spin

HSV 6.3 – Cue ball kicked off a rail at an angle, with bottom spin

HSV 6.4 – Cue ball kicked off a rail at an angle, with normal roll

HSV 6.5 – Cue ball kicked off a rail at an angle, with stun

technical proof

TP 6.3 – Increase in bank rebound angle due to the rail coefficient of restitution

Figure 6.20 shows an example where you can use the bank low-speed-roll effect to your advantage to execute a bank shot. Due to the stripes on the table the solid has no direct path to a pocket. The only option is to try to execute a bank shot or to play a safety. The stripe labeled as "obstacle ball" makes it impossible to execute an equal rail-distance bank shot where the rebound angle is the same as the approach angle. However, a possible solution is to shoot clear of the obstacle ball with slow enough speed so the rebound angle is larger than the approach angle, as shown in the figure. Again, the tough part is having a feel for how little speed to use. This intuition can come only with a great deal of practice and experience, but it does help to be aware of the facts presented in **Principle 6.7**.

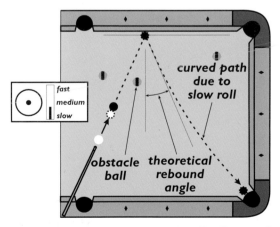

Figure 6.20 Using the bank low-speed-roll effect to help avoid an obstacle ball

The amount of increase or decrease in the rebound angle due to rail throwback and roll effects is also affected by how close the object ball is to the rail to begin with (see **Principle 6.8**). The closer the object ball is to the rail, the less time it has to develop forward roll. Therefore, the rebound path does not curve as much (see **Figure 6.21**).

Principle 6.8 **Smaller rebound angle when close to a rail**

*When banking an object ball that is close to a rail, the rebound angle will be smaller than expected (see **Figure 6.21**).*

- The object ball does not have enough distance to build up roll (see **Principle 6.7**). Instead, the object ball slides into the rail and there is little or no increase in rebound angle. In fact, the rebound angle can even be shortened due to rail throwback (see **Principle 6.6**).
- For kick shots, topspin can be used to counteract the cue-ball rebound-path roll effect.

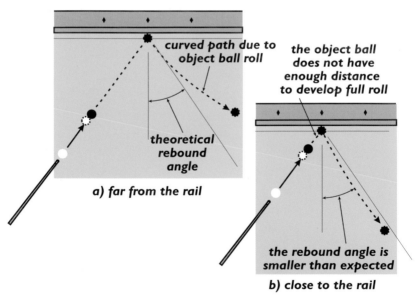

Figure 6.21 Effect of distance from the rail on rebound angle

Principle 6.6 showed that as the speed of a banked ball increases, the amount of throwback increases; and **Principle 6.7** showed that as the speed decreases, the amount of rebound curve increases. Fortunately, as summarized in **Principle 6.9** and shown in **Figure 6.22**, with medium speed and no sidespin, the banked ball does rebound off the rail as expected where the rebound angle is equal to the approach angle. Therefore, for balls banked or kicked with medium speed and no sidespin, the aiming methods presented in Section 1.02 and Section 1.03 work perfectly. Again, knowing how much speed to use comes only with practice.

Principle 6.9 **Ideal bank speed**

*With an appropriate medium speed, the bank throwback and roll curve effects (see **Principle 6.6** and **Principle 6.7**) cancel, resulting in a bank shot that agrees with the theoretical bank geometry, where the rebound angle is equal to the approach angle (see **Figure 6.22**).*

• If the ball hitting the rail has sidespin, the rebound angle will deflect in the direction of the spin (see the next section).

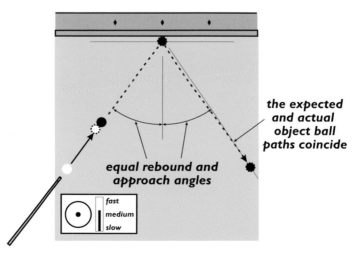

Figure 6.22 Ideal bank speed

Section 6.05   *English effects*

Sidespin has a dramatic effect on kick and bank shots. For a kick shot, the source of the sidespin is cue ball English. With a bank shot, object-ball sidespin is predominantly caused by cut angle effects (see Section 6.06). **Figure 6.23** and **Figure 6.24** illustrate the effects of the two directions of sidespin. When the sidespin is in the rolling direction along the rail (see **Figure 6.23**), the sidespin is referred to as **natural English** or **running English**. This type of sidespin results in an increase or lengthening in the rebound angle (see NV 6.8). The term "natural" is used because the spin is in the rolling direction along the rail (see the spin arrow in the figure). The term "running" is used because the sidespin causes the cue ball to speed up (run) slightly after rebounding off the rail. When the sidespin is opposite the rolling direction along the rail (see **Figure 6.24**), the sidespin is referred to as **reverse English**. This type of sidespin results in a decrease in or shortening of the rebound angle (see NV 6.9). With reverse English, the ball slows down slightly when it makes contact with the rail.

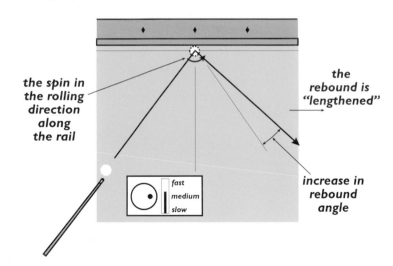

Figure 6.23 Natural-English effect

normal video

NV 6.8 – Kick shot with natural English

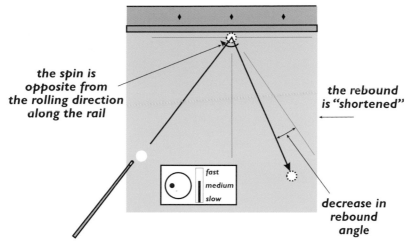

Figure 6.24 Reverse-English effect

NV 6.9 – Kick shot with reverse English

normal video

Principle 6.10 **Bank and kick English**

*With bank and kick shots, sidespin changes the rebound angle in the direction of the spin. Natural English increases the rebound angle (see **Figure 6.23**), and reverse English decreases the rebound angle (see **Figure 6.24**).*

- Sidespin can cause a large variance in the theoretical rebound angle.
- This effect is very difficult to control, so be careful using it.
- Object-ball sidespin caused by cut shot collision-induced spin (see the next section) is often not accounted for by inexperienced players.
- Understanding sidespin is particularly important in multiple-rail bank shots (see **Section 7.06**).

Figure 6.25 and **Figure 6.26** illustrate two examples where English can be used to help execute kick shots. In the first case, sidespin is used to cause a straight-on kick shot to rebound at an angle. In the second case, reverse English is used to caused an angled kick shot to rebound straight off the rail. In both cases, the sidespin is used to execute kick shots that would not have otherwise been possible due to the obstacle balls (see NV 6.10 and NV 6.11).

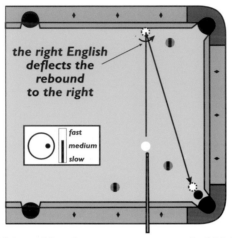

Figure 6.25 Using sidespin to create an angled kick shot

normal video

NV 6.10 – Using sidespin to create an angled kick shot

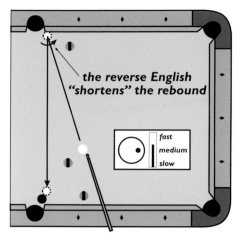

Figure 6.26 Using reverse English to straighten a kick shot

normal video

NV 6.11 – Using reverse English to straighten a kick shot

high-speed video

HSV 6.6 – Cue ball kicked off a rail with fast speed and reverse English

HSV 6.7 – Cue ball kicked off a rail with fast speed and natural English

HSV 6.8 – Cue ball kicked off a rail with slow speed and reverse English

HSV 6.9 – Cue ball kicked off a rail with slow speed and natural English

HSV 6.10 – Cue ball kicked straight into a rail with side English

HSV 6.11 – Cue ball kicked off a rail with reverse English

HSV 6.12 – Cue ball kicked off a rail with natural English

Section 6.06 *Cut angle effects*

In **Section 4.05** (starting on page 105), it was shown that when the cue ball hits an object ball with a cut angle, the throwing action gives the object ball a small amount of sidespin, called collision-induced English (see **Principle 4.15** on page 109). This sidespin can normally be neglected; but with bank shots it must be taken into consideration because sidespin-rail interaction produces a significant effect. **Figure 6.27** shows what happens with an **outside cut**, where the cue ball strikes the object ball on the side opposite the banking direction (see NV 6.12). The cue-ball throwing action imparts reverse English to the object ball (in this case, left sidespin) causing the rebound angle to be smaller than expected (see **Principle 6.10**). **Figure 6.28** shows an **inside cut,** where the cue ball strikes the object ball on the same side as the banking direction (see NV 6.13). An inside cut imparts natural English to the object ball (in this case, right sidespin) causing the rebound angle to be larger than expected (see **Principle 6.10**). With inside-cut bank shots, you must also be careful to avoid collision of the cue ball with the rebounding object ball, because their paths can cross. When shooting a bank shot with a cut angle on the object ball, you must compensate for the sidespin effects by either adjusting your aim or your speed, as summarized in **Principle 6.11**.

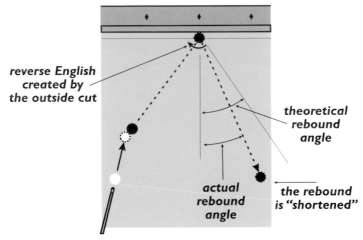

Figure 6.27 Bank outside cut, creating reverse English

normal video

NV 6.12 – Bank outside cut, creating reverse English

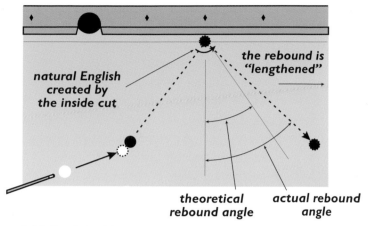

Figure 6.28 Bank inside cut, creating natural English

NV 6.13 – Bank inside cut, creating natural English

normal video

Principle 6.11 **Bank cut angle compensation**

*When shooting a bank shot with a cut angle on the object ball, you must compensate for the sidespin effects by adjusting either your aim (see **Figure 6.27** and **Figure 6.28**) or your speed (see **Principle 6.6** on page 187 and **Principle 6.7** on page 190).*

- With an outside cut (see **Figure 6.27**), you need to increase your cut angle (and bank approach angle) to achieve the expected rebound angle. With an inside cut (see **Figure 6.28**), you need to decrease your cut angle (and bank approach angle) to achieve the expected rebound angle.
- Object ball sidespin due to English transfer (see **Section 4.04**, starting on page 95) can also contribute to rebound angle deflection (see HSV 6.13 and HSV 6.14).
- Understanding the effects of sidespin is particularly important when planning multiple-rail bank shots (see **Section 7.06**).

high-speed video

HSV 6.13 – Ball banked fast into the rail with a cut angle and English

HSV 6.14 – Ball banked slowly into the rail with a cut angle and English

Section 6.07 *Bank- and kick-shot advice*

Some books, and many instructors, advise just practicing a variety of bank shots over and over again, until you develop intuition for using speed and angles appropriately. There is nothing better for your game than frequent practice; however, I believe that your bank- and kick-shot success can be greatly improved if you try to understand and utilize the principles in this chapter. Because of all of the factors that can come into play with bank and kick shots, your intuition might often be wrong. You would need to practice bank shots for a lifetime to develop your intuition completely. Applying an understanding of the fundamentals can greatly improve upon your level of intuition. In this case, science is worth the effort and can help improve your intuition.

When planning a bank or kick shot it is wise to follow a methodical procedure to ensure that you take everything into consideration.

Following is my recommended procedure:

1. Use one of the geometric aiming methods described in Section 6.02 and Section 6.03 to **find the theoretical aiming line and rail-contact point**. For bank shots, I recommend the equal rail-distance methods (see **Figure 6.4** on page 174 and **Figure 6.10** on page 180). For kick shots where the object ball is close to the kick rail, I recommend the mirror-image method (see **Figure 6.14** on page 184). Otherwise, use the equal separation-distance method (see **Figure 6.15** on page 186).

2. **If there are obstacle balls in the path of the cue ball or object ball, adjust your aim slightly, if possible, and compensate with speed,** based on the effects described in Section 6.04. In the case of kick shots, English can also be used to compensate (see Section 6.05). **Figure 6.18** on page 189 and **Figure 6.20** on page 191 show examples of how to use speed to alter the theo-

retical rebound angle. **Figure 6.25** on page 196 and **Figure 6.26** on page 197 show examples of how to use English to alter the rebound angle for kick shots.

3. Adjust your aim or adjust your shot speed to **compensate for cut-shot spin effects,** as described in Section 6.06.

Unfortunately, it is difficult to know exactly how much speed or English to use to compensate for changes in aiming direction, but you will develop this intuition with practice and experience. If you practice with the procedure above and make it part of your routine, your success with bank and kick shots should improve dramatically. With frequent practice, you will develop intuition and might not need to think about these shots as much. But it is still prudent to check your intuition with your understanding of principles, especially if you are facing a critical shot in a game.

Chapter 7
Advanced Techniques (Shot Making)

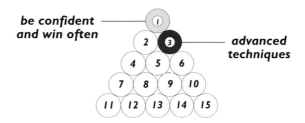

be confident and win often

advanced techniques

In this chapter, you will learn a variety of advanced shots and techniques that are sometimes required if you want to become a competitive pool player and win regularly. Just as with all previous chapters, you should not work on these things until you are completely comfortable with the more fundamental material presented early in the book. To play at the top of your game, you must have the ability to execute the basics so well that you never need to make the difficult shots discussed in this chapter, unless an opponent or an unfortunate circumstance forces you to.

Section 7.01 *Combination shots*

With a **combination shot**, an object ball is hit into one or more other object balls, to pocket a ball. **Figure 7.1** shows an example two-ball combination where first the cue ball strikes the 1-ball, then the 1-ball hits the 2-ball and sends it into the corner pocket. This shot is not easy, but there are no other reasonable offensive options in this case. A safety might be more appropriate in this situation (see **Section 5.06**, starting on page 152). To aim a combination shot, you apply the cut-shot aiming method (see **Section 3.02**, starting on page 35) twice. In

Figure 7.1, you first visualize the ghost-ball location for the 1-ball to create the required impact line with the 2-ball. Then, you visualize the required ghost-ball aiming location for the cue ball to create the necessary impact line between the 1-ball and its ghost-ball target (see NV 7.1). This technique might sound simple (or maybe not), but combination shots are usually much more difficult than they appear (see **Principle 7.1**). The one exception is when all of the balls are fairly close together and lined up fairly straight with your target.

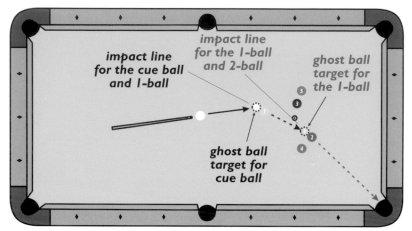

Figure 7.1 Aiming a combination shot

normal video

NV 7.1 – Aiming a combination shot

A combination shot can be very difficult, because any error with the first impact (the cue ball with the 1-ball in **Figure 7.1**) compounds to the second impact (the 1-ball and 2-ball contact in **Figure 7.1**). As was shown in Chapter 3 (see **Principle 3.17** on page 64), a small error in the cut angle produces a much larger error in the impact-line direction. Therefore, a very small error in the cut angle on the 1-ball grows to a larger error in the first impact-line direction, creating an even larger error in the cut angle for the 2-ball—which grows to an even larger error in the final 2-ball path direction. This compounding of the error is illustrated in **Figure 7.2**. The level of difficulty increases dramatically with distance between the cue ball, the object balls, and the target pocket; and with larger cut angles.

Principle 7.1 **Combinations are tough**

If the balls in a combination shot are not close together and aligned with your target, the shot margin of error is extremely small (i.e., it is easy to miss the shot).

- Because a combination shot involves successive impacts, the errors from both impacts compound resulting in a much larger error with the final ball path (see **Figure 7.2**).
- The level of difficulty increases dramatically with distance between the balls and with the sizes of the cut angles involved (see **Principle 3.17** on page 78).

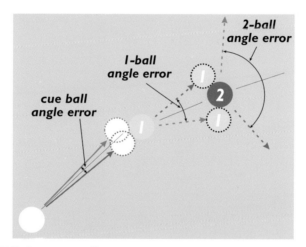

Figure 7.2 Compounding errors in a combination shot

Section 7.02   *Carom and billiard shots*

With carom and billiard shots, also known as **kiss shots**, the cue ball or an object ball is deflected off another object ball to help make a shot. **Figure 7.3** shows an example **billiard shot** where the cue ball is deflected off one object ball to pocket another. **Figure 7.4** shows an example **carom shot** where an object ball is deflected off a second object ball to pocket a third. These shots seem complicated, but they really are not that difficult if you have a solid understanding of the 90° rule (see **Principle 3.3** on page 51). In **Figure 7.3**, bottom English is used to achieve cue ball stun at the first object-ball contact. This results in the cue ball deflecting off the first object ball perpendicular to (i.e., exactly 90° away from) the impact line with the first object ball. Therefore, the cue ball travels along the tangent line to pocket the second object ball (see NV 7.2). Given the ball layout in **Figure 7.3**, this shot is the only one with a reasonable chance of pocketing a ball. Fortunately, if you can visualize the impact line and cueball ghost-ball position required to create the cue-ball tangent-line path, the shot is easy to execute. To aim the shot, first visualize the postimpact cue-ball tangent line to the target ball (e.g., using your cue stick), then visualize the required impact line perpendicular to that line (see NV 7.2). Then aim at the first object ball to drive the cue ball along this line.

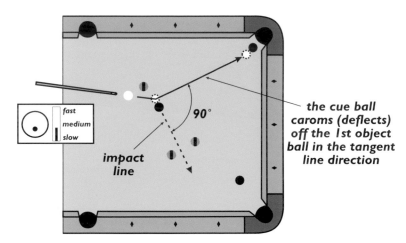

Figure 7.3 Cue-ball billiard shot

NV 7.2 – Cue-ball billiard shot

normal video

Figure 7.4 shows a carom shot where an object ball, instead of the cue ball, is deflected off another object ball, to pocket a third object ball. This shot sounds complicated, but it really is not much more difficult than the billiard shot shown in **Figure 7.3**. It would be much more difficult if the cue ball were farther away from the 1-ball, and if a larger cut angle were required on the 1-ball (see Chapter 3). The aiming procedure is the same as above. First visualize the 1-ball tangent-line path, next visualize the perpendicular impact-line for the 5-ball, and then aim the 1-ball at the 5-ball, to send the 1-ball along the tangent line (see NV 7.3). One major difference with object-ball carom shots versus cue ball billiard shots is that you do not have as much control over the spin of the carom object ball (e.g., the 1-ball in **Figure 7.4**). With the cue ball billiard shot, you have total control over the cue ball English; but with an object-ball carom shot, the only way to ensure stun for the carom ball impact (e.g., the 1-ball impact with the 5-ball in **Figure 7.4**) is to hit the shot hard, especially if there is significant separation distance between the carom object ball (the 1-ball) and the first impact ball (the 5-ball). In **Figure 7.4**, because the 1-ball is fairly close to the 5-ball, the speed does not need to be excessive, but it still needs to be fairly fast. If the shot were hit much softer, the 1-ball would be rolling by the time it gets to the 5-ball and the 1-ball would deflect away from the tangent line (see Section 3.04, starting on page 48, and Section 4.07, starting on page 115).

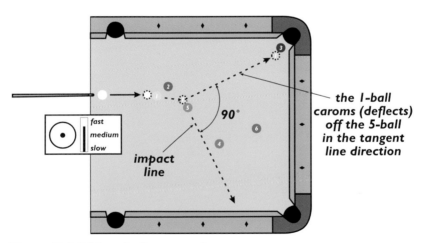

Figure 7.4 Object-ball carom shot

NV 7.3 – Object-ball carom shot

The 30° rule (see **Principle 3.5** on page 49) can also be invaluable in planning carom and billiard shots. **Figure 7.5** shows a good example from a 9-ball game, where a cue-ball billiard shot, off the 1-ball, can result in a victory. Remember, the 30° rule predicts that the cue ball path deflects from its original path approximately 30°, over a fairly wide range of cut angles. That means that the shot in **Figure 7.5** is easy to make (i.e., there is a wide margin of error) as long as you are careful with speed. In **Figure 7.5**, the cue ball is hit a little above center to make sure it is rolling when it hits the 1-ball; otherwise, the 30° rule does not apply. Also, the shot is hit fairly slowly, so the cue ball deflects immediately after impact with the 1-ball (see NV 7.4). If the shot were hit harder, the cue ball would deflect along the 1-ball tangent line first, before turning to the 30° direction (see Section 4.07, starting on page 115), probably resulting in a missed shot.

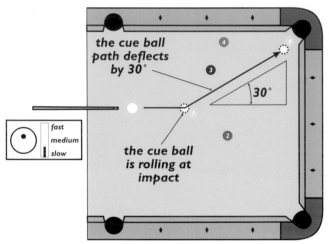

Figure 7.5 30° rule cue-ball billiard example

    NV 7.4 – 30° rule cue-ball billiard shot

normal video

In **Figure 7.5**, because the 9-ball is a "duck" in the mouth of the pocket, the billiard shot is an obvious choice because it results in victory. However, even if some other ball was in the 9-ball's place, the billiard shot would still be more attractive than the difficult 1-ball-2-ball combination. This is because the margin of error for a 30° rule billiard shot is so much larger than the small margin of error for a combination shot. Furthermore, even if the 2-ball was not blocking the path of the 1-ball to the corner pocket, the billiard shot might still be preferable (easier to execute) than the 1-ball cut shot in the bottom corner pocket. Again, this is because the margin of error for a 30° rule billiard shot is still larger than the small margin of error for a large cut-angle cut shot (see Chapter 3). **Principle 7.2** summarizes these conclusions concerning billiard shots.

Principle 7.2 **A billiard shot is sometimes better than a combo or a tough cut**

A billiard shot with normal roll is usually a better option than a difficult combination shot or an extreme cut shot.

- The margin of error for a rolling billiard shot is fairly large (see **Section 3.04**, starting on page 48), provided the speed is slow (see **Section 4.07**, starting on page 115).
- Combination shots can be much more difficult than they seem (see **Principle 7.1**).
- The margin of error for a large cut-angle cut shot can be extremely small (see **Principle 3.17**, starting on page 78).

Section 7.03   *Frozen-ball throw shots*

The term **frozen** is used to describe two balls that are touching. The cue ball could be frozen to an object ball, or two object balls could be frozen together. In these cases, you need to be aware of the effects of ball throwing, where the departing ball can leave in a direction other than the impact line between the two balls.

Figure 7.6 shows the case of two frozen object balls, where the 1-ball is touching the 2-ball. Notice that the impact line through the 1-ball and 2-ball is not aimed toward the target pocket (see NV 7.5). Many inexperienced players would think that because the balls are touching, the 2-ball would leave along the 1-ball-2-ball impact line, regardless of how you hit the 1-ball. As illustrated in **Figure 7.7**, this is true if the cue ball hits the 1-ball in-line with the 1-ball-2-ball impact line, where the impact angle is 0°. However, if the cue ball hits the 1-ball away from the impact line, as shown in **Figure 7.6**, where there is an impact angle, the 1-ball slides against the 2-ball during impact, creating a throw effect (see Section 4.05, starting on page 105). The throw direction of the 2-ball does not depend upon the approach angle of the cue ball. Both cue ball directions shown in **Figure 7.6** (directions A and B) result in throw of the 2-ball in the tangent line (sliding) direction of the 1-ball. This effect can help you make shots that inexperienced players might think are not possible. **Principle 7.3** summarizes the main points concerning this type of shot.

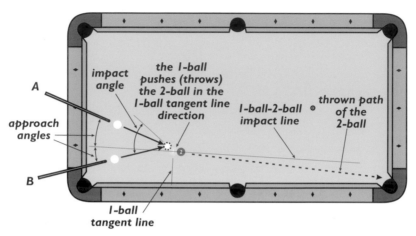

Figure 7.6 Throw due to frozen object balls

NV 7.5 – Frozen-object ball throw

normal video

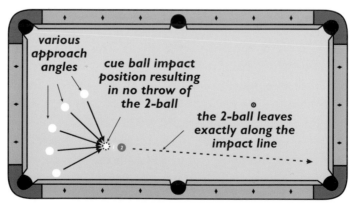

Figure 7.7 Cue-ball impact position resulting in no object-ball throw

Principle 7.3 **Frozen object ball throw**

*When two object balls are touching, if the first ball is hit at an angle to the impact line between the two object balls, the second ball will be thrown off the impact line in the direction of the first ball's motion (see **Figure 7.6**).*

- The throwing action is due to the sideways sliding friction between the two object balls, which is the same effect that causes English throw (see **Principle 4.11** on page 102) and cut-shot throw (see **Section 4.05**, starting on page 105).
- The amount of the throw increases at slower speeds (see HSV 7.1 and HSV 7.3).
- If the cue ball hits the first object ball in-line with the impact line (see **Figure 7.7**), the second ball leaves along the impact line (i.e., there is no throw in this case).
- The amount of throw increases with the impact angle (see **Figure 7.6**).
- The throw direction is independent of the approach angle (see directions "A" and "B" in **Figure 7.6**).
- When the approach angle differs from the impact angle (see **Figure 7.6**), there is a small amount of collision-induced English (see **Principle 4.15** on page 109) that can reduce the throw angle slightly if its direction opposes the impact-angle throwing direction. Also, if there is English on the cue ball, a small amount can be transferred to the object ball (see Section 4.04, starting on page 95), which can affect the throwing action slightly (see HSV 7.2 and HSV 7.4). These effects are usually not significant enough to warrant attention and can usually be neglected.

high-speed video

HSV 7.1 – Throw of a frozen object ball at slow speed
HSV 7.2 – Throw of a frozen object ball at slow speed, with English
HSV 7.3 – Throw of a frozen object ball at fast speed
HSV 7.4 – Throw of a frozen object ball at fast speed, with English

Figure 7.8 illustrates another type of frozen-ball shot, where the cue ball is frozen to an object ball. Again, in this case, many inexperienced players would think that you do not have much control over the object ball's path. They might think that the object ball will leave along the impact line regardless of how you hit the cue ball. However, as with the frozen object-ball case above, you can create a throw effect to help you make the shot. As with a nonfrozen throw shot (see **Principle 4.11** on page 102), the object ball is thrown opposite the direction of the English. In **Figure 7.8**, right English throws the object ball to the left (see NV 7.6). Because the cue ball is frozen to and pushed into the object ball, a larger throw can be achieved than with a nonfrozen throw shot. **Figure 7.9** shows how cut angle can also be used (instead of English) to throw a frozen object ball. **Principle 7.4** summarizes the important points concerning frozen cue-ball throw shots.

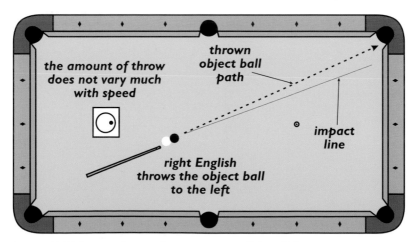

Figure 7.8 Throw due to frozen cue-ball English

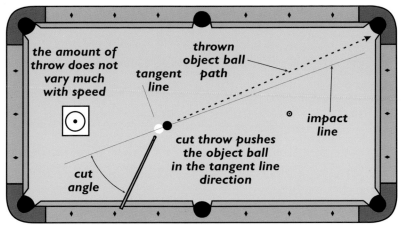

the amount of throw does not vary much with speed

tangent line

thrown object ball path

cut throw pushes the object ball in the tangent line direction

impact line

cut angle

Figure 7.9 Throw due to frozen cue-ball cut angle

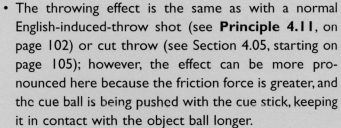

Principle 7.4 **Frozen cue-ball throw**

When the cue ball is touching the object ball, English (see ***Figure 7.8****) or cut angle (see* ***Figure 7.9****) can be used to throw the object ball away from the impact-line path.*

- The throwing effect is the same as with a normal English-induced-throw shot (see **Principle 4.11**, on page 102) or cut throw (see Section 4.05, starting on page 105); however, the effect can be more pronounced here because the friction force is greater, and the cue ball is being pushed with the cue stick, keeping it in contact with the object ball longer.
- Unlike with a nonfrozen throw shot, the amount of throw does not vary significantly with shot speed (see **Principle 4.12**, on page 103).
- According to the rules (see Section 1.03, starting on page 6), you are allowed to "push" the cue ball only in this case, when the cue ball is frozen to an object ball (see HSV 7.5).

normal video

NV 7.6 – Frozen cue-ball throw

high-speed video

HSV 7.5 – Frozen cue-ball throw

Section 7.04 *Using throw for position*

In previous sections, we saw how throw can be used to deflect the path of an object ball, to help avoid an obstacle ball (see **Figure 4.24** on page 104), and to execute frozen-ball shots (see the previous section). A more subtle application of throw is using it to help "cheat a pocket" (see **Principle 5.8** on page 137) in order to achieve improved cue ball position for the next shot. "Cheating a pocket" works well by itself when the object ball is close to a pocket; but when the object ball is far from the pocket, there is not as much room to "cheat." In these cases, English throw can be used to increase the amount of cue ball deflection. **Figure 7.10** shows an example where pocket cheating and English throw are both required to achieve decent and safe position for making the 8-ball and winning the game.

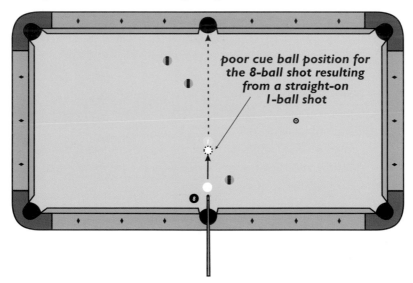

Figure 7.10 Example shot requiring cheat and throw

In **Figure 7.10**, the cue ball is lined up for a square hit on the 1-ball, which is unfortunate, because we need to be able to achieve position on the 8-ball. If the cue ball were farther to the right, there would be a favorable angle, creating a cut shot that would naturally lead to good cue ball position for the 8-ball (see Principle 5.4 on page 129). If the cue ball were aimed at the 1-ball for a square hit, it would be impossible to leave the cue ball in good position for the 8-ball. With a square hit, the cue ball would remain on the aiming line after impact with the 1-ball, regardless of what type of English is used. As illustrated in **Figure 7.11**, to achieve better position for the 8-ball, you can cheat the pocket (see **Principle 5.8** on page 137) by aiming the 1-ball to the right of the pocket center. The 1-ball is still pocketed, but the cue ball drifts to the left after impact, creating better position for a shot on the 8-ball.

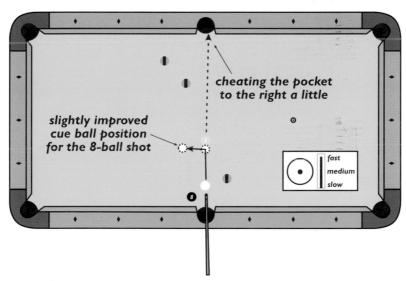

Figure 7.11 Using pocket cheating to help position

In **Figure 7.11**, fast speed is necessary to create significant cue ball motion. As shown in **Figure 7.12**, an alternative is to use slower speed and throw to allow the aim to be adjusted even more, making it easier to move the cue ball off the line to the pocket. In this case, the 1-ball is aimed farther to the right, and right English is used to throw the 1-ball back on course to the left. Again, the result is better position for a shot at the 8-ball in the side pocket. This shot cannot be hit as hard, because significant throw only occurs at lower speeds (see **Principle 4.12** on page 64). This limits the amount of cue ball motion you can achieve. However, because the effective target size of the pocket increases with slower speed (see **Principle 3.14** on page 64), the pocket can be cheated even more than with the faster shot in **Figure 7.11**.

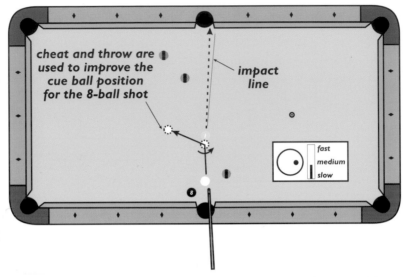

Figure 7.12 Using English throw and pocket cheating to achieve better position

Principle 7.5 **Cheat and throw for position**

Pocket cheating and English-induced throw can be used to create cue-ball tangent-line motion in straight-in shots (see Figure 7.12).

• An alternative is to just "cheat" the pocket and use faster speed (see **Figure 7.11**).

Section 7.05 *Power break*

The first shot of a game is called the **break**. A break that is hit very hard is called **power break**. A good power break is important and can give a player a tremendous advantage. The purpose of a power break is to create as much object-ball motion as possible to increase the chances of making balls on the break, allowing retained control of the table. As stated in **Principle 7.6**, the most important attribute of a good power break is solid contact with the lead ball. Another important attribute is control over the motion of the cue ball. Ideally, the cue ball delivers all of its energy and comes to rest close to the center of the table, without too much motion after hitting the pack of balls. This means that all the cue ball energy is delivered to the ball pack. Also, the center-table position affords the greatest number of options for shots after the break.

> Principle 7.6 **Break efficiency**
>
> *The most important attribute of a good break is a square hit, so all of the cue ball energy is delivered to the rack of balls.*
>
>
>
> - See **Principle 7.7** for a list of best practices for a power break.
> - Side English should never be used, because the cue ball path will deflect from the aiming direction (see **Principle 4.9** on page 99).

Figure 7.13 illustrates the recommended changes in your stance, grip, and bridge for executing an effective power break. You should use a longer bridge distance than normal, to allow for a longer stroke. Use a closed bridge for more cue-stick stability, and place the cue ball on the head string, as close as possible to the rack. Some people prefer a rail bridge (see **Figure 2.7b** on page 22), but the cue ball will be farther from the rack, and the cue stick might be elevated more. Both of these factors can decrease your accuracy. You should use a firmer grip than normal, and grip the cue stick farther back, to allow more power over the longer stroke. Your upper body should be more upright than usual, with your weight more forward and your back leg straighter and firmly planted, to allow more power. **Principle 7.7** summarizes all of the recommended "best practices" for executing a good power break. The reason for using a heavier cue stick is that it will generally be stiffer, allowing it to deliver force to the cue ball more reliably, with less cue-stick deflection and vibration. However, as with baseball-bat selection, the extra weight will allow you to generate more ball speed only if you can generate stick speed with the heavier weight. Even if you choose the same weight cue that you use for normal play, use a different cue for the break. A power stroke compresses and hardens the cue tip, which can reduce its effectiveness for normal play. A harder, compressed tip is acceptable (and actually better) for a break stick.

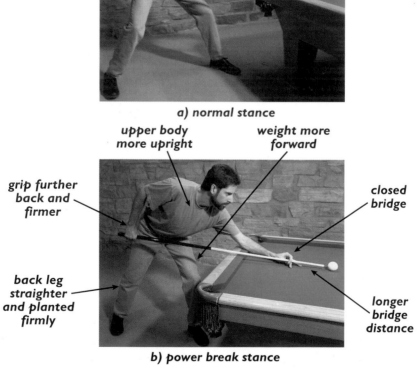

a) normal stance

upper body more upright

weight more forward

grip further back and firmer

closed bridge

back leg straighter and planted firmly

longer bridge distance

b) power break stance

Figure 7.13 Differences in power-break stance, grip, and bridge

Principle 7.7 **Power break "best practices"**

A good power break should generally comply with the following list of "best practices" (see **Figure 7.13** and NV 7.7):

- Shoot from the head string, close to the center of the table, so the cue ball is as close as possible to the racked balls.
- Use a heavier cue stick, if you can stroke it comfortably at high speed.
- Use a longer bridge distance than normal, to allow for a longer stroke.
- Use a closed bridge for more cue-stick stability.
- Use a firmer grip than normal, farther back on the cue stick, to allow more power over a longer stroke.
- Keep your upper body more upright than usual, with your weight more forward, to allow more power transfer to the cue stick.
- Keep your back leg straighter than normal, and firmly planted, to create more stability and to allow more power.
- Use a slight follow stroke, so the cue ball will come to rest near the center of the table after it rebounds off the rack.
- Most importantly, aim to hit the lead ball as squarely as possible (see **Principle 7.6**).
- Use only as much power and speed as you can control. You should sacrifice some power if it will improve your accuracy.
- Take several fast practice strokes to ensure your aim is true.
- Move your weight more forward during the final stroke to increase power.
- Keep the cue stick as level as possible during the stroke to prevent the cue ball from bouncing off the slate (see Section 7.10). Jumping the cue ball off the

table during a break, a common occurrence with inexperienced players, is usually caused by hitting down on the cue ball, which causes the cue ball to bounce slightly and hit the lead ball above center.

- Follow all of the other normal stroke "best practices" summarized in **Principle 2.10** on page 28.

normal video

NV 7.7 – Power-break stance and stroke

high-speed video

HSV 7.6 – 8-ball break with a square, center hit

HSV 7.7 – 9-ball break with a square, oblique hit

When playing 8-ball under rules that award a victory for making the 8-ball on the break, try the method illustrated in **Figure 7.14** and described in **Principle 7.8**. Just be careful not to scratch, which would result in a loss under some rules, if the 8-ball were also pocketed. A side benefit of this break method is that it results in good dispersion of the balls, where all of the balls usually leave the rack area. Also, with a square hit, one or more object balls (sometimes the 8-ball) are usually pocketed. When the 8-ball is pocketed, it most often goes in the opposite side pocket, but sometimes goes in the upper corner or near side pocket (see HSV 7.8 through HSV 7.11). The 8-ball can also sometimes get deflected into other pockets, due to the good motion of all the balls. With a standard lead-ball break, the 8-ball almost never moves (see HSV 7.6) unless it is hit in secondary collisions.

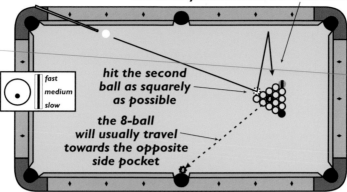

Figure 7.14 Making the 8-ball on the break

Principle 7.8 **8-ball-break victory**

*To make the 8-ball on the break, which results in a victory under some rules, shoot from the head string, adjacent to the rail, and strike the second ball squarely (see **Figure 7.14**).*

- The 8-ball will most often head toward the far side pocket (see **Figure 7.14**), but it sometimes heads towards the other side pocket or the near corner pocket (see HSV 7.8 through HSV 7.11). Notably, if the rack is solid, the 8-ball moves significantly when the second ball is hit squarely.
- The 8-ball will be pocketed about 10% of the time (i.e., in 1 in 10 breaks) when the rack is good (i.e., all balls are touching) and the hit is square.
- If you do not hit the second ball squarely, you risk scratching in the near bottom-corner pocket. A scratch could be disastrous if you happen to also pocket the 8-ball, and you are playing under rules that would count this as a loss.
- Use a small amount of draw to help prevent a scratch and create a secondary collision, after the cue ball rebounds off the side rail (see **Figure 7.14**).

high-speed video

HSV 7.8 – Making the 8-ball on the break in the near side pocket

HSV 7.9 – Making the 8-ball on the break in the near corner pocket

HSV 7.10 – Making the 8-ball on the break in the near side pocket (with deflection assist)

HSV 7.11 – Making the 8-ball on the break in the far side pocket

In the game of 9-ball, there is no trick to making the 9-ball on the break (which results in a victory under some rules). However, there is an effective 9-ball break that is used by most good players. As shown in **Figure 7.15**, the 1-ball can often be pocketed in the side pocket, on the break, by positioning the cue ball close to the side rail, using a rail bridge (see **Figure 2.7b** on 22), and hitting the 1-ball squarely. Hitting the rack squarely with good force also results in good motion of all the other balls. The ideal position for the initial cue ball placement depends on the properties and condition of the balls, so it will take some experimenting. Obviously, if the rack is not tight and consistent, this or any other breaking method will not produce consistent results. The reason why professionals on TV often pocket a ball on the break, besides the fact that they regularly hit the 1-ball squarely, with a lot of force, is that mechanical racking devices are frequently used (e.g., the Sardo Tight Rack, described at *www.tightrack.com*). These devices produce a tight rack that helps eliminate some of the uncertainties involved with the break. If the balls are consistently racked tightly with all balls touching, a professional player can routinely pocket the 1-ball on the break in the side pocket (and often other balls) using the technique shown in **Figure 7.15**.

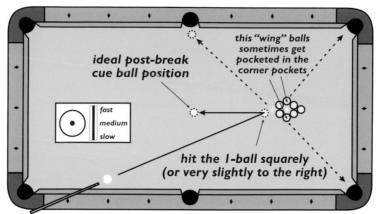

Figure 7.15 Power 9-ball break

Principle 7.9 **The best 9-ball break**

⑨

*To consistently make a ball on a 9-ball break, position the cue ball close to a side rail and hit the 1-ball squarely with a power break (see **Figure 7.15** and HSV 7.7). With some practice and cue-ball position adjustment, the 1-ball can be pocketed in the side pocket fairly consistently.*

- The balls must be racked tightly (with all balls touching) and aligned properly, with the 1-ball on the foot spot and the 9-ball directly behind.
- The ideal placement of the cue ball needs to be determined through trial and error, because it depends on the ball properties and other conditions. Ideally, before playing a match, you would practice on a table to settle on a position. Also, over a multiple game match, you can tweak the position from one game to the next, based on what you see. Regardless of your angle to the pocket, hit the 1-ball squarely to transfer as much speed as possible from the cue ball to the rack.
- A soft 9-ball break (see **Figure 7.16**) is sometimes used as an alternative to a power break. As with the power break, the primary goal is to pocket the 1-ball in the side pocket.

Some professional players use a softer 9-ball break, as illustrated in **Figure 7.16**. As with the power break, the main goal is to pocket the 1-ball in the side pocket. It is easier to control the postbreak cue-ball position with a softer break (see NV 7.8). This type of break is only a good choice if a mechanical racking device is used (e.g., the Sardo Tight Rack) and if you can consistently make the 1-ball in the side pocket. When you do make a ball on the break, the resulting table layout is usually very good, and you have a decent chance to run the table. With a power break, because the balls move around the table so much, the postbreak table layout is very unpredictable and can have ball clusters and unequal dispersion. With a softer break, the balls move a controlled amount and usually disperse fairly evenly. A downside is that the balls are not moving as much and the likelihood of making multiple balls on the break is very slim. Also, if you do not pocket a ball on the break, and you leave the cue ball in the center of the table with good ball dispersion, your opponent is presented with an excellent opportunity to run the table. Now it should be clear why you do not want to attempt this type of break unless you are fairly confident you will pocket the 1-ball in the side pocket. Most players should probably stick to a good, solid power break, where you will often pocket one or more balls on the break, retaining control of the table (even if the resulting ball layout might not be ideal).

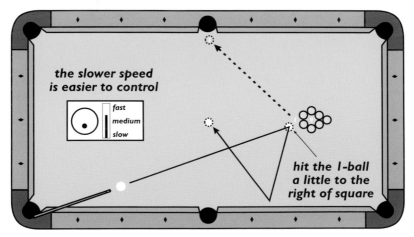

Figure 7.16 Soft 9-ball break

Section 7.06   *Two-rail kick and bank shots*

Chapter 6 presented all of the basics concerning single-rail bank and kick shots. This section presents more advanced multiple-rail bank and kick shots, where the cue ball or object ball deflects off more than one rail during a shot. The most basic multiple-rail shot is the 2-rail kick shot illustrated in **Figure 7.17**. The two striped obstacle balls prevent a direct shot or a single-rail kick shot, so the only option is a two-rail kick shot. Several effects come into play with a two-rail shot. Because the shot has to be hit fairly hard, the rebound angle off the first rail will be smaller than the approach angle, due to rail throwback (see **Principle 6.6** on page 187). Also, when a ball hits a rail at an angle, the rail imparts some sidespin to the ball. This sidespin is called **rail-induced English** (see **Principle 7.10**). In **Figure 7.17**, the sidespin is counterclockwise, which reduces the rebound angle off the second rail (see **Section 6.05**, starting on page 194). Finally, because some speed is lost in the kick off the first rail, and because the ball might be rolling when it hits the second rail, the second rebound angle could increase, due to the low-speed roll effect (see **Principle 6.7** on page 190). For a faster shot, both rebound angles would be smaller, and you would need to adjust your aim to the right. For a slower shot, both rebound angles would be larger (especially the second one) and you would need to adjust your aim to the left. Two-rail kick shots are very difficult because of their sensitivity to changes in speed. Also, any unintentional English put on the cue ball has a dramatic effect (see **Principle 6.10** on page 195). Therefore, if you are not planning for English, you should be very careful not to hit left or right of the cue ball center.

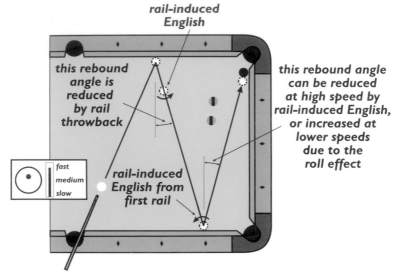

rail-induced
English

this rebound
angle is
reduced
by rail
throwback

this rebound angle
can be reduced
at high speed by
rail-induced English,
or increased at
lower speeds
due to the
roll effect

fast
medium
slow

rail-induced
English from
first rail

Figure 7.17 Two-rail kick shot

Principle 7.10 **Rail-induced English**

When a ball rebounds off a rail, the rail imparts sidespin to the ball (see **Figure 7.17**).

• The sidespin is caused by friction and throwback forces resulting from the rail opposing the ball's sideways motion (see HSV 6.4 and HSV 6.5). The side spin is in the running (natural) English direction. For the first rail rebound in **Figure 7.17**, the running English direction is counterclockwise.

• The amount of rail-induced English increases with shot speed and for larger approach angles.

high-speed video

HSV 6.4 – Cue ball kicked off a rail at an angle, with normal roll

HSV 6.5 – Cue ball kicked off a rail at an angle, with stun

Figure 7.18 illustrates a two-rail bank shot. These shots can be even more difficult than two-rail kick shots because you do not have as much control over the spin of the object ball. This is true for topspin and bottom spin, because the object ball is skidding after cue ball impact, and gradually builds up normal roll (see **Figure 4.6a** on page 84). The amount of roll depends on distance to the rail and ball speed. If the object ball is not rolling completely when it hits the rail, the rebound angle will be smaller than expected (see **Principle 6.8** on page 192). With a kick shot, you can hit the cue ball so it is rolling immediately (see **Principle 4.2** on page 86), so you do not need to worry about this effect. Sidespin English is an even bigger concern. If there is a cut angle between the cue ball and object ball, the cue ball imparts a small amount of sidespin to the object ball (see **Principle 4.15** on page 109). In **Figure 7.18** the cut angle creates clockwise spin on the object ball that reduces the first rebound angle.

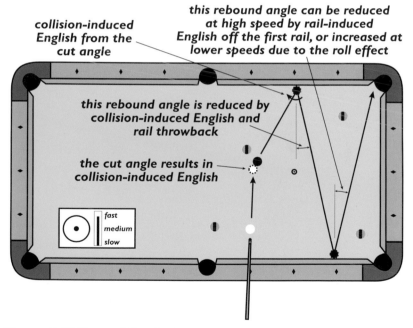

Figure 7.18 Two-rail bank shot

Hopefully, you will not be forced to execute two-rail kick and bank shots very often, because they are very difficult to execute. However, if you want to attempt a two-rail shot, practice a lot to figure out how to aim. When practicing kick shots, try to use a consistent speed with slight follow (to ensure normal roll), and be careful not to use any side English. A good way to estimate where to hit the first rail is to use the one-rail equal rail-distance method (see **Principle 6.2** on page 174) as a reference point, as illustrated in **Figure 7.19**. First visualize where you would hit the rail for a one-rail kick as shown. The aim point for the two-rail kick needs to be a larger distance from the target (e.g., 10% to 20% larger than the one-rail kick half-distance). The exact distance required depends on the shot speed and the approach angle. Use less distance for faster shots and for smaller approach angles.

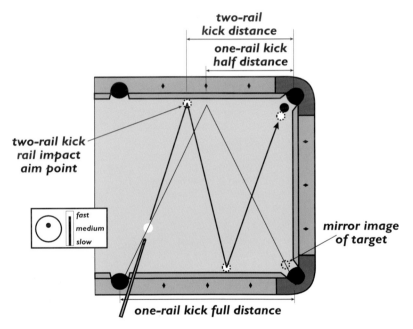

Figure 7.19 Two-rail-kick shot aiming method

Figure 7.20 shows another type of two-rail kick shot, where the ball is kicked against the two rails adjacent to a corner pocket (see NV 7.9). The two-rail kick is required in this example because the obstacle stripes prevent a direct shot or a one-rail kick shot. Ignoring all speed and English effects, the leaving path would be parallel to (at the same angle as) the entering path (see TP 7.1), as shown in the figure. Also, the distance between the entering path and the pocket centerline would be the same as the distance between the leaving path and the pocket centerline.

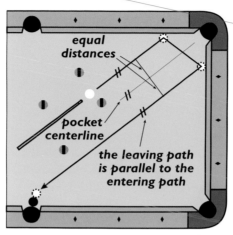

Figure 7.20 Two-rail parallel-line kick-shot method

normal video

NV 7.9 – Two-rail parallel-line kick-shot method

technical proof

TP 7.1 – Two-rail parallel-line kick-shot geometry

Figure 7.21 illustrates the effect rail-induced English (see **Principle 7.10** on page 226) has on the path of the two-rail corner kick shot. The first rail contact produces running English that flattens the path a little away from the parallel-line direction. **Figure 7.22** illustrates the effect that speed has on the shot. Fortunately, speed has very little effect on the final target direction of the shot, because the speed effects tend to cancel out over the two-rail contacts. For a slower shot, the rebound angle off the first rail is larger, but the approach angle to the second rail is smaller. Likewise, for a faster shot, the rebound angle off the first rail is smaller, creating a larger approach angle on the second rail. Therefore, the final-path direction is fairly independent of speed.

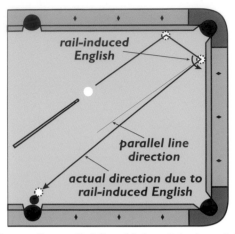

Figure 7.21 Two-rail parallel-line kick rail-induced-English effect

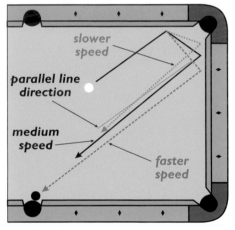

Figure 7.22 Two-rail parallel-line kick speed effect

There are several methods for planning three-rail bank and kick shots. They include the **Corner-5**, or 5-System, and the **Plus System**. These techniques are useful in carom billiard games like "three-cushion," but I think they have little application in pocket billiard games like 8-ball and 9-ball. They also involve multiple-diamond numbering systems and formulas (see TP 7.2) that are difficult to remember and apply. Most people would be better off using one of the two-rail methods described above, or just raw intuition.

TP 7.2 – Multiple-rail diamond-system formulas

Section 7.07   *Frozen-ball bank shots*

When an object ball is frozen to a rail, or very close to a rail, you must be careful to avoid a secondary cue-ball collision after object ball rebound. As illustrated in **Figure 7.23**, for a straight-on bank shot with no cut angle, the approach angle should be at least 45°, to be safe from a secondary collision (e.g., see HSV 7.12). If the cut angle is much smaller than 45°, the cue ball will double kiss the object ball, resulting in a radically different rebound angle for the object ball (see NV 7.10).

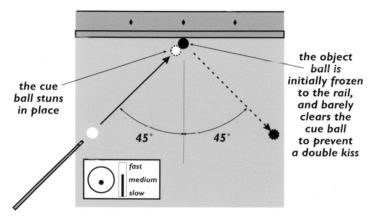

Figure 7.23 Straight-on bank of a ball frozen to a rail

HSV 7.12 – Ball frozen to a rail, banked with a double-kiss near miss

NV 7.10 – Double kiss of a ball frozen to a rail

As illustrated in **Figure 7.24**, when there is a cut angle the rebound angle can be much smaller than 45°. With a cut angle, the cue ball departs along a tangent line perpendicular to the impact line with the object ball. At the same time, the object ball compresses the rail cushion immediately after impact (see **Figure 6.17** on page 188). This compression gives the cue ball time to clear from the rebound path of the object ball. Also, the compression displaces the object ball away from the cue ball slightly, creating more clearance between the balls. In **Figure 7.24**, as long as the cue ball is hit hard and the cut angle is more than about 25°, the object ball will rebound without double kissing the cue ball. The resulting rebound angle can be quite small (about 15°) due to rail throwback (see **Principle 6.6** on page 187). This will allow you to bank the frozen ball even when you have very little room with which to work. **Principle 7.11** summarizes the important points from **Figure 7.24**.

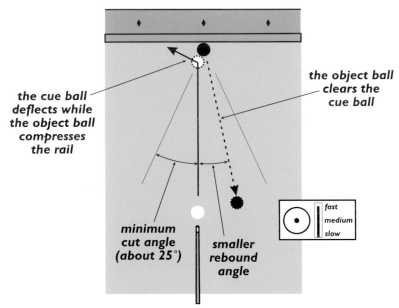

Figure 7.24 Cut-angle bank of a ball frozen to a rail

Principle 7.11 **Frozen ball banked off a rail**

*When a ball is frozen to a rail, to create a small rebound angle without double kissing, you can use a smaller-than-expected cut angle if the cue ball is hit hard (see **Figure 7.24**).*

- For a shot where the cue ball approaches the rail straight-on (see **Figure 7.24**), the smallest cut angle that will not result in a double kiss at high speed is about 25°. This cut angle can result in a much smaller rebound angle (about 15°) due to rail throwback (see **Principle 6.6** on page 187).

Section 7.08 *Kick-shot vertical-plane spin*

Sometimes it is useful (or just interesting) to know how the rail affects the topspin or bottom spin of a kicked or banked ball. **Figure 7.25** illustrates the geometry of a typical rail, showing the heights that are important in understanding ball-rail interaction. The impact height of ball-rail contact can vary slightly among table manufacturers, but it is usually located slightly below the normal-roll impact height (see Section 4.01, starting on page 80). Because of this, when a ball hits the rail with normal roll, it will not rebound with normal roll (see **Principle 7.12**). Instead, it will slide away from the rail with stun, or with slight bottom spin (see HSV 7.13 through HSV 7.16). Understanding this effect could be important if the post-rebound spin can affect your shot. A good example is a kick shot where you want to control the path of the cue ball after contact with the kicked object ball. This is especially important when the object ball is close to the rail, and the cue ball has not yet had enough time or distance to achieve normal roll (see Section 4.01, starting on page 80). **Figure 7.26** shows an example where this applies. To get position on the 2-ball after kicking the 1-ball into the corner pocket, a stun stroke is used, so the cue ball will have topspin on the rebound (see HSV 7.17 and HSV 7.18). This allows the cue ball to follow the 1-ball, resulting in good position for the 2-ball. This shot is fairly advanced and difficult, so hopefully you will never be forced to attempt it. But if the need arises, it is good to understand the principles involved.

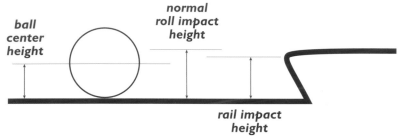

Figure 7.25 Rail-impact height

Principle 7.12 **Rail spin**

A ball's vertical-plane spin is changed when it bounces off a rail (see TP 7.3 and TP 4.2).

- Topspin on the approach results in bottom spin on the rebound (see HSV 7.13 and HSV 7.14).
- Normal roll on the approach results in stun or in slight bottom spin on the rebound (see HSV 7.15 and HSV 7.16).
- Stun on the approach usually results in topspin on the rebound (see HSV 7.17 and HSV 7.18).
- Bottom spin on the approach usually results in stun on the rebound (see HSV 7.19 and HSV 7.20).
- The actual vertical-plane rebound spin depends on the condition of the balls (surface finish and cleanliness), but the above statements are true in most cases.

high-speed video

HSV 7.13 – Cue ball kicked off the rail with top spin
HSV 7.14 – Cue ball kicked off the rail with top spin (side view)
HSV 7.15 – Cue ball kicked off the rail with roll
HSV 7.16 – Cue ball kicked off the rail with roll (side view)
HSV 7.17 – Cue ball kicked off the rail with stun

high-speed video

HSV 7.18 – Cue ball kicked off the rail with stun (side view)

HSV 7.19 – Cue ball kicked off the rail with bottom spin

HSV 7.20 – Cue ball kicked off the rail with bottom spin (side view)

technical proof

TP 7.3 – Ball-rail interaction and the effects on vertical-plane spin

TP 4.2 – Center of percussion of the cue ball

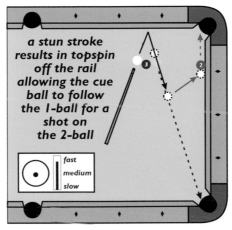

Figure 7.26 Example kick shot requiring control of vertical-plane spin

Section 7.09 *Massé shots*

A **massé shot**, also called a curve shot, is a shot where the cue stick is elevated, to give the cue ball a significant amount of side and bottom English, causing the cue ball's path to curve. Elevating the cue imparts significant English without giving the cue ball too much forward speed. The combination of the sidespin skidding of the ball and the slow forward motion allows the cue ball to curve quite dramatically. **Figure 7.27** shows an example where a massé shot is required. There is neither a direct path to the 1-ball nor a reasonable kick shot opportunity. Instead, a massé shot is used to curve the cue ball path around the obstacle 2-ball. To execute the shot, the cue stick is elevated and the cue ball is struck from above, with bottom-left English (see NV 7.11). **Figure 7.28** illustrates several different stances and hand bridges you can use to achieve the necessary cue stick motion. With each method, bridge stability is key. The elevated V-bridge technique (see **Figure 7.28a**) involves a highly elevated open bridge; it is comfortable because it is familiar to most people. But it is limited by a very small stroke length, because the bridge is so close to the cue ball. **Figure 7.28b and c** show alternative bridges using a closed bridge, where the hand is supported by part of your body. These bridges allow a longer stroke distance but are useful only when the cue ball is close to a rail. The keys to executing an effective massé shot are summarized in **Principle 7.13**.

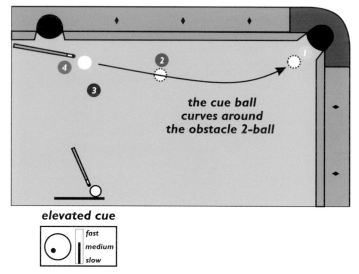

Figure 7.27 Large-curve massé shot example,

a) elevated open bridge

b) closed bridge against the body

c) closed bridge against the leg

Figure 7.28 Large-curve massé shot stance and bridge options

normal video

NV 7.11 — Large curve massé shot

Principle 7.13 **Massé curve shot**

To cause the cue ball path to curve, elevate the cue stick and stroke down on the cue ball with bottom and side English.

- The amount of curve increases with cue stick elevation and the amount of English.
- The amount of curve decreases with increased cue ball speed. The cue ball speed decreases with cue stick elevation, and increases with stroke force.
- The curve is delayed with more cue ball speed (i.e., faster shots take longer to curve).
- The cue tip must be in good condition (see Section 2.01 on page 16) to achieve significant English and curve.
- Drive the cue stick firmly into the cue ball (i.e., do not chop at the ball).

As implied in **Principle 7.13**, the cue stick needs to be elevated only a small amount to achieve a small amount of curve. **Figure 7.29** illustrates an example where a small amount of curve can make for a relatively easy shot. In this case, the small curve is used to avoid the obstacle 2-ball. Without cue ball curve, there is no direct shot at the 1-ball, and any alternative shot (e.g., a kick shot) would be much more difficult. **Figure 7.30** shows that a normal elevated open bridge can be used, because the cue stick is not elevated very much. This type of shot is fairly easy to execute with a little practice (see NV 7.12), and it is a much better alternative than attempting a long or multiple-rail kick shot.

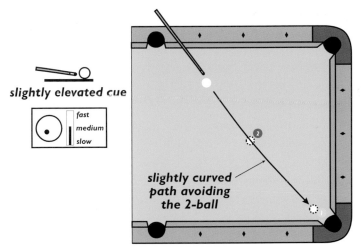

Figure 7.29 Small-curve massé shot example

Figure 7.30 Small-curve massé shot stance and bridge

normal video

NV 7.12 — Small-curve massé shot

high-speed video

HSV 7.21 — Slight massé curve around a ball

HSV 7.22 — Massé curve around a ball adjacent to a rail

Section 7.10   *Jump shots*

A **jump shot** is used to bounce the cue ball off the table, to clear an obstacle ball. **Figure 7.31** illustrates and **Principle 7.14** summarizes how to execute a legal jump shot. The cue stick must be elevated close to 45° and the cue ball must be struck through its center (or close to center) with fast stick speed (see HSV 7.23, HSV 7.24, and HSV 7.25). **Figure 7.32** shows an example where a jump shot is the best option. The 2-ball blocks the direct path to the 1-ball, and other obstacle balls block reasonable kick-shot possibilities. Even if the other obstacle balls (besides the 2-ball) were not present, the jump shot still might be a higher percentage shot than a kick shot. The jump shot is a good alternative only if you are practiced enough to be able to execute it with confidence. Also, the table cloth must be thick enough (not thin, worn, or compressed) to enable the cue ball to bounce high enough to clear the 2-ball. An alternative to pocketing the 1-ball in **Figure 7.32** with a jump shot is to use a massé shot, but you would need substantial curve to clear the 2-ball. A large-curve massé shot is extremely difficult to execute consistently, even for an experienced player with much practice.

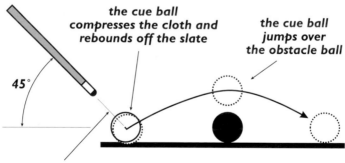

Figure 7.31 Executing a legal jump shot

HSV 7.23 – Jump shot (slight bottom spin)
HSV 7.24 – Jump shot (slight top spin)
HSV 7.25 – Jump shot (tip slip and stun)

Principle 7.14 **Jump shot**

To legally jump the cue ball over an obstacle ball, strike down through the cue ball's center at close to a 45° angle (see **Figure 7.31** *and NV 7.13).*

- For the best action, use a light cue stick or a special-purpose jump cue. The lighter weight allows you to get the cue stick up to speed faster. It also allows the cue stick to more easily rebound away from the cue ball, to avoid interference with the motion of the cue ball. Some manufacturers provide cue sticks specifically designed for executing jump shots (e.g., see the Bunjee Jumper on the Internet at *www.bunjeejump.com*).
- Use a throwing motion with a lighter grip. Do not try to drive the cue stick through the cue ball with a firm grip. This prevents the cue stick from bouncing back, and the cue ball might not clear the cue tip on the bounce. You can use a normal stroke (see **Figure 7.34a**) or a dart-throwing grip and stroke (see **Figure 7.34b**).
- Use more speed for a higher and longer jump.
- Elevate the cue stick more for a quicker and shorter jump (e.g., to clear an obstacle ball closer to the cue ball).
- A jump shot is easier on new, heavy, fuzzy felt because the cloth compression allows the cue ball to strike the slate with more downward speed. A jump shot is extremely difficult on a very thin or worn cloth.
- When practicing jump shots on a table that you care about, place a small, loose piece of spare cloth under the cue ball and over the table's cloth. This will prevent the shots from permanently marking the table's surface. You can get a spare piece of cloth from any local billiards retailer that installs or repairs tables.

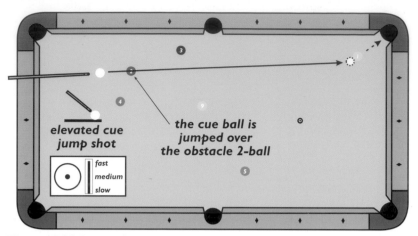

Figure 7.32 Jump-shot example

Figure 7.33 shows what many inexperienced players think is proper technique for a jump shot, where you hit well below the center of the cue ball, and scoop it into the air over the obstacle ball. Unfortunately, this rather easy-to-execute shot is illegal (see Section 1.03, starting on page 6) because the resulting miscue causes a secondary impact of the cue stick with the cue ball. **Figure 7.34** shows the proper technique. **Figure 7.34a** shows a normal grip and stroke with a regular stick. **Figure 7.34b** shows an alternative grip and stroke, called a **dart stroke**. The dart stroke allows you to achieve a "throwing" motion, with a light grip, which allows the cue stick to easily rebound off the cue ball. With practice, either stroke can be used to achieve good cue-ball height fairly consistently.

obstacle ball

scooping the ball into the air is illegal

Figure 7.33 Illegal jump shot

a) normal grip and stroke

b) dart grip and stroke

the cue stick is
elevated about 45°

strike through the
center of the cue ball

c) side view

Figure 7.34 Legal jump shot

normal video

NV 7.13 – Jump shot

NV 7.14 – see Bunjee Jumper demonstrations online at
www.bunjeejump.com

Refer to the Bunjee Jumper website at *www.bunjeejump.com* for detailed advice and instructions on how to execute various types of advanced jump shots. Using different strokes, English, and cue-stick elevation, you can vary the jump shot characteristics quite a bit.

Section 7.11   *That's all, folks*

This chapter concludes the book. I hope you found the book interesting and useful, and I hope you will continue to find it valuable as a reference. Make sure you bookmark the book website (**www.engr.colostate.edu/pool**) in your Internet browser, so you can have easy access to resources posted there. I will continue to maintain and enhance the website over time. A CD-ROM is also available for purchase on the website, if you want to be able to access all of the resources quickly, and without an Internet connection. Good luck with your game and have fun!!!

Bibliography

Books:

Billiards Congress of America. *Billiards: The Official Rules and Records Book.* Colorado Springs: BCA, 2001.

Billiards Congress of America. *How to Play Pool Right.* Colorado Springs: BCA, 2001.

Byrne, R. *Advanced Technique in Pool and Billiards.* San Diego: Harvest Book, Harcourt Brace & Company, 1990.

Byrne, R. *Byrne's New Standard Book of Pool and Billiards.* San Diego: Harvest Original, Harcourt Brace & Company, 1998.

Capelle, P. *Play Your Best Pool—Secrets to Winning 8-ball and 9-ball.* Midway City, CA: Billiards Press, 1995.

Elephant Balls. *Practice Balls Instructional System.* Elephant Balls, 1997.

Fels, G. *Advanced Pool: Techniques and Strategies for Mastering the Game.* Chicago: Contemporary Books, Tribune New Media, 1995.

Koehler, J. *The Science of Pocket Billiards.* Laguana Hills, CA: Sportology Publications, 1989.

Laurance, E., and T. Shaw. *The Complete Idiot's Guide to Pool & Billiards.* Indianapolis: Alpha Books, 1999.

Martin, R., and R. Reeves. *The 99 Critical Shots in Pool.* New York: Times Books, Random House, 1993.

Videos:

Mike Siegel 9-Ball, Straight Pool, and 8-Ball. Joss Productions. Video.

How to Play Pool Right, with Jerry Briesath. Billiards Congress of America. Colorado Springs: BCA, 2002. Video.

Magazines and Nontechnical Articles:

Billiards Digest. www.billiardsdigest.com. Chicago: Luby Publishing Inc., 2002.

Pool and Billiard Magazine. www.poolmag.com. Summerville, SC: Sports Publications Ltd., 2002.

Simpson, T. "Using Your Bunjee Jumper: Why Balls Jump." www.bunjeejump.com (2002).

Technical Articles and Books:

Alciatore, D., and M. Histand. *Introduction to Mechatronics and Measurement Systems.* 2d ed. New York: McGraw-Hill, 2003.

Barnes, G. "Study of Collisions—Part I: A Survey of the Periodical Literature." *American Journal of Physics.* 26, no. 1 (1958).

Bayes, J. and W. Scott. "Billiard-Ball Collision Experiment." *American Journal of Physics.* 31, no. 3 (1963).

Beer, F. and E. Johnston. *Vector Mechanics for Engineers – Dynamics.* 5th ed. New York: McGraw-Hill, 1988.

Daish, C. *The Physics of Ball Games.* The English Universities Press, 1972.

Greenwood, D. Principles of Dynamics. 2d ed. Englewood Cliffs, NJ: Prentice-Hall, Inc., 1988.

Griffing, D. *The Dynamics of Sports.* Loudonville, OH: Mohican Publishing Company, 1982.

Onada, G. "Comment on 'Analysis of Billiard Ball Collisions in Two Dimensions'." *American Journal of Physics.* 57, no. 5 (May 1989).

Walker, J. "The Physics of the Follow, the Draw, and the Massé (in billiards and pool)." *Scientific American.* (July 1983).

Wallace, R. and M. Schroeder. "Analysis of Billiard Ball Collisions in Two Dimensions." *American Journal of Physics.* 56, no. 9 (September 1988).

Witters, J. and D. Duymelinck. "Rolling and sliding resistive forces on balls moving on a flat surface." *American Journal of Physics.* 54, no. 1 (January 1986).

Websites:

See links on the book website at: *www.engr.colostate.edu/pool*

Glossary

Glossary

30° rule: the principle stating that a rolling cue ball's path deflects by approximately 30° after impact with an object ball (provided the ball-hit fraction is close to ½).

8-ball: the pool game where the objective is to pocket the 8-ball after pocketing all seven of your designated balls (stripes or solids).

9-ball: the pool game played with only the first nine balls (1–9). The lowest numbered ball must always be hit first. The person who pockets the 9-ball wins the game.

90° rule: the principle stating that the cue ball and object ball will separate at 90° after impact, provided the cue ball strikes the object ball with no vertical-plane spin (i.e., stun).

aiming line: the imaginary line through the cue stick, in the direction of the center of the ghost-ball target, that results in contact with the object ball at the desired contact point.

aiming point: the center of the imaginary ghost-ball target resulting in contact with the object ball at the desired contact point.

angle of incidence: same as "approach angle."

angle of reflection: same as "rebound angle."

angle to the pocket: a ball's angle of approach to a pocket, measured relative to the pocket centerline. A straight-in shot has a 0° angle to the pocket.

approach angle (aka "angle of incidence"): the angle at which a ball approaches a rail, measured from the perpendicular to the rail. A ball driven directly into (perpendicular to) a rail has an approach angle of zero.

avoidance shot: a shot where the cue ball path is controlled, to avoid hitting surrounding balls.

backspin: same as "bottom spin."

ball grouping: two or more balls of the same type (stripes or solid) in the same general area of the table.

ball–hit fraction: for a cut shot, the fraction of the object ball covered by the projected cue ball. For a square hit (0° cut angle), the ball-hit fraction is 1. For a half-ball hit, the ball-hit fraction is ½. For a glancing hit (close to a 90° cut angle), the ball fraction is close to 0.

ball–in–hand: situation in which the cue ball can be placed anywhere on the table as a result of a foul or scratch by your opponent.

bank shot: a shot in which the object ball is bounced off one or more rails before being pocketed.

billiard shot: a shot where the cue ball is deflected off an object ball to strike a second object ball.

billiards: term for all cue games, including pool (pocket billiards), snooker, and carom games.

BCA: Billiards Congress of America. The BCA is an organization supporting the development of and participation in billiard sports. They publish the "World Standardized Rules" for pool and billiards. Their website is located at *www.bca-pool.com*.

body English: contorting your body in a feeble attempt to change the path of balls in motion.

bottom English: same as "draw English."

bottom spin (aka "backspin" or "draw English"): reverse rotation of the cue ball resulting from a below-center hit on the cue ball (see draw shot).

break: the first shot of a pool game, where the cue ball is hit from behind the head string (i.e., in the "kitchen") into the racked balls.

break–up shot: a shot where the cue ball is directed, after striking an object ball, to strike a ball cluster to scatter the balls into more favorable positions.

bridge: the support for the shaft end of the cue stick during a shot stroke, either the left hand (for a right-handed player) or an implement (see "mechanical bridge").

butt: the handle or grip end of the cue stick.

called shot: a shot for which you specify the ball being targeted and the target pocket (e.g., "9-ball in the corner pocket").

carom shot (aka "kiss shot"): a shot where an object ball is deflected off an incidental ball before being pocketed or striking another object ball.

center of percussion: technical term used to describe the "normal-roll impact height."

chalk: the dry, abrasive substance applied to the cue tip to help prevent slipping by increasing friction between the tip and the cue ball.

cheat the pocket: aim an object ball away from the center of a pocket, to alter the path of the cue ball.

closed bridge: hand bridge where the index finger is curved over the cue stick, providing solid support.

cloth: (aka "felt"): wool or wool-nylon blend material covering the table's playing surface.

cluster: two or more balls close together or touching.

coefficient of restitution: technical term used to quantify the "rail rebound efficiency."

collision-induced English: sidespin imparted to the object ball during a cut shot, caused by sliding friction between the cue ball and the object ball.

collision-induced throw: deflection of the object-ball path away from the impact line of a cut shot, caused by sliding friction between the cue ball and the object ball.

combination shot: a shot where the cue ball hits an incidental object ball, which then hits and pockets a different object ball, possibly after other intermediate ball collisions.

contact point: the point of contact between the cue ball and the object ball at impact.

Corner-5 System: a Diamond System for aiming three-rail kick shots.

crutch: slang term for "mechanical bridge."

cue: same as "cue stick."

cue ball: the white ball, struck by the cue stick.

cue-ball angle error: the angle between the actual cue ball aiming line and the desired aiming line.

cue stick (aka "cue"): the tapered wooden implement used to strike the cue ball.

cue tip: the fibrous or pliable end of the cue stick that comes in contact with the cue ball.

curve shot: a shot using a slightly elevated cue stick and bottom side English to create massé action to curve the cue ball a small amount around an obstacle ball.

cushion (aka rail): the cloth-covered triangular-cross-section strip of rubber bordering the playing surface, off which the balls rebound.

cut angle: the angle between the cue-ball aiming line and the object-ball impact line, for a cut shot.

cut-induced spin: same as "collision-induced English."

cut-induced throw : same as "collision-induced throw."

cut-throat: a casual pool game played with three people. Each person is assigned five balls to protect (1–5, 6–10, or 11–15). The objective of the game is to pocket your opponents' balls. The last person with one or more balls remaining on the table wins the game.

cut shot: a shot where the cue ball impacts the object ball at an angle to the impact line (i.e., the shot is not "straight-in").

dart stroke: a stroke, similar to the throwing motion for a dart, used to execute a jump shot, usually with a shorter, lighter cue stick.

dead stroke: when you are in a state ("in the zone") where you can make no mistake and your play seems effortless, automatic, and confident.

defensive shot: a shot where you try to pocket a ball, but if you miss the shot you try to leave the cue ball or object ball in a difficult position for your opponent.

deflection (aka "squirt"): displacement of the cue ball path away from the cue-stick stroking direction, caused by the use of English. The effect increases with cue stick speed and the amount of English.

diamonds (aka "spots"): inlays or markings adjacent to the table cushions (on the top surface of the table rails) used as target or reference points. There are three diamonds equally spaced between each pocket.

Diamond System: a multiple-rail kick and bank shot method that uses the diamonds as aiming targets.

dirty pool: unsportsmanlike conduct or play.

double hit: an illegal shot where the cue stick hits the cue ball twice during a stroke (e.g., when the cue ball bounces back from a nearby object ball during the stroke).

double kiss: double hit of the cue ball and object ball during a bank shot of an object ball frozen or close to a rail.

draw English: bottom spin (backspin) put on the cue ball by a draw shot.

draw shot: a shot in which the cue ball is struck below center to impart bottom spin to the cue ball, causing the cue ball to pull back from the object ball, after impact, farther than it would otherwise.

duck: slang term for a ball sitting close to a pocket that is virtually impossible to miss (i.e., a "sitting duck").

effective pocket center (aka "target center"): the target line to a pocket that has the same margin of error on both sides. For a straight-on shot, the effective pocket center goes through the center of the pocket opening.

effective pocket size (aka "target size"): the total margin of error left and right of the pocket center that still results in pocketing a ball.

elevated bridge: a hand V-bridge where the heel (base) of the hand is lifted off the table to raise the cue stick (e.g., to clear an obstacle ball close to the cue ball).

end rail: a short rail between two corner pockets.

English: term usually used to refer to sidespin applied to the cue ball, but can also be used to refer to any type of spin applied to the cue ball (e.g., with draw and follow shots).

English-induced throw: deflection of the object ball path away from the impact line, resulting from sidespin of the cue ball. It is caused by sliding friction between the cue ball and the object ball.

English transfer: the imparting of a small amount of spin from the cue ball to the object ball, in the opposite direction of the cue ball spin (e.g., left spin on the cue ball results in transfer of a small amount of right spin to the object ball).

felt: the cloth that covers the table surface.

ferrule: the sleeve, usually plastic, on the end of the cue stick shaft to which the cue tip is attached (with adhesive).

follow English: topspin put on the cue ball by a follow shot.

follow shot: a shot in which the cue ball is struck above center to impart topspin to the cue ball, causing the cue ball to roll forward, after impact, more than it would otherwise.

follow-through: the movement of the cue stick through the cue ball position during the end of your stroke in the direction of the aiming line, after making contact with the cue ball.

foot rail: the short rail at the far end of the table where the balls are racked.

foot spot: the point on the table surface over which the lead ball of a rack is centered. It lies at the intersection of imaginary lines passing through the second diamonds on the long rails, and the center diamonds on the short rails.

foul: a violation of the rules of the game.

frozen ball: a ball in contact with (touching) another ball.

ghost ball: imaginary aiming target for the cue ball, where the cue ball needs to impact the object ball so the line through their centers (the impact line) is in the direction of the desired object-ball path.

grip: the clutch of the right hand (for a right-handed player) on the butt of the cue stick, used to support and impart force to the cue stick during a stroke.

half-ball hit: a shot where the cue-ball aiming line passes through the edge of the object ball. It results in a cut angle of 30°.

hand bridge: the sliding support created with your hand to guide the cue stick.

head rail: the short rail at the end of the table from where you break.

head string: the imaginary line at the head of the table, behind which you must break.

high-speed video (HSV): video clip shot with a special high-frame-rate video camera that can be played back in super slow motion.

hooked: same as "snookered."

horizontal plane: the imaginary plane parallel to the table surface passing through the cue ball. Adjusting the cue-stick position left and right of the cue ball center, in the horizontal plane, creates side English.

HSV: see "high-speed video."

impact height: the height of the part of the rail cushion that contacts a rebounding ball.

impact line: the imaginary line through the cue-ball and object-ball centers at impact. The object ball moves along this line after impact (unless throw is involved).

impact point: the point of contact between the cue ball and object ball during impact.

in-and-safe: a special safety shot in the game of 8-ball, where you declare "in-and-safe" or "safety" before the shot, and you return control of the table to your opponent after your shot, even if you legally pocket one of your object balls. The purpose is to leave the cue ball in a difficult position for your opponent.

inside cut: term used to describe a bank shot where the cue ball hits the object ball on the side toward the bank direction, relative to the aiming line. The cue ball imparts natural (running) collision-induced English to the object ball.

inside English: sidespin in the direction of the object ball, in a cut shot (e.g., when the cue ball strikes an object ball on the left side, creating a cut shot to the right, right sidespin would be called "inside English" and left sidespin would be "outside English").

insurance ball: An easily pocketed ball (e.g., a ball in the jaws of a pocket) that you leave untouched until you need it to get out of trouble (e.g., when you create poor position after a shot).

jacked up: slang term used to refer to an elevated cue stick.

jaws: the inside walls of a pocket.

joint: the mechanical connection (usually threaded) between the butt and shaft ends of a two-piece cue stick.

jump shot (legal): a shot in which the cue ball is bounced off the table surface, with a downward stroke, to jump over an obstacle ball.

jump shot (illegal) : an illegal shot in which the cue ball is lifted off the table surface to jump over an obstacle ball by hitting the cue ball well below center.

jump stick: a special cue stick, usually shorter and lighter, designed specifically for shooting jump shots.

kick shot: a shot in which the cue ball bounces off one or more rails before contacting the object ball.

kill shot: a shot where you use draw or reverse English to limit the cue ball's motion after object ball or rail contact.

kiss (aka "carom"): contact between balls.

kiss shot: same as a "carom shot" or "billiard shot."

kitchen: slang term for the area behind the head string, from where the cue ball is shot during a break.

lag for break: a skill shot used to determine which player will break. Each player must shoot a ball from behind the head string and return it as close as possible to the head rail after bouncing off the foot rail.

leave: the position of the balls after a player's shot. A "good" leave is one in which the ball positions for the next shot are desirable.

leave an angle: control cue ball position after a shot so there is a cut angle on the next target object ball, creating more opportunities for controlling cue ball position for the follow-on shot.

left English: clockwise sidespin imparted to the cue ball by striking it to the left of center.

left spin: same as "left English."

legal shot: shot in which the cue ball strikes a legal object ball first, and either an object ball is pocketed or some ball hits a rail after contact with the object ball.

line of action: same as the "impact line."

long rail: same as "side rail."

makable region: the area within which you can leave the cue ball after the current shot, to be able to pocket the next target ball.

margin of error: a measure of how much angle or position error you can have in your shot, while still pocketing the object ball.

massé shot: a shot where an elevated and firm stroke is used with extreme bottom-side English, to significantly curve the path of the cue ball (e.g., around an obstacle ball).

mechanical bridge (aka "crutch," "rake," or simply "bridge"): a special stick with an end attachment that helps guide the cue stick, in place of a hand bridge. A mechanical bridge is used when the cue ball cannot be reached comfortably with a hand bridge.

miscue: a stroke in which the cue tip does not establish good contact with the cue ball, resulting in poor transmission of force and an unpredictable cue ball path.

miss: failure to pocket the intended ball.

money shot: a key shot in a game that, if pocketed, will usually result in a victory.

natural: a shot easy to execute with a normal stroke, requiring no English.

natural English: same as "running English."

natural roll: same as "normal roll."

near point: the pocket rail cushion point closest to the object ball.

near rail: the rail cushion adjacent to a pocket along which the object ball is approaching.

normal roll: topspin resulting from natural rolling motion of a ball where there is no sliding between the ball and the table cloth.

normal-roll impact height (aka "center of percussion"): the height at which you can strike the cue ball so it rolls without slipping (i.e., it has normal roll) immediately. This height is at 7/10 of the cue ball's diameter above the table surface.

normal video (NV): video clip, shot with a digital-video camera, played back at regular speed.

NV: see "normal video."

object ball: the ball to be legally struck by the cue ball, or the ball to be pocketed.

object–ball angle error: the angle between the actual object-ball impact line (path) and the desired target line direction.

object balls: the balls other than the cue ball.

offset: same as "pocket center offset."

one-pocket: a pool game where each player has a designated pocket in which he or she must pocket more than half of the balls to win.

on the hill: a slang term used to indicate that you only have one more game to win for a match play victory.

open bridge: a hand bridge that has no finger over the top of the cue stick. The cue stick glides on a V-shape formed by the thumb and the base of the index finger.

open table: the condition in 8-ball (e.g., after the break), when no player has pocketed a called shot yet and stripes and solids are not yet assigned.

outside cut: term used to describe a bank shot where the cue ball hits the object ball on the side away from the bank direction, relative to the aiming line. The cue ball imparts reverse collision-induced English to the object ball.

outside English: the opposite of "inside English."

over cut: hitting the object ball with too large of a cut angle, hitting the ball too thin.

pill pool: a 15-ball game played with three or more players. Each player draws a small bead ("pill") numbered 1–15 from a bottle. The drawn numbers are kept secret. If you pocket your numbered ball before an opponent does, you win. As with 9-ball, the lowest numbered ball must be hit first and you remain at the table as long as you pocket balls.

Plus System: a Diamond System for aiming multiple-rail kick shots where an end-rail is hit first.

pocket a ball: cause an object ball to go into a pocket.

pocket billiards: same as "pool."

pocket center offset (aka "offset"): the distance between the effective pocket center and the actual pocket center.

pocket centerline: the imaginary line through the center of the pocket in the straight-in direction.

pocket speed: the slowest you can hit a shot and still pocket an object ball. The object ball is given just enough speed to reach and drop into the pocket.

point: the tip of a rail cushion bordering a pocket.

pool (aka "pocket billiards"): billiard games that use a table with pockets.

position (aka "shape"): the placement of the balls (especially the cue ball) relative to the next planned shot.

position play: using controlled cue ball speed and English to achieve good cue ball position for subsequent shots.

power break: a break shot, hit with a lot of force, resulting in active scatter of the racked balls.

powder: talc or other fine particle substance used to reduce friction between a hand bridge and the cue stick.

problem ball: a ball that is difficult or impossible to pocket unless it or some other ball is moved first.

push-out shot: a special shot allowed after the break in 9-ball where you can hit the cue ball anywhere on the table and your opponent has the option to shoot the next shot or have you shoot instead.

push shot: a shot in which the cue tip remains in contact with the cue ball longer than is appropriate for a normal stroke and legal shot.

Pyramid of Progress: the term I use to describe the pool-skills-development pyramid, used to illustrate the successive levels of competencies required to become a good pool player.

rack: triangle- or diamond-shaped device used to position the balls prior to a break. The term can also refer to the group of balls after they have been racked.

rack of skills: the term I use to refer to the pool skills rack-of-balls illustration corresponding to the "Pyramid of Progress."

rail: the side of the table's upper frame (usually decorative wood) that supports the cushions that border the playing surface. The term "rail" is also used to refer to the cushion off which the balls rebound.

rail bridge: a hand bridge where the cue stick slides on the top of the rail, with fingers used to support the stick sideways.

rail impact height: the height at which the rail cushion makes contact with a rebounding ball. This height is usually slightly lower than the "normal roll impact height."

rail-induced English: sidespin imparted to a ball by a rail when the ball approaches and rebounds off the rail at an angle.

rail rebound efficiency: the ability of the rail cushion to spring back and preserve a banked ball's speed.

rail cut shot: a cut shot where the object ball is frozen to the rail cushion along which the ball is cut.

rail-first shot: a shot where the cue ball is kicked off a rail in close proximity to the object ball, instead of hitting the object ball directly.

rail grove: an imaginary line that is parallel to a rail, half a ball diameter away from the rail. It is sometimes visible on a worn table.

rail throwback: the term I use to describe the reduction in bank rebound angle due to sideways compression of the rail, especially evident at high speed.

rail track: same as "rail grove."

rake: slang term for "mechanical bridge."

rattle: the multiple rail cushion collisions that can occur against the inner walls of a pocket that can prevent an object ball from being pocketed. It occurs when the object ball glances the near rail or rail point bordering the pocket.

rebound angle (aka "angle of reflection"): the angle at which a ball rebounds from a rail, measured from the perpendicular to the rail. A ball heading straight away from a rail has a rebound angle of zero.

reverse English: sidespin where the cue ball slows and has a smaller rebound angle, after hitting a rail (i.e., the opposite of "natural" or "running" English). The spin is in the direction opposite the "rolling" direction along the rail during contact.

right English: counterclockwise sidespin imparted to the cue ball by striking it to the right of center.

right spin: same as "right English."

roll: same as "normal roll."

run: a series of balls pocketed in succession during one turn.

run the table: to make all of the required balls and win the game before giving your opponent a turn at the table.

running English (aka "natural English"): sidespin that causes the cue ball to speed up after bouncing off a rail, also resulting in a larger rebound angle. The spin is in the direction that results in "rolling" along the rail during contact.

safety: defensive position play shot where you leave your opponent in a difficult situation.

scratch: pocketing the cue ball by accident during a shot.

shaft: the bridge end of the cue stick, to which the ferrule and tip are attached.

shape: same as "position."

shark: an unscrupulous player that disguises his or her ability with the goal of making money from an unsuspecting gambler.

short rail: same as "end rail."

shot: the action of hitting the cue ball into an object ball with the goal of pocketing a ball.

shot maker: a person good at making difficult shots.

side rail (aka "long rail"): a long rail having a side pocket between two corner pockets.

sidespin: clockwise or counterclockwise horizontal-plane rotation of a ball.

skill shot: a difficult shot requiring more ability than a typical shot.

slate: the material (usually machined metamorphic rock slate) beneath the table cloth providing the base for the playing surface.

slop shot: a shot with no clear objective, usually hit hard in the hopes that something might go in.

snooker: the billiards game played with 21 object balls on a special snooker table, which is larger than a regulation pool table. The balls and pockets are smaller. The pockets are also shaped differently.

snookered (aka "hooked"): the condition when the cue ball is positioned behind an obstacle ball, usually creating the need for a kick or jump shot.

solid: a ball numbered 1–7 that has no stripe.

speed control: using the correct amount of cue ball speed to achieve good position for the next shot.

spot a ball: place an illegally sunk object ball on the foot spot. If there is no room to spot the ball directly on the foot spot without moving an obstacle ball, it is spotted as close a possible behind the foot spot on a line through the foot spot, perpendicular to the end rail.

spots: alternative term for "diamonds."

squirt: slang term for "deflection."

stance: the body position and posture during a shot.

steering: term used to describe a non-straight follow-through where the cue stick is pivoted toward the object ball or target pocket, away from the aiming line. Obviously, this is bad technique—you should follow through straight.

stick: same as "cue stick."

stop shot: a shot where the cue ball stops immediately after hitting the object ball. It results from a straight-on stun shot.

straight pool: a pool game in which any object ball can be pocketed at any time. A point is scored for each pocketed ball.

straight-in shot: a shot in which the cue ball is directly in-line with the object ball and the intended pocket (i.e., a shot where the cut angle is zero).

stripe: a ball numbered 9–15 that has a stripe through the number.

stroke: the cue-stick and arm motion required to execute a shot.

stroke steer: same as "steering."

stroking plane: the imaginary vertical plane containing the cue stick, dominant eye, cue-ball contact point, aiming line, and ghost-ball target.

stun shot: a shot where the cue ball has no topspin or bottom spin (i.e., it is sliding across the table cloth) when it hits the object ball.

tangent line: the imaginary line perpendicular to (90° away from) the impact line between the cue ball and an object ball. For a stun shot, the cue ball moves along this line after object-ball impact.

target size: same as "effective pocket size."

target center: same as "effective pocket center."

technical proof (TP): an analytical derivation of a principle using mathematics and physics.

thin cut: a shot requiring a large cut angle, where only a small fraction of the cue ball glances the object ball.

throw: object ball motion away from the impact line, due to relative sideways sliding motion between the cue ball and object ball caused by sidespin or a cut angle.

throw shot: a shot in which English is used to alter the path of the object ball.

top English: same as "follow English."

topspin: forward rotation of the cue ball, usually in excess of normal roll, resulting from an above-center hit on the cue ball (see follow shot).

TP: see "technical proof."

transfer of English: same as "English transfer."

trash: slang term used to describe balls pocketed by accident.

triangle: device used to rack all 15 balls into a triangle shape (e.g., for a game of 8-ball or straight pool).

turn: a player's stay at the table, which continues as long as the player continues to legally pocket object balls.

two-way shot: a shot where you attempt to pocket a ball and, at the same time, play for a safety in case you miss the shot.

V-bridge: same as "open bridge."

vertical plane: the imaginary plane perpendicular to the table surface passing through the cue ball. Adjusting the cue stick height above and below the cue ball center, in the vertical plane, creates follow (topspin) or draw (bottom spin).

wing balls: the two balls adjacent to the 9-ball (towards the side rails) in a 9-ball rack.

Index

Index

30 degree rule 48-56
  carom shot 207
  for avoidance shot . . . 147-152
  speed effects 52
8-ball 1, 249
  ball groupings 143-147
  blocking a pocket 154-155
  break-up shot 147-152
  making the 8 ball
    on the break 220-224
  rules 6-11
  safety 162
90 degree rule 41-48, 249
  carom shot 205
  cut angle effects 116
  for break-up shot 148
9-ball 1, 249
  power break 222
  rules 6-11
  soft break 223
aiming line 27, 33, 249
  bank shot 171, 173
  kick shot 182-186
  using the cue stick
    to visualize 39
aiming pint 35, 249
angle of incidence 169, 249
angle of reflection 169, 249
angle to the pocket . 60, 128, 249
approach angle 169, 249
avoidance shot 147-152, 249
backspin 80, 249
ball grouping 143-147, 249
ball-hit fraction 49-51, 249
ball in hand 8, 131, 165-166, 250
bank shot 128, 149-201, 250
  advice 200-201

aiming methods 171, 173
cut angle effects 197-200
English effects 194-197
frozen ball 231-233
sidespin effects 193-197
speed effects 186-192
two-rail 225-231
**Billiard Congress
of America (BCA)** 6
  World Standardized Rules 6
billiard shot 205, 250
billiards 6, 250
blocked pocket 93, 154-155
body English 28, 130, 250
bottom English 250
bottom spin 80, 250
  conversion to normal roll 83-85
break 3, 5, 250
  making the 8 ball 220-224
  power 217-224
break-up shot 147-152, 250
bridge 21, 250
  masse shot 235-237
  power break 218-224
Bunjee Jumper 241, 244-245
butt 5, 250
called shot 9, 250
carom 3, 250
  shot 56, 205-209, 250
center of percussion 85, 235, 251
chalk 17-18, 251
cheat the pocket . . 126, 136-137,
               214-216, 251
closed bridge 21, 251
cloth 251
cluster 251

coefficient of
   restitution 189, 191, 251
collision-induced
   English 105, 109, 251
collision-induced
   throw 105, 107-108, 251
   eliminating 107-108
combination shot . . 203-205, 251
contact point 35-39, 58, 251
Corner-5 System 230, 251
corner pockets 63
crutch 251
cue 251
cue ball 5, 251
   angle error 76, 251
curve delay 118
cue ball path 115
cue ball speed 45-47
cue tip 7, 11, 252
curve shot 235-239, 252
cushion 5, 251
cut angle 33, 252
   bank shot effects 169,
            183-185, 194, 197-200
   effect on cue ball path   115-116
   favorable 68
   kick shot 197-200
   margin of error 73
   rail cut shot 109-114
   speed effects 45-46
cut shot 33, 36, 105, 252
   along a rail 109-114
   effects on bank shots 195
   overcutting 106
   speeds 45-47
   throw effects 105
cut-induced spin 109, 252
cut-induced throw 105, 108, 252
cut-throat 252
dart stroke 242, 252

dead stroke 252
defensive shot 152-153, 252
deflection 98-100, 252
diamond 5, 176-179, 252
Diamond System 252
dirty pool 252
double hit 252
double kiss 252
draw 80, 253
   for position control 131
   speed effects 83-84
   technique 80
draw shot 86-88, 253
duck 91, 208, 253
effective pocket center 253
effective pocket size 253
Elephant Practice Balls . . . 37, 82
elevated bridge . 21, 100-101, 253
   jump shot 240-245
   masse shot 235-239
end rail 253
English 79-123, 253
   advice and examples, 120-122
   collision-induced, 105, 109
   curve 101
   deflection 98-100
   for position
      control 87, 115, 131
   inside 107
   kick shot effects 194-197
   natural 109, 194, 257
   outside 107
   persistence 98
   pitfalls 98
   rail-induced 225-231
   reverse 109, 133, 194, 260
   running . . . 109, 133, 194, 260
   squirt 98
   throw 97, 101-102, 105
   transfer 105

English transfer 105, 253
English-induced throw . 105, 253
equal extended rail
   distance bank method . . . 180
equal rail distance
   method 173-179
equal separation distance
   kick shot method . . . 185-186
felt   253
ferrule 253
follow 42, 48, 52, 80, 85
   for position control 131
   rail dribble 94
   speed effects 83-84
   technique 93-94
follow shot 90-94, 253
follow through . . 29, 87-88, 254
following a ball into a pocket . 91
foot rail 254
foot spot 5, 8, 254
foul 7, 254
frozen ball 158, 254
frozen ball bank shots . . 231-233
frozen ball throw 209-214
ghost ball 33, 35, 254
   carom shot 205-209
   combination shot 203-205
grip 3-5, 254
   power break 217-224
half-ball hit 49, 254
hand bridge 21, 254
hand visualization 44, 53
head rail 254
head string 5, 7, 254
high-speed video 13, 254
hooked 254
horizontal plane 254
horizontal plane English 80
impact height 254
impact line 33, 254

carom shot 205-209
combination shot 203-205
frozen ball 209-210
using the cue
   stick to visualize 39
impact point 36, 255
in-and-safe 9, 162, 255
inside cut 198, 255
inside English 107, 255
insurance ball 147, 255
jacked up 255
jaws 255
joint 255
jump shot 8, 240-245, 255
jump stick 242, 255
kick shot 149-201, 255
   advice 200-201
   aiming methods 182-186
   cut angle effect 197-200
   English effects 194-197
   speed effects 186-192
   two-rail 225-231
   vertical plane spin 233-235
kill shot 89, 255
kiss 255
kiss shot 205, 256
kitchen 5, 7, 256
lag for break 256
leave 256
leave an angle 128, 256
left English 80, 256
left spin 256
legal shot 7, 8, 244, 256
line of action 33, 256
   frozen balls 209-210
long rail 256
makable region 137-143
   overlap 147
margin of error 60, 256
   30 degree rule 60

allowable 60-61, 72-78
ball grouping 143-147
carom shot 208-209
combination shot 203-205
cut shot 105, 111
makable region 137-143
rail cut shot 111
masse shot 235-239, 256
large curve 235-239
small curve 235-239
mechanical bridge 21, 256
technique 24-25
mirror image kick
shot method 183-185
miscue 8, 16-17, 24,
82, 121, 256
miss 153, 257
money shot 257
natural 257
natural English ... 109, 194, 257
natural roll 257
near point 63-65, 257
near rail 61-65, 257
normal roll 83, 84, 209, 257
normal roll impact
height 85, 233, 257
normal video 13, 257
object ball 5, 257
angle error 72, 76, 257
offset 61, 71, 257
on the hill 257
one-pocket 257
open bridge 21, 23, 257
open table 9, 258
outside cut 198, 258
outside English 107, 258
over cut 106, 258
parallel midpoint line
bank method 180-182
pill pool 258

planning shots 56-59
Plus System 230, 258
pocket a ball 258
pocket billiards 258
pocket center 58, 72
pocket center offset 258
pocket centerline 60, 258
pocket selection 33, 57-58
pocket size 60-63
angle to the pocket 57
speed effect 59
pocket speed 154, 258
point 35-37, 63, 258
pool 6, 258
position 115, 125-168
position plan 125-168, 258
position safety 156
powder 258
power break 217-224, 258
practice balls 37, 81
problem ball 259
push out 10, 259
push shot 259
Pyramid of Progress 2, 259
rack 5, 259
mechanical 222
proper 506
rack of skills 4, 259
rail 259
rail bridge 22, 31, 259
rail cut shot 109-114, 259
rail dribble 94
rail-first shot 134, 259
rail grove 169-170, 259
rail impact height 233, 259
rail-induced English ... 225, 259
rail rebound efficiency 259
rail throwback 186, 260
rail track 260
rake 260

rattle 66, 260
rebound angle 169, 189-192, 260
reverse English 109, 133, 194, 260
right English 80, 260
right spin 260
roll 260
rules 6
run 260
run the table 260
running English . . 109, 113-114,
133, 194, 260
safety 9, 125-168, 260
8-ball 162
frozen-ball 158
position 156-158
two-way shot 160-162
Sardo Tight Rack 222
scratch 7, 104, 260
prevention 48, 86, 220
shaft 5, 21, 260
shape 260
shark 260
short rail 261
shot 261
shot maker 261
shot planning 56-59
side pockets 63
side rail 261
sidespin 63, 80, 95-105, 261
bank and kick
shot effects . . . 171, 186-193
rail interaction 95
skill shot 261
slate 261
sliding 83
sliding force 83-84, 102,
slop shot 261
snooker 6, 158, 261
snookered 261
solid 6, 7, 261

speed control 59, 127, 261
spin 79-123
cut-induced 109
spot a ball 8, 261
spots 261
squirt 98, 261
stance . 15, 25-27, 41, 58-59, 261
masse shot 235-239
power break 217-218
steer 28, 261
stick 261
stop shot 47, 89, 261
straight pool 262
straight-in shot 262
strategy 115, 125-168
stripe 6, 7, 262
stroke 27, 29, 262
jump shot 241-245
masse shot 235-239
power break 217-224
stroke steer 28, 30, 262
stroking plane 31, 262
stun shot 42-45, 80, 87, 262
tangent line 33, 262
carom shot 206
English independence 97
persistence 117
target center 60-64, 72, 262
target size 61-64, 72, 262
technical proof 13, 262
thin cut 262
throw 97, 101-102, 262
collision-induced 105
English 97, 101
English-induced 105
for position 214-216
frozen ball 209-214
throw shot 262
top English 262
topspin . . . 41, 43, 47-52, 80, 262

transfer of English 105, 262

trash 10, 262

triangle 263

turn 263

two-rail kick and
    bank shots 225-231

two-way shot 160-162, 263

undercutting 37

V-bridge 21, 263

vertical plane 80, 263

vertical plane English 80, 233-235

wing balls 263

David G. Alciatore, PhD, PE ("Dr. Dave")

Dr. Dave is a mechanical engineering professor at Colorado State University in Fort Collins, Colorado. He is also a devoted pool and billiard enthusiast and an expert in understanding the physics of pool and billiards. Dr. Dave has many years of teaching experience and has written university level textbooks. The textbook experiences helped him develop skills for presenting and illustrating difficult concepts in a concise and understandable way. His inspiration and knowledge have also come from his experience teaching advanced dynamics to engineering graduate students. For more than ten years, he has often used pool examples to motivate his students to learn some very difficult motion analysis techniques.

normal video

technical proof

high-speed video

Contained within:
- over 250 illustrations and photographs.
- over 80 clearly presented principles of the game.

Also, over 150 video clips and 20 technical proofs
are accessible via the Internet or an optional CD-ROM.

More information and other resources are available on
the book website at:

www.engr.colostate.edu/pool